NihonGO NOW! Level 2 is an intermediate-level courseware package that takes a performed-culture approach to learning Japanese. This approach balances the need for an intellectual understanding of structural elements with multiple opportunities to experience the language within its cultural context.

From the outset, learners are presented with samples of authentic language that are context-sensitive and culturally coherent. Instructional time is used primarily to rehearse interactions that learners of Japanese are likely to encounter in the future, whether they involve speaking, listening, writing, or reading.

Level 2 comprises two textbooks with accompanying activity books. These four books in combination with audio and video files allow instructors to adapt an intermediate-level course, such as the second or third year of college Japanese, to their students' needs. They focus on language and modeled behavior, providing opportunities for learners to acquire language through performance templates. Online resources provide additional support for both students and instructors. Audio files, videos, supplementary exercises, and a teachers' manual are available at www.routledge.com/9781138305304.

NihonGO NOW! Level 2 Volume 1 Activity Book provides a wealth of communicative exercises for students following the *Level 2 Volume 1 Textbook*.

Mari Noda is Professor of Japanese at The Ohio State University.

Patricia J. Wetzel is Emerita Professor of Japanese at Portland State University.

Ginger Marcus is Professor of the Practice of Japanese Language at Washington University in St. Louis.

Stephen D. Luft is Lecturer of Japanese at the University of Pittsburgh.

Shinsuke Tsuchiya is Assistant Professor of Japanese at Brigham Young University.

日本語 NOW!
NihonGO NOW!
Performing Japanese Culture
Level 2 Volume 1
Activity Book

Mari Noda, Patricia J. Wetzel, Ginger Marcus,
Stephen D. Luft, and Shinsuke Tsuchiya

Routledge
Taylor & Francis Group
LONDON AND NEW YORK

First published 2021
by Routledge
2 Park Square, Milton Park, Abingdon, Oxon OX14 4RN

and by Routledge
52 Vanderbilt Avenue, New York, NY 10017

Routledge is an imprint of the Taylor & Francis Group, an informa business

© 2021 Mari Noda, Patricia J. Wetzel, Ginger Marcus, Stephen D. Luft, and Shinsuke Tsuchiya

The right of Mari Noda, Patricia J. Wetzel, Ginger Marcus, Stephen D. Luft, and Shinsuke Tsuchiya to be identified as authors of this work has been asserted by them in accordance with sections 77 and 78 of the Copyright, Designs and Patents Act 1988.

All rights reserved. No part of this book may be reprinted or reproduced or utilised in any form or by any electronic, mechanical, or other means, now known or hereafter invented, including photocopying and recording, or in any information storage or retrieval system, without permission in writing from the publishers.

Trademark notice: Product or corporate names may be trademarks or registered trademarks, and are used only for identification and explanation without intent to infringe.

British Library Cataloguing-in-Publication Data
A catalogue record for this book is available from the British Library

Library of Congress Cataloging-in-Publication Data
Names: Noda, Mari, author.
Title: Nihongo now! : performing Japanese culture / Mari Noda, Patricia J. Wetzel, Ginger Marcus, Stephen D. Luft, Shinsuke Tsuchiya, Masayuki Itomitsu.
Description: New York : Routledge, 2020. | Includes bibliographical references. | Contents: Level 1, volume 1. Textbook—Level 1, volume 1. Activity book—Level 1, volume 2. Textbook—Level 1, volume 2. Activity book. | In English and Japanese.
Identifiers: LCCN 2020026010 (print) | LCCN 2020026011 (ebook) | ISBN 9780367509279 (level 1, volume 1 ; set ; hardback) | ISBN 9780367508494 (level 1, volume 1 ; set ; paperback) | ISBN 9781138304123 (level 1, volume 1 ; textbook ; hardback) | ISBN 9781138304147 (level 1, volume 1 ; textbook ; paperback) | ISBN 9781138304277 (level 1, volume 1 ; activity book ; hardback) | ISBN 9781138304314 (level 1, volume 1 ; activity book ; paperback) | ISBN 9780367509309 (level 1, volume 2 ; set ; hardback) | ISBN 9780367508531 (level 1, volume 2 ; set ; paperback) | ISBN 9780367483241 (level 1, volume 2 ; textbook ; hardback) | ISBN 9780367483210 (level 1, volume 2 ; textbook ; paperback) | ISBN 9780367483494 (level 1, volume 2 ; activity book ; hardback) | ISBN 9780367483364 (level 1, volume 2 ; activity book ; paperback) | ISBN 9780203730249 (level 1, volume 1 ; ebook) | ISBN 9780203730362 (level 1, volume 1 ; ebook) | ISBN 9781003051855 (level 1, volume 1 ; ebook) | ISBN 9781003039334 (level 1, volume 2 ; ebook) | ISBN 9781003039471 (level 1, volume 2 ; ebook) | ISBN 9781003051879 (level 1, volume 2 ; ebook)
Subjects: LCSH: Japanese language—Textbooks for foreign speakers—English. | Japanese language—Study and teaching—English speakers.
Classification: LCC PL539.5.E5 N554 2020 (print) | LCC PL539.5.E5 (ebook) | DDC 495.682/421—dc23
LC record available at https://lccn.loc.gov/2020026010
LC ebook record available at https://lccn.loc.gov/2020026011

ISBN: 978-1-138-30531-1 (hbk)
ISBN: 978-1-138-30532-8 (pbk)
ISBN: 978-0-203-72932-8 (ebk)

Typeset in Times New Roman
by Apex CoVantage, LLC

Access the Support Material: www.routledge.com/9781138305304

Contents

Act 13 「困ったときはお互い様」です。
They say, "We're all in the same boat." 1

シーン 13-1　練習 2

 ♫13-1-1C Discussing the division chief's activities
 部長の活動について話す (BTS 1) 2
 ♫13-1-2C Which perspective? どんな見方？ (BTS 3) 2
 ♫13-1-3P Suggesting an alternative した方がいいと勧める (BTS 1, 4) 3
 ♫13-1-4P Responding with a personal observation
 私見を交えて答える (BTS 3) 3
 13-1 腕試し 4

シーン 13-2　練習 5

 ♫13-2-1C What is being suggested? どんな助言？ (BTS 4, 7) 5
 ♫13-2-2P Saying "no" 「だめ」と言う (BTS 7) 5
 ♫13-2-3P Reminding the boss about the limitation imposed
 限られた範囲について (BTS 3, 7) 6
 ♫13-2-4P Accepting and declining 受け入れる、断る (BTS 6) 6

シーン 13-3　練習 7

 ♫13-3-1C According to what? 何の通り？ (BTS 9) 7
 ♫13-3-2C What happened to that? 例の、どうなった？ (BTS 8) 7
 ♫13-3-3P Agreeing out loud 従う意思表示をする (BTS 5, 6, 9) 7
 13-3 腕試し 8

シーン 13-4　練習 9

 ♫13-4-1C Scanning for 気 「気」を探そう (BTS 13) 9
 ♫13-4-2C When does the event occur? いつの話？ (BTS 14) 9
 ♫13-4-3P Endorsing the suggested trait 提案を支持する (BTS 10) 10
 ♫13-4-4P Responding to an objection 問題に対応する (BTS 11, 12) 10

v

シーン 13-5　練習 11
    🎧13-5-1C What's wrong? どこが悪いのでしょう。(BTS 15) 11
    🎧13-5-2P Connecting a phone call 電話を取り次ぐ 11

シーン 13-6　練習 12
    🎧13-6-1C What did they do? 先輩がしたことは？ (BTS 16) 12
    🎧13-6-2C Why not? なぜ？ (BTS 16) 12
    🎧13-6-3P Describing multiple activities
        どんなことをするか伝える (BTS 14, 16) 12

シーン 13-7R　練習 14
    13-7-1R Person or comparison? 人？比較？ 14
    13-7-2R Inventory count 在庫を調べる 14
    13-7-3R Half-full or half-empty? だけ？しか？ 15
    🎧13-7-4W Using mnemonics お客様の特徴を記す 15

シーン 13-8R　練習 16
    13-8-1RW Expressing concerns and prohibitions 気をつけること 16
    13-8-2RW "When" statements こんなときは…… 16
    🎧13-8-3RW Potluck party assignments 持ち寄り品の割り当て 17

シーン 13-9R　練習 18
    13-9-1R Family hobbies 家族の趣味 18
    13-9-2R How is everyone in the family? ご家族は？ 19
    13-9-3W Describing family members 家族の紹介 20

評価 21
    🎧聞いてみよう 21
    🎧使ってみよう 22
    読んでみよう 24
    🎧書き取り 25
    書いてみよう 26
    知ってる？ 27

Act 14　一緒にお好み焼き作ろう！
Let's make *okonomiyaki* together! 31

シーン 14-1　練習 32
    🎧14-1-1C Transitive or intransitive? 他動詞？自動詞？ (BTS 1) 32
    🎧14-1-2C Action to exert change or not? したこと？起こったこと？ (BTS 1) 33

🎧 14-1-3P Telling what the target of the action is
　　　　　何(なに)に対(たい)して行動(こうどう)する？ (BTS 1) 33
　　　🎧 14-1-4P Confirming with additional information
　　　　　情報(じょうほう)を加(くわ)えて確認(かくにん)する (BTS 1, 2) 34
　　　14-1 腕試し 35

シーン 14-2　　練習 36
　　　🎧 14-2-1C Hearsay or not? 聞(き)いたこと？ (BTS 4) 36
　　　🎧 14-2-2P Reporting what you heard 聞(き)いたことを伝(つた)える (BTS 1, 4) 36
　　　🎧 14-2-3P Responding with reservation ためらいながら認(みと)める (BTS 5) 37
　　　🎧 14-2-4P Encouraging someone to do their best 努力(どりょく)を促(うなが)す (BTS 7) 37
　　　14-2 腕試し 38

シーン 14-3　　練習 39
　　　🎧 14-3-1C When did it happen? いつのこと？ (BTS 9, 10) 39
　　　🎧 14-3-2P Requesting approval for timing
　　　　　タイミングについて許可(きょか)を求(もと)める (BTS 9, 10)..39
　　　🎧 14-3-3P Stating a self-imposed deadline
　　　　　いつまでにするつもりか伝(つた)える (BTS 11) 40
　　　🎧 14-3-4P Let's cook! 料理(りょうり)しよう！ 41
　　　14-3 腕試し 41

シーン 14-4　　練習 42
　　　🎧 14-4-1C When did it happen? いつの話(はなし)？ (BTS 9, 10, 13, 14) 42
　　　🎧 14-4-2P It's starting to get that way. そうなってきました。 (BTS 12)...........42
　　　🎧 14-4-3P Recalling when it happened いつのことか思(おも)い出(だ)す (BTS 9, 13)...........43
　　　🎧 14-4-4P Suggesting we do it before it's too late
　　　　　早(はや)めのタイミングを示唆(しさ)する (BTS 14) 44
　　　14-4 腕試し 44

シーン 14-5　　練習 45
　　　🎧 14-5-1P Finding out what to do next 次(つぎ)のステップは…… (BTS 15).............45
　　　🎧 14-5-2P Suggesting a sense of imminent disaster
　　　　　危機感(ききかん)を表現(ひょうげん)する (BTS 16) 46
　　　🎧 14-5-3P Stating the obvious わかりきったことを言う (BTS 17) 46
　　　14-5 腕試し 47

シーン 14-6　　練習 48
　　　🎧 14-6-1C Necessity or prohibition? 必要(ひつよう)？禁止(きんし)？ (BTS 18).............................48
　　　🎧 14-6-2C What's going on? 何があったの？ 48
　　　🎧 14-6-3P Correcting a friend's misunderstanding
　　　　　思(おも)い違(ちが)いを指摘(してき)する (BTS 18, 19) 50

vii

- 14-6-4P Reminding a friend about what the teacher said
  先生の言葉を思い出させる (BTS 17, 18) 50
- 14-6-5P Suggesting a course of action
  すべきか否かを言う (BTS 18) 51
- 14-6 腕試し 52

シーン 14-7R　練習 53
- 14-7-1R Transitive or intransitive? 対象のある行動？ない行動？ 53
- 14-7-2R Resulting state or action? 結果の状況？過程？ 53
- 14-7-3W Writing down what to buy 買い物リスト 54

シーン 14-8R　練習 55
- 14-8-1R Transitive or intransitive? 対象のある行動？ない行動？ 55
- 14-8-2R When? いつ？ 55
- 14-8-3W Adding a time frame タイミングを明らかにする 56

シーン 14-9R　練習 57
- 14-9-1R Transitive or intransitive? 対象のある行動？ない行動？ 57
- 14-9-2R Should or should not? するべきか否か 57
- 14-9-3W Writing names for a game 名前を書く 58

評価 59
- 聞いてみよう 59
- 使ってみよう 61
- 読んでみよう 62
- 書き取り 66
- 書いてみよう 66
- 知ってる？ 68

Act 15　教えてもらえますか？
Can I have you explain it to me? 73

シーン 15-1　練習 74
- 15-1-1C Can you do it? できますか？ (BTS 1) 74
- 15-1-2P Reassuring Nozaki-san that it'll work out!
  大丈夫と力づける (BTS 1) 75
- 15-1-3P Asking if Asano-san can do it?
  できるかどうか確認する (BTS 1) 75
- 15-1 腕試し 76

| シーン 15-2 | 練習 | 77 |

♪15-2-1P Talking about a weekend trip 旅行の予定について話す (BTS 2)............77
♪15-2-2P Compass directions 方向を正す..77
15-2 腕試し 78

| シーン 15-3 | 練習 | 79 |

♪15-3-1C Hearsay or not? 伝言か否か (BTS 5)...79
♪15-3-2P Confirming an arrival time 到着時間を確認する (BTS 5, 6)............80
♪15-3-3P Reporting a train issue 延着の伝言を伝える (BTS 5, 6)................81
15-3 腕試し 81

| シーン 15-4 | 練習 | 82 |

♪15-4-1C Follow the procedures 指示に従う (BTS 7, 8)..............................82
♪15-4-2P Adding deadlines to a request
　締め切り情報を加えて依頼する (BTS 7) 82
♪15-4-3P Making a request 依頼する (BTS 7) 83
♪15-4-4P Being modest about your abilities 謙遜する (BTS 1, 9) 84
15-4 腕試し 84

| シーン 15-5 | 練習 | 85 |

♪15-5-1C Intention or assumption? 意図？思い込み？ (BTS 2, 11)...............85
♪15-5-2P Describing a fictitious situation
　仮定に基づいて話してもらう (BTS 2) 86
♪15-5-3P Dealing with a gap in preparation
　しそびれたことをすぐする (BTS 11)..86
15-5 腕試し 87

シーン 15-6 練習 88

♪15-6-1P Making a suggestion with *enryo*
　遠慮がちに意見を述べる (BTS 12)..88
♪15-6-2P Being prepared for mishaps 予定の変更に備える (BTS 12)............89
15-6 腕試し 89

シーン 15-7R 練習 90

15-7-1R Potential or honorific passive? 可能？尊敬の受け身？......................90
15-7-2R Potential or intransitive? 可能形？自動詞？..................................90
15-7-3W Filling out a schedule 予定表に書き込む......................................91

| シーン 15-8R | 練習 | 92 |

🎧15-8-1RW Organizing explanations 手順を示す ... 92
15-8-2R する？なる？ ... 93
15-8-3W Convenient? Inconvenient? 便利か不便か ... 94

| シーン 15-9R | 練習 | 95 |

15-9-1R Intention or mistaken assumption? 意図？思い違い？ ... 95
15-9-2R Whose opinion matters? 誰の意見？ ... 95
15-9-3W Filling out a schedule 予定表に書き込む ... 96

評価 ... 97

🎧聞いてみよう ... 97
🎧使ってみよう ... 98
読んでみよう ... 99
🎧書き取り ... 101
書いてみよう ... 102
知ってる？ ... 103

Act 16　呼んでくれれば行ったのに……。
If only you had called me I would have gone 107

| シーン 16-1 | 練習 | 108 |

🎧16-1-1C Declining invitations 誘いを断る (BTS 2) ... 108
🎧16-1-2C A reflection session 反省会 (BTS 1) ... 108
🎧 16-1-3P Saying what should be done in a certain situation
　するべきことをアドバイスする (BTS 1) ... 109
🎧 16-1-4CP Acknowledging a thoughtful act 意外な手助け (BTS 3) ... 109
16-1 腕試し ... 110

| シーン 16-2 | 練習 | 111 |

🎧16-2-1C Enlisting help to continue
　話を続けるための助けを求める (BTS 6) ... 111
16-2-2P I'm about to do it するところ (BTS 5) ... 111
🎧16-2-3P ～たら or ～えば? (BTS 4) ... 112
🎧16-2-4P Stating a regret 後悔する (BTS 4) ... 113
16-2 腕試し ... 113

| シーン 16-3 | 練習 | 114 |

🎧16-3-1C Just happened or about to happen? どんなところ? (BTS 5, 7) ... 114
🎧16-3-2C Like what? たとえて言うと (BTS 8) ... 114
🎧16-3-3P It seems as if . . . はっきりとは言えないですが……。 (BTS 8) ... 115
🎧16-3-4CP Expressing envy うらやましさ (BTS 8) ... 115

| シーン 16-4 | 練習 | 117 |

- 🎧16-4-1C Just happened or about to happen?
  今あったこと？これから？(BTS 5, 7, 9) ... 117
- 🎧16-4-2P If I put my mind to it... 機会を逃して後悔する (BTS 3, 4) ... 117
- 🎧16-4-3P Just as I was about to...
  ちょうどしようとしたところに……(BTS 9) ... 118
- 🎧16-4-4P Presenting observation as evidence
  見たことを証拠として出す (BTS 5) ... 119

| シーン 16-5 | 練習 | 120 |

- 🎧16-5-1C Reason or purpose? 理由？目的？(BTS 10) ... 120
- 🎧16-5-2C Doing something for a purpose
  目的を持って行動する (BTS 10) ... 120
- 🎧16-5-3P Explaining the purpose of an item
  使用目的を説明する (BTS 10) ... 121
- 🎧16-5-4P Approaching a task collaboratively 一緒に取り組む ... 122

| シーン 16-6 | 練習 | 123 |

- 🎧16-6-1C Listening to opinions and taking notes
  意見を書き取る (BTS 11) ... 123
- 🎧16-6-2C Writing down opinions that you hear
  意見を聞いて書きとめる (BTS 11) ... 124
- 🎧16-6-3P Summarizing an opinion 意見をまとめる ... 124
- 🎧16-6-4P Expressing an opinion 意見を言う (BTS 11) ... 125
- 16-6 腕試し ... 125

| シーン 16-7R | 練習 | 126 |

- 16-7-1R Contrast or reason? 逆接？理由？ ... 126
- 16-7-2RW Things that I should do or should have done...
  やるべきこと、後悔してること。... 126
- 16-7-3W Writing down reminders 忘れないよう記録する ... 127

| シーン 16-8R | 練習 | 128 |

- 16-8-1R Provisional expressions 仮の表現 ... 128
- 16-8-2R Explaining what happened 何が起こったか説明する ... 128
- 16-8-3W Asking a favor by leaving a note お願いをメモする ... 129

| シーン 16-9R | 練習 | 130 |

- 16-9-1R Expressing cause, reason, and purpose 原因、理由、目的の表現 ... 130
- 16-9-2R Which statement is softer? より柔らかい表現は？ ... 131

16-9-3RW Softening your statements and opinions
供述・意見を和らげる 131

評価 133

🎧聞いてみよう 133
🎧使ってみよう 134
読んでみよう 136
🎧書き取り 139
書いてみよう 139
知ってる？ 141

Act 17　この記事によると……
According to this article 145

シーン 17-1　練習 146
🎧17-1-1C Meanings of ながら (BTS 1) 146
🎧17-1-2P Stating that you are multi-tasking
　　同時にしていると伝える (BTS 1) 146
🎧17-1-3P Apologizing for not being prompt
　　遅れていることを謝罪する (BTS 1) 147
🎧17-1-4P Affirming solidarity 仲間意識を高める (BTS 2) 147
17-1 腕試し 148

シーン 17-2　練習 149
🎧17-2-1C What's the expectation? 予想されていること (BTS 3) ... 149
🎧17-2-2P Giving assurance 確信を伝える (BTS 3) 149
🎧17-2-3P Stating that it's unlikely 可能性が低いことを伝える (BTS 3) 150
🎧17-2-4P Disagreeing partially 一部を否定する (BTS 3) 150
17-2 腕試し 151

シーン 17-3　練習 152
🎧17-3-1C Who did it? したのは誰？ (BTS 5) 152
🎧17-3-2P Suggesting that someone else do it 他の人にさせる (BTS 5) 152
🎧17-3-3P Volunteering an expert できる人を勧める (BTS 5) 153
🎧17-3-4P Committing to get it done right away
　　すぐ行うよう約束する (BTS 6) 153

シーン 17-4　練習 154
🎧17-4-1C Who did it? したのは誰？ (BTS 7) 154
🎧17-4-2C According to what? 何によると？ (BTS 7) 154

- 🎧17-4-3P Accepting an invitation 促されたことをする (BTS 7)....................155
- 🎧17-4-4P Making a conjecture from a graph グラフを読み取る (BTS 8)........155
- 17-4 腕試し 156

シーン 17-5　練習 157
- 🎧17-5-1C Qualified responses 〜次第？情報源？ (BTS 8, 11) 157
- 🎧17-5-2P Predicting a gradual change 緩やかな変化を予測する (BTS 10)..........157
- 🎧17-5-3P Describing a collaborative effort
  協働したことを伝える (BTS 9) 158
- 🎧17-5-4P Saying that it depends 状況によることを指摘する (BTS 11).........158
- 17-5 腕試し 158

シーン 17-6　練習 159
- 🎧17-6-1C When? いつ？ (BTS 13) 159
- 🎧17-6-2P Encouraging to do as much as possible
  出来るだけするようアドバイスする (BTS 12) 159
- 🎧17-6-3P Suggesting that the situation is limited
  状況が限られていると示唆する (BTS 12) 159
- 🎧17-6-4P Defending the blamed person 弁護する (BTS 14)............................160

シーン 17-7R　練習 161
- 17-7-1R "Time" or "notwithstanding"? 並行か矛盾か 161
- 17-7-2R Reasonable expectations 妥当な予想 161
- 17-7-3RW Responding ambiguously 曖昧に答える 162

シーン 17-8R　練習 163
- 17-8-1R Making requests 依頼の内容 163
- 17-8-2R Identifying the source 情報源は？ 163
- 17-8-3RW Using causatives 使役表現 164
- 17-8-4RW Thank you messages 感謝のことば 164

シーン 17-9R　練習 166
- 17-9-1R To or with each other? 〜合う 166
- 17-9-2R Depending on what? 何によって？ 166
- 17-9-3RW Writing short memos メモを書く 167

評価 168
- 🎧聞いてみよう 168
- 🎧使ってみよう 170

読んでみよう 171
　　　🎧書き取り 174
　　　書いてみよう 174
　　　知ってる？ 176

Act 18　怒(おこ)られた。
I got reprimanded. 181

シーン 18-1　　練習 182
　　　🎧18-1-1C Who did it? 誰(だれ)がした？ (BTS 1) 182
　　　🎧18-1-2C Listening to the weather forecast 天気予報(てんきよほう)を聞(き)く (BTS 4) 182
　　　🎧18-1-3P Describing a negative experience 嫌(いや)な経験(けいけん)を伝(つた)える (BTS 1) 183
　　　🎧18-1-4P Describing based on expectations 期待(きたい)と比(くら)べて伝(つた)える (BTS 2) 184
　　　18-1 腕試し 184

シーン 18-2　　練習 185
　　　🎧18-2-1C What's going on? どういうこと？ (BTS 6) 185
　　　🎧18-2-2P Acknowledging lack of care
　　　　うっかりしていたことを認(みと)める (BTS 5) 185
　　　🎧18-2-3P Requesting to follow up
　　　　やりっぱなしにしないよう念(ねん)を押(お)す (BTS 5) 185
　　　🎧18-2-4CP Adding a conjecture 推測(すいそく)を加(くわ)える (BTS 6) 186
　　　18-2 腕試し 186

シーン 18-3　　練習 187
　　　🎧18-3-1C Meanings of noun + らしい (BTS 6, 8) 187
　　　🎧18-3-2P Doing things out of responsibility 責任上(せきにんじょう)仕方(しかた)なく行(おこな)う (BTS 7) 187
　　　🎧18-3-3P Doing some damage control 失言(しつげん)から立(た)ち直(なお)る (BTS 8, 9) 188
　　　🎧18-3-4RP Giving mild correction 少(すこ)し言(い)い変(か)える(BTS 9) 188
　　　18-3 腕試し 190

シーン 18-4　　練習 191
　　　🎧18-4-1C Who is she talking about? 誰(だれ)のこと？ (BTS 10) 191
　　　🎧18-4-2P Responding to unreasonable demands
　　　　無理(むり)な要求(ようきゅう)に対応(たいおう)する (BTS 10, 1) 191
　　　🎧18-4-3P Adding an observation about Kato-san
　　　　加藤(かとう)さんについて気(き)づいたことを加(くわ)える (BTS 10) 192
　　　🎧18-4-4P Modifying the description of the situation
　　　　状況(じょうきょう)が違(ちが)うことを伝(つた)える (BTS 1, 9, 10) 192
　　　18-4 腕試し 193

シーン 18-5	練習	194
	♬18-5-1C What are they talking about? 話題は？ (BTS 12)	194
	♬18-5-2P Describing the type of place どんなところを選んだか伝える (BTS 11)	194
	♬18-5-3P Giving reassurance of satisfactory performance 満足度を示す(BTS 11)	195
	♬18-5-4P Identifying the issue 問題点を挙げる (BTS 12)	195
	18-5 腕試し	195

シーン 18-6	練習	196
	♬18-6-1C Even supposing that... 条件の不足を指摘する (BTS 13)	196
	♬18-6-2P Being critical of others' behavior 言動を批判する (BTS 13)	196
	♬18-6-3P Summarizing in a word 一言でまとめる	197
	♬18-6-4RCP Making an observation 観察を述べる (BTS 6)	197
	18-6 腕試し	199

シーン 18-7R	練習	200
	18-7-1R Passive? Honorific? Potential? 受け身？尊敬？可能？	200
	18-7-2R It seems that... 様子の表現	200
	18-7-3RW Journal entries about weather 気候について記述する	201

シーン 18-8R	練習	202
	18-8-1R Expressions associated with temperature 温度の表現	202
	18-8-2R 俳句？川柳？	202
	18-8-3W Warm or cold? 温度について言及する	203
	18-8-4W What season? 季節を限定する	203

シーン 18-9R	練習	204
	18-9-1R What particle? 疑問文の助詞を使いこなす	204
	18-9-2R Even if... 条件・状態に関わらず	204
	18-9-3RW How many? 数の表現	205
	18-9-4RW Expressing apology and disappointment 謝罪や残念な気持ちを述べる	205

評価		206
	♬聞いてみよう	206
	♬使ってみよう	209

読んでみよう	210
🎧書き取り	213
書いてみよう	214
知ってる？	215

Appendix A: 文字練習 Symbol practice 218
Appendix B: Assessment answer sheets 251
Appendix C: Answer keys 256

第 13 幕
Act 13

「困[こま]ったときはお互[たが]い様[さま]」です。

They say, "We're all in the same boat."

困[こま]ったときはお互[たが]い様[さま]。
When in need, we're all in the same boat.

◆ シーン 13-1 練習

13-1-1C Discussing the division chief's activities
部長の活動について話す (BTS 1)

What activity by the division chief is mentioned in each of the conversations? Select from the collection below.

例1. 仕事 _____

例2. 準備 _____

3. _____

4. _____

5. _____

6. _____

案内　心配　仕事　準備　面接　運転　説明

13-1-2C Which perspective? どんな見方？ (BTS 3)

Two members of a project team are talking to each other before their meeting begins. What quantities are mentioned? Is the speaker's perspective that the quantities are abundant or limited?

		Abundant	Limited
例1.	7 hours of sleep	○	
例2.	1 course		○
3.			
4.			
5.			
6.			
7.			
8.			

2

13-1-3P Suggesting an alternative した方(ほう)がいいと勧(すす)める (BTS 1, 4)

Gently disagree with your boss, Ohta-san, by suggesting the alternative action as being better. You should use in your suggestions the expression provided below.

例1.
大田さん	誰にも連絡しなくてもいいよね。	It's okay not to let anyone know, right?
あなた	いや、ご家族には連絡された方がいいですよ。	No, you should let your family know.

例2.
大田さん	ちょっと腰が痛いだけだから、別に、クリニックに行く必要ないよね。	My back only hurts a little, so I don't really need to go to the clinic, right?
あなた	いや、今回はいらっしゃった方がいいですよ。	No, you should go this time.

例 1. ご家族(かぞく)　例 2. 今回(こんかい)は　3. 今日中(きょうじゅう)に　4. いい席(せき)
5. ちょっと　6. 会議(かいぎ)まで　7. 今週中(こんしゅうちゅう)に　8. もう一回(かい)だけ

13-1-4P Responding with a personal observation
私見(しけん)を交(まじ)えて答(こた)える (BTS 3)

Respond to an inquiry by a colleague, Hotta-san, using the information in the illustration and suggesting whether you feel that the quantity you provide is below or above the perceived expectation. You should use in your suggestions the expression provided below.

例1.
堀田さん	５匹ぐらい飼ってるのかな？	Does she have about five, maybe?
あなた	猫ですか？いやいや、１０匹も飼ってるんですよ。	Do you mean cats? No, no, she has *ten*.

例 2.
堀田さん	７つぐらい必要なのかな？	Do we need about seven, maybe?
あなた	椅子ですか？いやいや、２つしか必要じゃないんですよ。	Do you mean chairs? No, no, we only need two.

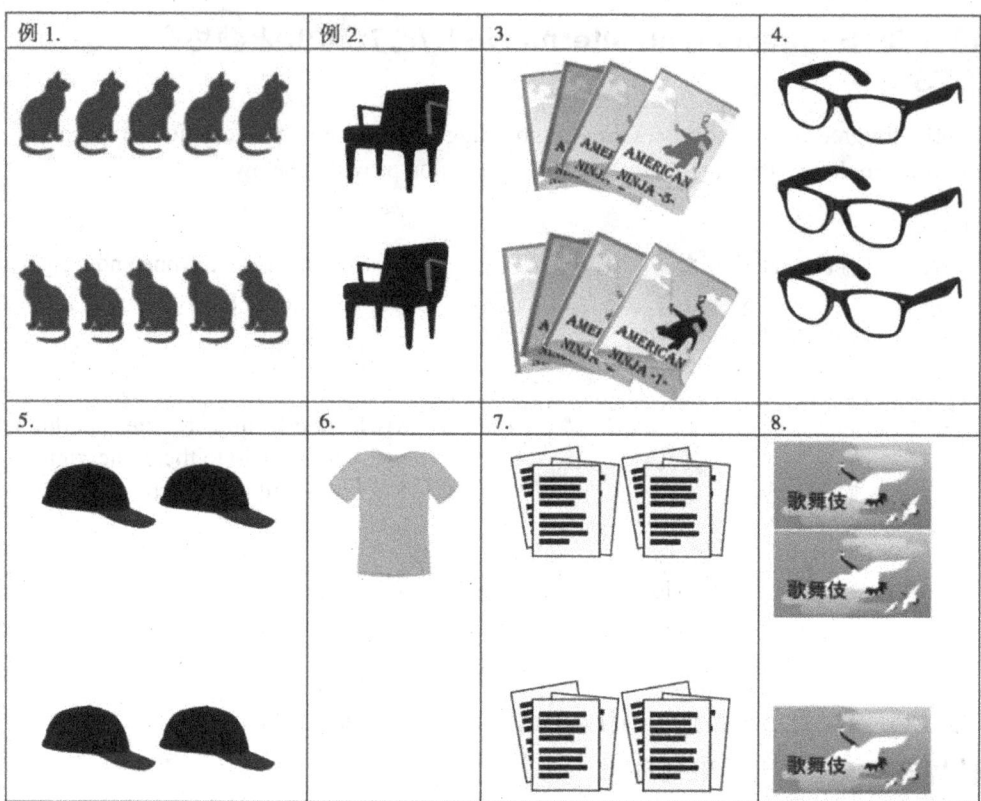

13-1 腕試し

1. Being careful not to sound too aggressive, suggest a course of action to a Japanese *senpai* or superior.
2. When you see someone having some kind of difficulty, show *omoiyari* by doing things like asking how they are doing, advising them to do something that would be good for them (e.g., taking a break), or offering some kind of assistance.

◆ シーン 13-2 練習

13-2-1C What is being suggested? どんな助言？ (BTS 4, 7)

Tsukada-san is your *senpai* who likes to give advice, such as what one shouldn't do, what would be better if one did or didn't do, etc. Listen to him and write down what he suggests.

例 1. One shouldn't use the office supplies in this room.

例 2. It'd be better to delete this segment.

3. _____
4. _____
5. _____
6. _____
7. _____
8. _____
9. _____
10. _____

13-2-2P Saying "no" 「だめ」と言う (BTS 7)

You are looking after a friend's son, Akira, for the day. When he makes various demands firmly say no, at least for now. You might not understand everything that he is talking about, but you should still be able to refuse his requests.

例 1.
| 明 | ねえ、この文房具、1,000円だよ。買いたいなあ。だめ？ | Hey, this stationery is 1,000 yen. I sure want to buy it. Can I? |
| あなた | 今は買っちゃダメ。 | Not right now. |

例 2.
| 明 | ねえ、すっごくかわいいよね、この猫。飼ってみたいなあ。いけない？ | Hey, this cat is so cute! I sure want to keep it. Can I? |
| あなた | 今は飼っちゃダメ。 | Not right now. |

13-2-3P Reminding the boss about the limitation imposed
限られた範囲について (BTS 3, 7)

Your boss, Shiratori-san, seems to have forgotten she said that Tanaka-san would be the only person permitted to do various things. When she asks questions about who would do those things, respond to her by reminding her of her earlier directives.

例 1.
白鳥さん	何人ぐらい休むの？来週。	How many people will be taking time off next week?
あなた	何人ぐらいって、来週は田中さんしか休んじゃいけないっておっしゃってませんでした？	How many? Didn't you say that no one but Tanaka-san was allowed to take time off next week?

例 2.
白鳥さん	みんなに頼んだ？教授のお世話。	Did you ask everyone to help the professor?
あなた	みんなにって、教授のお世話は田中さんにしか頼んじゃいけないっておっしゃってませんでした？	Everyone? Didn't you say that I wasn't allowed to ask anyone but Tanaka-san to help the professor?

13-2-4P Accepting and declining 受け入れる、断る (BTS 6)

Respond to invitations and suggestions by Umeda-bucho, accepting or declining according to the illustrations.

例 1.
上田部長	無理しちゃダメですよ。ちょっと休憩した方がよくないですか？１０分ぐらいありますから。	Don't overdo it. Shouldn't you take a break? We have 10 minutes.
あなた	１０分ぐらいですか？じゃあ、せっかくですから休憩します。すみません。	10 minutes? Then I'll take a break, since you've gone to such trouble. Thanks.

例 2.
上田部長	この本、読んでみませんか？歴史的なもの興味あるでしょう？	Why don't you try reading this book? You're interested in historical things, right?
あなた	歴史的なものですか？あ、でもすみません。せっかくですが、今回は遠慮しておきます。また別のときに是非。	Historical things? Oh, but, sorry, I know you've gone to a lot of trouble, but I'll hold back this time. But definitely some other time.

例 1. 😊　例 2. 😣　3. 😣　4. 😊

5. 😊　6. 😊　7. 😣　8. 😣

◆ シーン 13-3 練習

13-3-1C According to what? 何の通り? (BTS 9)

Division chief Yagi and Kanda-san are discussing various items. Listen and complete the chart below with the information about the items and what has been done to them.

			according to what . . .
例 1.	A proposal	changed	according to Yagi-bucho's instructions
例 2.	A program	made	according to what was heard from Mr. Yamada
3.	_____	_____	_____
4.	_____	_____	_____
5.	_____	_____	_____
6.	_____	_____	_____
7.	_____	_____	_____

13-3-2C What happened to that? 例の、どうなった? (BTS 8)

Listen to Sakamoto-san ask his colleague, Yoshida-san, what happened to something that he assumes his colleague is familiar with. What does Sakamoto-san find out?

例 1. He quit part-time work and got married.

例 2. A man on the second floor took it.

3. _____

4. _____

5. _____

6. _____

13-3-3P Agreeing out loud 従う意思表示をする (BTS 5, 6, 9)

Your colleague, Oda-san, seems skeptical about the division chief's suggestion. Voice your thinking that you will follow the division chief's suggestion for the time being, given the opportunity.

例 1.

| 小田さん | 部長はもうしばらく休憩した方がいいって言うけど、どうかなあ。 | The division chief says we should rest a while, but I wonder. |
| あなた | とにかく部長の言う通り、もうしばらく休憩するか。せっかくそう言ってくれたんだから。 | Well, at any rate, I guess I'll rest a while like the division chief said. Since she went to the trouble to say so. |

例 2.

| 小田さん | 部長は一緒に帰った方がいいって言うけど、どうかなあ。 | The division chief said we should go home together, but I wonder. |
| あなた | とにかく部長の言う通り、一緒に帰るか。せっかくそう言ってくれたんだから。 | Well, at any rate, I guess we'll go home together like the division chief said. Since she went to the trouble to say so. |

13-3 腕試し

1. When an appropriate opportunity presents itself, comment to your friend/colleague that something turned out exactly as your friend/colleague has predicted.
2. Thank someone for the advice they gave you, and tell them how things turned out when you followed their advice.

◆ シーン 13-4 練習

🎧 13-4-1C Scanning for 気「気」を探そう (BTS 13)

Listen to two people talk and see if you can pick out all expressions that include 気 and write them out. Write the full phrase (Noun + particle(s), Verb with an inflection, for example). You may use ひらがな for parts that you don't know the kanji for, but always use 気.

例 1. 元気に、病気した、元気に _____
例 2. 気になさらないで、平気でした _____
3. _____
4. _____
5. _____
6. _____
7. _____

🎧 13-4-2C When does the event occur? いつの話? (BTS 14)

Usui-san and his colleague are talking about an event. Write down what occurrence is mentioned in relation to the event. Also, select the general time frame of the event being discussed.

	Event	Occurrence	Past	Habitual	Future
例 1.	Phone call	When she completed it			○
例 2.	Being there	When he was in trouble	○		
3.	Drinking tea				
4.	Having someone look				
5.	Passing a test				
6.	Wanting something				
7.	Becoming cheap				

13-4-3P Endorsing the suggested trait
提案を支持する (BTS 10)

You and Usui-san are on the same product design team. When Usui-san assesses the situation and makes a suggestion, endorse her suggestion.

例 1.

| 臼井さん | これでは、小さすぎますか？もっと大きくできますよね。 | Is this too small? They can make it bigger, you know. |
| あなた | そうですね。少し大きめにお願いしましょう。 | That's true. Let's ask for one that's a little on the big side. |

例 2.

| 臼井さん | この時間じゃ、ちょっと早いかもしれませんね。もう少し遅くしてもらったらどうでしょう。 | This timing might be a bit early. How about we have them do it a little later? |
| あなた | そうですね。少し遅めにお願いしましょう。 | That's true. Let's ask them to do it a little on the late-ish side. |

13-4-4P Responding to an objection
問題に対応する (BTS 11, 12)

Umehara-san, a team member of your project team, points out various issues with the proposals you have made. Respond by accepting his suggested bottom-line.

例 1.

| 梅原さん | え？明日ですか？いや、この仕事は今日やらないと間に合いませんよ。 | What? Tomorrow? No, if this job isn't done today it won't be on time. |
| あなた | そうですか。やっぱり明日じゃ無理ですか。わかりました。今日やりましょう。 | Okay. Tomorrow's no good after all. That's fine. Let's do it today. |

例 2.

| 梅原さん | え？アルバイトですか？いや、この計画は部長にお願いしないとはっきりしませんよ。 | What? A part-time worker? No, if we don't ask the division chief to go over this plan it'll be unclear. |
| あなた | そうですか。やっぱりアルバイトじゃ無理ですか。わかりました。部長にお願いしましょう。 | Okay. A part-time worker's no good after all. That's fine. Let's ask the division chief. |

◆ **シーン 13-5 練習**

13-5-1C What's wrong? どこが悪いのでしょう。(BTS 15)

Listen to Ichiro talk to his mother and write down what symptoms are identified.

例 1. Has diarrhea. _____

例 2. Has a cough. _____

3. _____

4. _____

5. _____

6. _____

13-5-2P Connecting a phone call 電話を取り次ぐ

You happened to take an incoming phone call in your office. Announce that you'll connect it to the person requested.

例 1.

| 臼井さん | すみません。水野課長さん、いらっしゃいますか？ | Excuse me. Is section chief Mizuno available? |
| あなた | はい、水野と代わりますので、少々お待ちください。 | Yes, I'll connect you with Mizuno, so please wait a moment. |

例 2.

| 臼井さん | えっと、部長さん、いらっしゃったらお話ししたいんですが。 | Um, if the *bucho* is in, I'd like to speak to her, but . . . |
| あなた | はい、部長と代わりますので、少々お待ちください。 | Yes, I'll connect you with the *bucho*, so please wait a moment. |

◆ **シーン 13-6 練習**

🎧 13-6-1C What did they do? 先輩がしたことは? (BTS 16)

Kanda-san is talking to his various *senpai*. What two activities does each *senpai* mention?

例 1. Walking around historical places,   eating tasty fish
例 2. Eating ramen,   going shopping with friend(s)
   3. _____   _____
   4. _____   _____
   5. _____   _____
   6. _____   _____
   7. _____   _____

🎧 13-6-2C Why not? なぜ? (BTS 16)

Yamada-san works for an event company and is discussing some issues with her co-workers. What does Yamada-san's colleague suggest as the potential reasons for the issues at hand?

例 1. No time,   the teacher is strict
例 2. The topic was uninteresting,   the discussion was difficult
   3. _____   _____
   4. _____   _____
   5. _____   _____
   6. _____   _____
   7. _____   _____

🎧 13-6-3P Describing multiple activities
どんなことをするか伝える (BTS 14, 16)

Your *senpai* asks what you do under various circumstances. Respond, using the information in the illustrations.

「困ったときはお互い様」です。

例 1.
先輩　暇な時はどうしてたの？　　　What did you do in your free time?
あなた　そうですね。寝たり、音楽聞い　Hmm, I was doing things like sleeping and
　　　　たりしてました。　　　　　　listening to music.

例 2.
先輩　困った時は誰に相談するの？　　Who do you talk to when you have a problem?
あなた　そうですね。先輩に相談したり、Hmm, I do things like talking to my *senpai*
　　　　先生に相談したりします。　　and talking to a teacher.

◆ シーン 13-7R 練習

13-7-1R Person or comparison? 人？比較？

Read the following sentences and identify whether 方 refers to a person or is a comparison.

例 1.	赤いの買われる方、いらっしゃいますか。	☒ person	☐ comparison
例 2.	バスで来られた方がはやいですよ。	☐ person	☒ comparison
3.	青と黄色しかないんだったら、青の方にするか。	☐ person	☐ comparison
4.	今こちらは通ってはいけないので、銀行に行かれる方はあちらからお通りください。	☐ person	☐ comparison
5.	白なんかより黒にした方がよくない？	☐ person	☐ comparison
6.	せっかくだから少ししか食べていない方に食べていただきたいと思ってまして……。	☐ person	☐ comparison

13-7-2R Inventory count 在庫を調べる

The following is a list of office supplies at Ogaki Trading.

アイテム	色	先月	今月
ホワイトボードマーカー	黒	９７	２５
ホワイトボードマーカー	赤	２５	１０
ホワイトボードマーカー	青	１５	０
ポストイット	青	２４	１２
ポストイット	黄	０	４５
ポストイット	白	２８	２８

例 1.	How many red whiteboard markers do they have left this month?	10
例 2.	Which item was out of stock last month?	yellow sticky notes
3.	How many blue sticky notes did they have last month?	_____
4.	Which item is out of stock this month?	_____
5.	Which item had no change in its inventory from last month to this month?	_____
6.	Which item is used the most in the office?	_____

13-7-3R Half-full or half-empty? だけ？しか？

Circle either だけ or しか as most appropriate in the following sentences.

Ex. 1. 水はもう半分(だけ・(しか))ないよ。
Ex. 2. じゃあ半分((だけ)・しか)いただきます。
   3.   銀行で(だけ・しか)やってくれませんよ。
   4.   青いの(だけ・しか)使いましょう。
   5.   あのバスは東京から(だけ・しか)出てませんよ。
   6.   白も黒もあとはこれ(だけ・しか)です。
   7.   これ(だけ・しか)はやっておかないといけないと思って……。
   8.   黄色のポストイット、これ(だけ・しか)買ってもらわなかったの？

13-7-4W Using mnemonics お客様の特徴を記す

Sasha is trying to remember the names of clients at Ogaki Trading. Write down an object and color that will help her remember the person.

例 1.   山本さん   _____メガネ(青)_____
例 2.   田口さん   _____ネール(赤)_____
   3.   青木さん   _____
   4.   村上さん   _____
   5.   東さん   _____

◆ シーン 13-8R 練習

13-8-1RW Expressing concerns and prohibitions
気(き)をつけること

Fill in the blanks in the following statements by choosing the appropriate expression from the selection.

もらわないと	気分	部長
行っていないと	通って	やっておかない
自分一人	言っちゃ	3万円

例1.　明日までには＿＿やっておかない＿＿と……。
例2.　例の話、友だちに＿＿言っちゃ＿＿だめだよ。
　3.　ここは人の家だから、＿＿＿＿＿＿＿はいけないよ。
　4.　例のプロジェクト、＿＿＿＿＿＿＿ではできないからなあ。
　5.　彼には本当に気をつけて＿＿＿＿＿＿＿困るよ。
　6.　こんな＿＿＿＿＿＿＿では何もしたくないよ。
　7.　名古屋には早目に＿＿＿＿＿＿＿だめだから……。
　8.　＿＿＿＿＿＿＿じゃないと分からないことだから、白井さんに聞いても仕方がないよ。
　9.　＿＿＿＿＿＿＿じゃちょっと高目かなあ。

13-8-2RW "When" statements こんなときは……

Complete the following statements by choosing one of the phrases from the selection below.

本当にうれしかったですね	お電話くださいね
おたがい様ですよ	ちゃんと話を聞かないとだめですよ
全部やってしまいましたよ	友だちに来てもらってくださいね
例の話でもしようか	ちゃんと休まないといけませんよ

例1.　困った時は＿おたがい様ですよ＿＿＿＿＿＿＿＿＿＿。
例2.　名古屋にいらっしゃる時は＿お電話くださいね＿＿＿＿＿＿。
　3.　ライブのチケットが当たった時は＿＿＿＿＿＿＿＿＿＿。

4. 白井さんが来ていた時に＿＿＿＿＿＿＿＿＿＿＿＿＿＿＿＿＿＿＿＿。
5. 自分一人じゃできない時は＿＿＿＿＿＿＿＿＿＿＿＿＿＿＿＿＿＿＿。
6. 気分がよくない時は＿＿＿＿＿＿＿＿＿＿＿＿＿＿＿＿＿＿＿＿＿＿。
7. 先生が話されている時は＿＿＿＿＿＿＿＿＿＿＿＿＿＿＿＿＿＿＿＿。
8. せっかくだから彼が来てない時に＿＿＿＿＿＿＿＿＿＿＿＿＿＿＿＿。

13-8-3RW Potluck party assignments 持ち寄り品の割り当て

Suzuki-san is planning a potluck party and asking others to bring something. She asks you to write down the names next to the assignments. If the assignment is yours, write "self" in the memo.

例 1.	ご飯	川村さん
例 2.	おかず	友子さん
3.	サラダ	＿＿＿＿＿＿＿＿＿
4.	飲みもの	＿＿＿＿＿＿＿＿＿
5.	デザート	＿＿＿＿＿＿＿＿＿
6.	ゲーム	＿＿＿＿＿＿＿＿＿
7.	おかし	＿＿＿＿＿＿＿＿＿
8.	ペーパープレート	＿＿＿＿＿＿＿＿＿

◆ シーン 13-9R 練習

13-9-1R Family hobbies 家族の趣味

You found the following descriptions of someone's family members on a blog.

家族、6人家族+10才のねこ。名前はニャンた。
父、休みが月1、2日しかない忙しさで、外食が多い。メタボを気にしててダイエット中。
母、セール大好き。でも買ってもあまり使わないことが多い。朝に弱い。
姉、会社のOL。サスペンスドラマ好きで、休みは一日中部屋でドラマ。彼はいない。
自分、電話会社でインターン中。本当はケーキ屋さんになりたい。時々作ったりするが、あまりおいしくはない。彼はいない。
弟、大学生。毎日ゲームしたりマンガ読んだりしてるのだが、スポーツも勉強もできるし、彼女もいる。
妹、女子高生。時間があったらSNS。インスタのフォロワー2000人。スマホがないとダメ。

例1.	How many people are there in the family?	6
例2.	What kind of pet do they have? What is the pet's name? How old is it?	cat; Nyanta; 10
3.	Which family member is the youngest? What obsession does the person have?	

4. Who spends a lot of time watching television dramas? What does the person do? _____
5. Who is on a diet? Why? _____
6. Who likes shopping? What does the person do with the things they buy? _____
7. Who wants to open a cake shop? What does the person actually do? _____
8. Who is dating someone? What special capabilities are noted about this person? _____

13-9-2R How is everyone in the family? ご家族は？

Read the following exchanges about family members.

ご家族は元気にしていらっしゃいますか。	おかげさまで父も母も元気にしております。
お姉さんの気分はどう？	まだ部屋で休んでいます。
お兄様はもう元気になられましたか？	昨日休んですっかり元気になりました。
妹さんは元気にしてる？	はい。先日は妹がお世話になりました。
弟くんはひま？	うん、一日中マンガ読んだり、テレビ見たりしてるよ。

例1. How is the younger sister? _____doing well_____

例2. How is the older brother? ___felt better after resting yesterday___

3. How is the older sister? _____

4. How are the parents? _____

5. How is the younger brother? _____

13-9-3W Describing family members 家族(かぞく)の紹介(しょうかい)

Imagine that you have a large family and describe them in Japanese.

> Dad (56): when he is home he only watches TV
> Mom (53): likes doing things like yoga, baking cakes, etc.
> Brother (27): favorite color is black; everything has to be black (nothing else will do but black)
> Sister (24): favorite color is red; everything has to be red (nothing else will do but red)
> Myself (22): likes doing things like studying Japanese, watching Japanese dramas, etc.
> Sister (18): constantly blogging (lit. 'does nothing but blog') when she is in her room
> Brother (13): likes playing games, playing soccer with friends, etc.

	In relation to you	Age	Descriptions
例 1.	父	56才	家にいる時はテレビしか見ない。
例 2.	母	53才	ヨガをしたり、ケーキを作ったりするのが好き。
例 3.	兄	27才	好きな色は黒。何でも黒じゃないとだめ。
4.			
5.			
6.			
7.			

13-9R 「困(こま)ったときはお互(たが)い様(さま)です。」

◆ Act 13 評価

 聞いてみよう

Read the context, listen to the audio, and then answer the questions. If you hear something unfamiliar, rely on what you know to choose the correct answer.

1. Eri is helping her friend clean his new apartment.
   a. What is Eri's friend thinking of doing with the item in question?
   b. What does Eri want to do with it?
   c. What two reasons does Eri mention for doing this?

2. Sasha has just learned that Kanda-san already completed a complex program.
   a. How long did it take Kanda-san to complete the program?
   b. Does Kanda-san feel this is a short time or a long time?
   c. What did Suzuki-san do for a week? What was the result?

3. Sasha is giving directives to a part-time worker, Yamano-kun.
   a. What does Sasha ask Yamano-kun to do?
   b. What was Yamano-kun thinking of doing? Why?
   c. Why does Yamano-kun say it's okay?

4. Sasha notices a document in her in-box and talks to Kanda-san.
   a. What does Sasha want to know?
   b. What information does Kanda-san give her?
   c. What is Sasha able to figure out based on Kanda-san's answer?

5. Yagi-bucho is entertaining an out-of-town guest at her home.
   a. What does Yagi-bucho offer to let her guest do?
   b. What are two reasons her guest might want to do this?
   c. Does her guest accept her offer?

6. Sasha is impressed by Kanda's work.
   a. What has impressed Sasha?
   b. Why does Kanda-san say "お互い様"?

7. Mizuno-san and Kanda-san are talking about another office worker, Yamaguchi-san.
   a. What are Yamaguchi-san's symptoms?
   b. What seems to be the reason for the symptoms?
   c. What did Mizuno-san say to Yamaguchi-san? How did he respond?
   d. What does Kanda-san think Yamaguchi-san should not do?

8. A couple came to look at a furniture display.

    a. How does the woman feel about the furniture?
    b. How does the man feel about the furniture?
    c. What does the woman think one could do with the chair?
    d. What does the man think one is likely to do?

9. A man approaches an information desk at a department store.

    a. What does the man learn? Be specific.

10. Sasha asks Kanda-san about some document.

    a. What type of document is it?
    b. What happened to it?
    c. What reason does Kanda-san suggest for this happening?
    d. What does Sasha think is a rare occurrence?

 使ってみよう

For each of the following, listen to the audio, and respond to what was said based on the context. Then listen to the sample response.

1. Explain to your co-worker that (a) you are sleeping too little (i.e., your sleeping hours are insufficient); (b) you are suffering from lack of sleep lately; (c) you pulled an all-nighter last night; (d) you are a little fatigued; (e) a little longer rest hours would be good, but . . .; (f) you didn't take a nap today; (g) the proposal you are reading now is chaotic.
2. Give advice to various people, using a polite wording: (a) to a new part-timer, that it might be better if he came on the early side on the first day; (b) to a client, that making a copy just in case would be a good idea; (c) to your supervisor, that transferring it to another location and saving it would be convenient; (d) to a neighbor, that throwing away things you don't need would tidy things up; (e) to a colleague, that taking this medicine when suffering a light headache will cure it right away.
3. Explain the situation that your friend asks about, using examples: (a) for example, when your cough won't stop and your fever is high, it'd be good to go see a doctor; (b) when, for example, you lack sleep continuously or pay attention to someone's needs, you get tired; (c) things that have gotten small or have colors that don't match, for example, you give away to your younger sister or brother; (d) at any rate, if your friend organized the bookshelves and desktop, for example, his room would become more functional (easy to use); (e) you take a nap when you've pulled an all-nighter or it's rough due to the onset of a cold, for example.
4. Tell your advisor that the task is extremely cumbersome.
5. You just fell by the bus station, and a man in line came to help you up. You are fine (i.e., it's nothing serious).

6. Show your concern to a *senpai* by saying that you (have to) pay attention (to their needs) when talking to an eminent person.
7. You are allergic to eggs.
8. You are willing to make it as close to the proposal as possible.
9. You feel there is no need for your colleague to apologize. When in need, we are all in the same boat. Besides, he helped you before.
10. Urge your guest to eat a lot without holding back.
11. There is no need to show the report to the section chief, since the section chief is already familiar with it.
12. You've been struggling in class, and your teacher is talking to you about it. You only studied for 30 minutes last night.
13. You are talking with a friend about what to do about a certain task. Your friend had previously said that you shouldn't ask Ichiro to do things like this.

Now it's your turn to start the conversation based on the given context. Listen to how the other person reacts to you. For some items, you may not get a verbal response. Don't be concerned if you hear things you have not yet learned.

14. Your boat is lopsided and you need help!
15. Ask a friend if she remembers the teacher who substitute taught for Sakamoto-sensei last week.
16. Announce that as the head of the club you will introduce a new member.
17. Tell an office staff member that you happened to be in the area (i.e., come near) for business, so you came by.
18. Suggest to two subordinates that they both stop being so concerned about the other person and talk more.
19. Ask a friend about various circumstances: (a) what she is doing when she has time; (b) whom she requests (for help) when in trouble; (c) whether she'd borrow money from a friend when she is short; (d) what was her happiest time so far.
20. Complain that your nose drip won't stop due to your pollen allergy.
21. Ask a friend to teach you some songs that are popular now.
22. Give various directives: (a) to a part-time worker to close the windows on the second floor at 5 p.m.; (b) to a secretary to transfer the third page of this document to a place near you; (c) to a part-time helper to delete pages 2 through 6; (d) to new employees to help those in need; (e) to your subordinates to be more conscientious about pleasing customers; (f) to a group of volunteers to rest for a while.
23. Tell a friend (a) this won't be enough; (b) he can't take a break right now; (c) they said that deleting it would be bad; (d) throwing it out would cause trouble; (e) one person won't get it done.
24. Ask a co-worker what happened to the documents (that you assume she knows about).
25. Make a comment to yourself about the following, which you are considering doing: (a) taking a break; (b) asking the teacher; (c) giving up already; (d) stopping (before you do too much); (e) taking a look one more time.

読んでみよう

Consider the context provided and read the passage to answer the questions that follow.

1. Here is a group chat about preparing for a school event. One of the group members is going through the group's supply inventory.

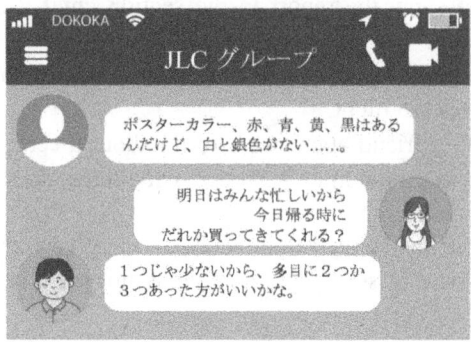

   a. What poster colors do they have? What colors are missing?
   b. What request is made? Why? What quantity is suggested? Provide details.

   [パフォーマンス] Your conversation partner is at a stationary store wondering what to buy. Answer their phone call and respond to their questions. Your conversation partner has not read the group chat.

2. Sasha is reading Eri's post.

a. Where did Eri go? With whom? How many people in total?
b. What did they eat? Can you guess what the dialectal expression でらうみゃ～ means?
c. Why is Eri tired? Note that イケメン stands for イケてるメン 'good-looking man.'

[パフォーマンス] Open a conversation by talking about Eri's blog with your conversation partner who has not seen the blog. Talk about your imagined trip to a city in Japan and talk about possible activities you can do while you are in that city.

3. Here is a short email message from Tomoda-san, who is coordinating a multi-family camping event.

> 件名: ファミリーキャンプ
>
> ご家族はお元気にしていらっしゃいますか。明日のファミリーキャンプですが、車で通ってはいけないところがあったり、せまくて入りにくかったりするところもあります。お父様とお母様、それに小さなご兄弟も来られるとお聞きしましたので、お気をつけていらしてください。何か困ったことがあったらお電話ください。
> 友田

a. What does Tomoda-san ask first?
b. What two things are mentioned about the family camp tomorrow that are related to getting to the destination?
c. What two requests are made? Provide details.

[パフォーマンス] Call Tomoda-san and ask for more details about the location of the event. Ask for permission to bring additional people.

書き取り

Listen to the audio, repeat silently what you hear, then write it down. What do you think the context is?

1. _____。
2. _____。
3. _____。
4. _____。
5. _____。

6. _____ 。

7. _____ 。

8. _____ 。

書いてみよう

Consider the context provided and compose a text according to the directions.

1. You are preparing for an event. Make a sign that tells people not to enter here.

2. Write a short memo asking Shirai-sensei whether he will attend tomorrow's event.

3. Following the models provided in 13-9-3W, describe three of your family members or friends in Japanese.

In relation to you	Age	Description

4. Imaging that you are in Japan on a class trip. Write an entry for the class blog.

This week, I did things like going to Nagoya and going to Kyoto. Since we came all the way to Japan, I went out with my friend and the two of us ate the ramen (that everyone was talking about). Just as everyone told us, it was really tasty! When I come to Japan next, I want to come with my family.

_____
_____
_____
_____
_____
_____
_____

知ってる?

Select the most appropriate option and write the letter on your answer sheet.

1. You ask your professor when she'll come to the meeting tomorrow.
   先生、あした何時に_____か。(BTS 1)

   a. 来(こ)られます
   b. 参(まい)ります
   c. 伺(うかが)います

2. You disagree with your friend who says that you must be embarrassed.
   ぜんぜん恥ずかしく_____ないよ。(BTS 2)

   a. とか
   b. じゃ
   c. なんか

3. You tell your friend that regrettably you only went to Miami on your vacation.
   あいにくマイアミに_____行かなかったんだ。(BTS 3)

   a. だけ
   b. しか
   c. は

4. You advise your friend not to go out alone late at night. 夜遅く一人で_____方がいいよ。(BTS 4)

   a. 出かけない
   b. 出かけていない
   c. 出かけなかった

5. You think that going by subway will be faster than by bus. バスで_____より、地下鉄で_____方が速いと思う。(BTS 4)

   a. 行った・行く
   b. 行く・行った
   c. 行った・行った

6. A question ending in the informal style followed by か is used when you_____. (BTS 5)

   a. disagree with a friend
   b. are certain about your opinion
   c. ask yourself a question

7. You can say 「せっかくですが」when you_____. (BTS 6)

   a. turn down an offer
   b. apologize for what you did
   c. extend an invitation

8. You want to know if you're not supposed to read a certain email. あのメール、_____ですか。(BTS 7)

   a. 読んでもいい
   b. 読んじゃダメ
   c. 読んでいただけない

9. 「その通(とお)りです。」 is an expression that can be used when you _____. (BTS 9)

   a. refuse an invitation
   b. seek more information
   c. debate an issue

10. You're sure that you won't be able to graduate if you don't take a history class.
    歴史(れきし)の授業(じゅぎょう)を_____、卒業(そつぎょう)できない。 (BTS 11)

    a. 取(と)らないと
    b. 取らないで
    c. 取らなくて

11. You tell your colleague that the way she wrote the email won't do.
    こんな書(か)き方(かた)_____いけないと思います。 (BTS 12)

    a. で
    b. じゃ
    c. には

12. You explain that you bought your suitcase before you came to Japan.
    日本に_____とき買(か)ったんです。 (BTS 14)

    a. 来る
    b. 来た

13. You explain that you want to buy a new cellphone when you get back to the U.S.
    アメリカに_____とき新(あたら)しい携帯(けいたい)を買(か)いたいんです。 (BTS 14)

    a. 帰(かえ)る
    b. 帰った

14. You comment that the temperature fluctuates from hot to cold in your office.
    _____ですね、ここ。 (BTS 16)

    a. 暑(あつ)くても寒(さむ)くても
    b. 暑かったり寒かったり
    c. 暑いし、寒い

15. It is sometimes hard to read the kanji for names and places because the readings _____. (BTL 1)

    a. change over time
    b. are determined by fixed rules
    c. can be variable

16. Which of the following is an appropriate expression for closing an email? (BTL 2)

    a. ありがとうございました。
    b. よろしくお願いします。
    c. 失礼(しつれい)します。

17. The negative of である is _____. (BTL 3)

    a. ではない
    b. でもない
    c. じゃない

18. Japanese people sometimes use 方言(ほうげん) to indicate that they_____. (BTL 4)

    a. are opposed to standard pronunciation
    b. share a connection with someone
    c. enjoy meeting people from other locales

19. When reporting information, family terms such as 父(ちち) and 母(はは) can be used _____. (BTL 5)

    a. neutrally
    b. honorifically
    c. humbly

20. When there are different characters for the same word (such as 辞(や)める and 止(や)める), the one that is used depends on the _____. (BTL 6)

    a. level of formality
    b. pitch pattern
    c. meaning in context

第 14 幕
Act 14

一緒にお好み焼き作ろう！
Let's make *okonomiyaki* together!

失敗は成功のもと。
Failure is the foundation of success.

◆ シーン 14-1 練習

14-1-1C Transitive or intransitive? 他動詞？自動詞？ (BTS 1)

Listen to each statement and select from the list the English that corresponds to what the speaker says.

例 1. __a__   例 2. __b__   3. _____   4. _____   5. _____
6. _____   7. _____   8. _____   9. _____   10. _____

例 1. a. Does that window open?
       b. Are you going to open the window?

例 2. a. Did the luggage arrive?
       b. Did you ship the luggage?

3. a. Is everything taken care of?
    b. Are you taking care of everything?

4. a. The students have gathered together.
    b. I'm gathering the students together.

5. a. Has that been decided?
    b. Did you make a decision on that?

6. a. It was a big help.
    b. I helped them out.

7. a. The schedule changed, right?
    b. You changed the schedule, right?

8. a. You can see it now.
    b. I'm looking at it right now.

9. a. It's in there.
    b. I'm putting it in there.

10. a. My Wednesday has opened up.
    b. I cleared my schedule on Wednesday.

14-1-2C Action to exert change or not? したこと？起こったこと？ (BTS 1)

In each of the statements you hear, identify the action and select whether it entails someone exerting change to an entity or not.

	Action	Exerts change to another entity?	
例 1.	Deciding	◯ Yes	No
例 2.	Separating	Yes	◯ No
3.	_____	Yes	No
4.	_____	Yes	No
5.	_____	Yes	No
6.	_____	Yes	No

14-1-3P Telling what the target of the action is
何に対して行動する？ (BTS 1)

You are supervising Yayoi, a new intern. Give her the information she needs, based on the illustrations.

例 1.
弥生　何を書きましょうか。　　　　　　What shall I write?
あなた　企画書です。企画書を書いてください。　The proposal. Please write the proposal.

例 2.
弥生　何を直しましょうか。　　　　　　What shall I fix?
あなた　本棚です。本棚を直してください。　The bookshelf. Please fix the bookshelf.

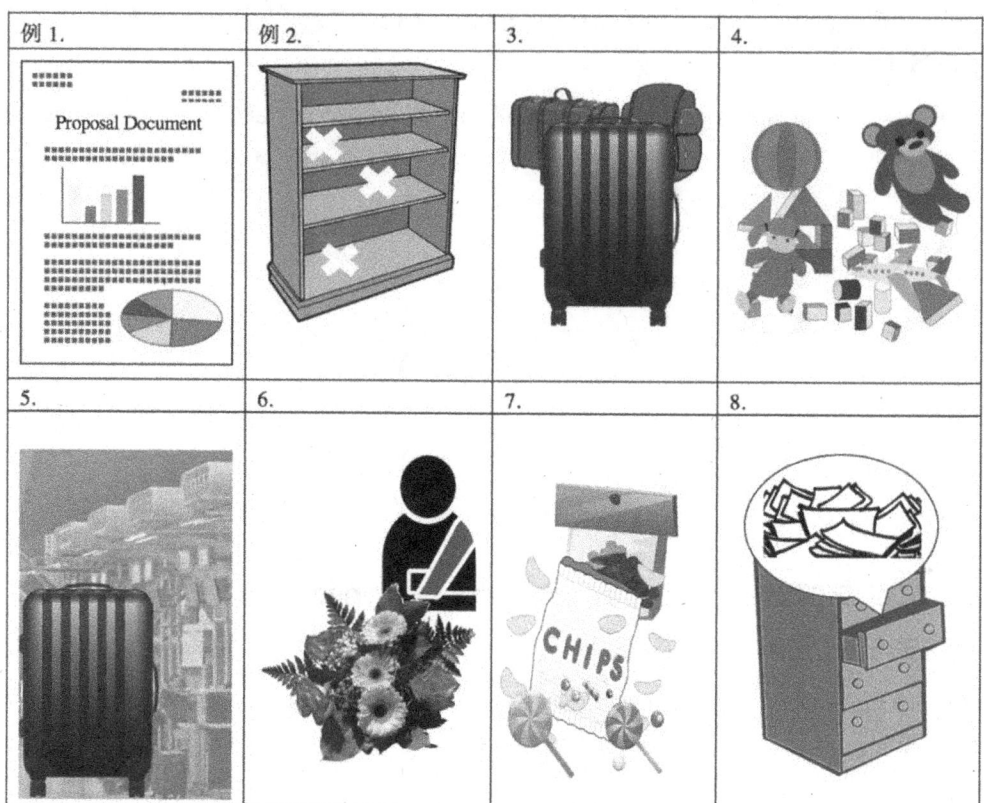

 14-1-4P Confirming with additional information
情報を加えて確認する (BTS 1, 2)

Respond affirmatively to your *senpai* as you prepare for a conference, adding the time when the critical situation started. Use the time information provided below.

例 1.
先輩　玄関、開いてますね？　　　　　　　　The entrance is open, right?
あなた　はい、１０時には開いたかと思います。　Yes, I trust it opened by 10:00.

例 2.
先輩　社長、起きておられますね？　　　　　　The president is awake, right?
あなた　はい、７時には起きられたかと思います。Yes, I trust she woke up by 7:00.

例 1. 10:00　　例 2. 7:00　　3. 8:30　　4. 9:30　　5. 8:00
　6. 9:00　　　7. 10:00　　　8. 10:15　　9. 5:00　　10. 8:30

14-1 腕試し

Ask your Japanese-speaking friends or associates some hypothetical questions. Try both past and future situations, such as what they would have done had they not pursued their current profession, or where they would like to go if they were to travel in the summer time.

◆ シーン 14-2 練習

 14-2-1C Hearsay or not? 聞いたこと？ (BTS 4)

Listen to the conversation. If one of the speakers is reporting information they heard from someone else, mark "hearsay"; if not, mark "not hearsay."

	Hearsay	Not hearsay
例 1.	○	
例 2.		○
3.		
4.		
5.		
6.		
7.		
8.		
9.		
10.		

 14-2-2P Reporting what you heard 聞いたことを伝える (BTS 1, 4)

When Murata-san, a co-worker, asks about what's going on, tell him that you heard Yoshida-san did it.

例 1.

村田さん　もう入っているんですか。　　It's already in here?
あなた　　はい、吉田さんが入れてくれた　Yes, I heard that Yoshida-san put it
　　　　　そうです。　　　　　　　　　　in there.

例 2.
| 村田さん | 来週のスケジュール、変わったんですね？ | Next week's schedule has changed, hasn't it? |
| あなた | はい、吉田さんが変えてくれたそうです。 | Yes, I heard that Yoshida-san changed it. |

14-2-3P Responding with reservation ためらいながら認める (BTS 5)

When Yoshida-san, a co-worker, asks you a question, respond based on the context. If there is nothing concerning about the situation, respond affirmatively. If there is something concerning about the situation, respond according to the pattern in a way that suggests the answer to her question is yes, but there are other things that should be considered.

例 1.		You rewrote the proposal, but you still don't think it's very good.
吉田さん	企画書、書き直したんですか。	Did you rewrite the proposal?
あなた	書き直すことは書き直したんですけど……。	I *did* rewrite the proposal, but . . .

例 2.		The printer started working again, and now it's working perfectly.
吉田さん	プリンター、直ったんですか。	Is the printer fixed?
あなた	はい、直りました。	Yes, it's fixed.

3. You increased the number of people, but the people you found don't seem very capable.
4. You saved the data without any problems.
5. You submitted the report, but there were a few things you forgot to include.
6. It looks nice, but you do not think it works very well.
7. You sent the schedule to Aoki-san, and she seemed pleased with it.

14-2-4P Encouraging someone to do their best 努力を促す (BTS 7)

When Tomoda-san, the intern, asks if he should do something, tell him to try his best to do it.

例 1.
| 友田さん | 古いのを使ったほうがいいんですか。 | Should I use an old one? |
| あなた | はい、なるべく古いのを使うようにしてください。 | Yes, please try your best to use the old ones. |

例2.

| 友田さん | 中谷さんに頼まないほうがいいんですか。 | Should I not ask Nakatani-san? |
| あなた | はい、なるべく中谷さんに頼まないようにしてください。 | Yes, please try your best not to ask Nakatani-san. |

14-2 腕試し

Find out (while also discussing your experience in the U.S. or elsewhere) where your Japanese associates and friends typically ate lunches when they were high school/college students and/or when they worked in Japan.

◆ シーン 14-3 練習

14-3-1C When did it happen? いつのこと? (BTS 9, 10)

Listen to the audio and indicate whether Action A happens before, during, or after Action B.

	Action A	before	during	after	Action B
例 1.	Cleaning the conference room	○			Mizuno-sensei coming
例 2.	Eating at an *okonomiyaki* restaurant		○		Being in Osaka
3.	Not being that terrible				Eating
4.	Going on a walk				Eating
5.	Cleaning a room				Coming home
6.	Doing a job				Murata-san writing a report
7.	Learning to use chopsticks				Coming to Japan
8.	Class ending				Talking to the teacher

14-3-2P Requesting approval for timing
タイミングについて許可を求める (BTS 9, 10)

Based on the schedule, respond to a superior's questions by indicating your plan to do the tasks before Tanaka-san arrives, while Tanaka-san is here, or after Tanaka-san leaves.

例 1.
神田さん　会議はいつするんですか。

あなた　　田中さんが来ている間にしようと思っているんですけど、よろしいでしょうか。

When are you going to hold the meeting?

I was thinking of doing it while Tanaka-san was here, but is that okay?

例 2.
神田さん　会議室はいつ片付けるんですか。

あなた　　田中さんが帰ってから片付けようと思っているんですけど、よろしいでしょうか。

When are you going to clean up the conference room?

I was thinking of doing it after Tanaka-san left, but is that okay?

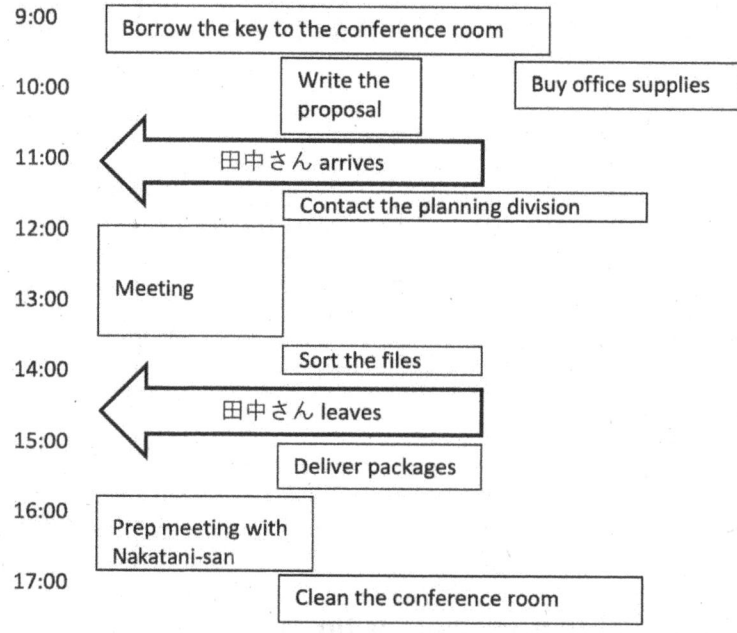

14-3-3P Stating a self-imposed deadline
いつまでにするつもりか伝える (BTS 11)

When your friend Ai asks you when you will do something, and reminds you about something that is going to happen, tell her that you will have it done by the time the thing she mentioned happens.

例 1.
| 愛 | これ、いつするの？田中さんはすぐ来るんでしょ？ | When are you going to do this? Tanaka-san is coming, right? |
| あなた | そう、田中さんが来るまでにしようと思っているんだ。 | Yeah, I'm going to do it by the time Tanaka-san gets here. |

例 2.
| 愛 | この部屋、いつ片付けるの？ミーティング、始まるんでしょ？ | When are you going to clean this room? The meeting is going to start, right? |
| あなた | そう、ミーティングが始まるまでに片付けようと思っているんだ。 | Yeah, I'm going to clean it by the time the meeting starts. |

 14-3-4P Let's cook! 料理しよう！

You found a recipe on the internet in English for a Chinese-style soup, and you and your friend Yuya decided to make it together. Based on the English recipe, tell Yuya what to do. Then check what you said with the sample.

1. Slice the onions and the carrots.
2. Boil 1 cup water in a pan and add the salt to it.
3. Heat some oil in the frying pan.
4. Put the sliced onions and carrots in the frying pan.
5. After about 2 minutes, add the salted hot water.
6. After about 1 minute, add an egg and mix together and it's done.

14-3 腕試し

1. Ask your Japanese friends about their favorite home dish. Get some details, such as whether the dish is from a particular region, what it contains, and whether it takes a lot of time to make.
2. Prepare to have a cooking session with your Japanese friends. Determine where you are going to cook, what ingredients are needed, and who will be responsible for getting them.

◆ シーン 14-4 練習

14-4-1C When did it happen? いつの話(はなし)？
(BTS 9, 10, 13, 14)

Listen to the audio and write down when the listed activities or situations happen(ed) relative to (i.e., before, during, after) another event/activity/situation.

例 1.	Not using French	After graduating
例 2.	Drinking	While it's hot
3.	Writing a report	
4.	Putting the phone somewhere	
5.	Going to the bookstore	
6.	Head starting to hurt	
7.	Taking medicine	
8.	Buying tickets	
9.	Realizing it's important	

14-4-2P It's starting to get that way. そうなってきました。
(BTS 12)

When your *senpai* Kawamura-san asks about the state of things, tell him that things didn't used to be that way, but they've started to get that way.

例 1.
川村さん	慣れた？	Are you used to it?
あなた	そうですね。前は全然慣れていなかったんですけど、ちょっと慣れてきました。	Yeah, before I wasn't used to it at all, but I've started to get used to it a little.

例 2.
川村さん	暑くなった？	Did it get hot?
あなた	そうですね。前は全然暑くなかったんですけど、ちょっと暑くなってきました。	Yeah, before it wasn't hot at all, but it's started to get hot a little.

14-4-3P Recalling when it happened　いつのことか思い出す (BTS 9, 13)

Yoshida-san is working on a report, and is confirming the relative timing of things you were involved with that happened yesterday. Answer her questions based on the list of things that happened yesterday, which is given below. In this list, events are given in the order in which they happened.

例1.
吉田さん	荷物が届いたのは、木村さんが帰る前だったんですか。	Did the package arrive before Kimura-san left?
あなた	いや、木村さんが帰った後だったと思うんですけど。	No, I think it was after he left.

例2.
吉田さん	大谷先生に本を借りたのは、山口研究所に行った後だったんですか。	Did you borrow the book from Otani-sensei after going to the Yamaguchi Research Institute?
あなた	はい、そうです。山口研究所に行った後で、大谷先生に本を借りたんです。	Yes, that's right. After going to the Yamaguchi Research Institute I borrowed the book from Otani-sensei.

Went to the bank

Visited the Yamaguchi Research Institute

Read an email from Mizuno-sensei

Kimura-san left early

Went to the library

Spoke to Mizuno-sensei

Read a new proposal

A package arrived

Borrowed a book from Otani-sensei

Cleaned room 305

14-4-4P Suggesting we do it before it's too late
早(はや)めのタイミングを示唆(しさ)する (BTS 14)

When Saori, your friend, says that something bad will happen if you don't act quickly, agree that you should act before the bad thing happens (or, in other words, while the bad thing hasn't yet happened).

例1.
沙織	早くしないと高くなっちゃうんだよね。	If we don't do it quickly, it's going to get expensive.
あなた	うん、高くならないうちにした方がいいね。	Yeah, we should do it before it gets expensive.

例2.
沙織	早くしないとみんな帰っちゃうんだよね。	If we don't do it quickly everyone's going to leave.
あなた	うん、みんな帰らないうちにした方がいいね。	Yeah, we should do it before everyone leaves.

14-4 腕試し

Apply what you practiced in 14-3 and have a cooking session with your Japanese friends. Keep good communication going about who is doing what when. Enjoy the food together!

◆ シーン 14-5 練習

 14-5-1P Finding out what to do next
次のステップは…… (BTS 15)

You are cooking with a friend, but you've forgotten what you're supposed to do next. Check with your friend about what you should do next, based on the illustrations below.

例 1.
あなた　次は、ええと、ソースをつけるんだっけ。　　So next, we, um, was it adding the sauce?
一郎　　そう、ソースつけて。　　　　　　　　　　　Yeah, add the sauce.

例 2.
あなた　次は、ええと、水を測るんだっけ。　　　　　So next, we, um, was it measuring the water?
一郎　　そうね。じゃ、ちょっと測っておいて。ちょっと少な目で。　Yeah, that was it. Okay, then measure the water. A bit on the littler side.

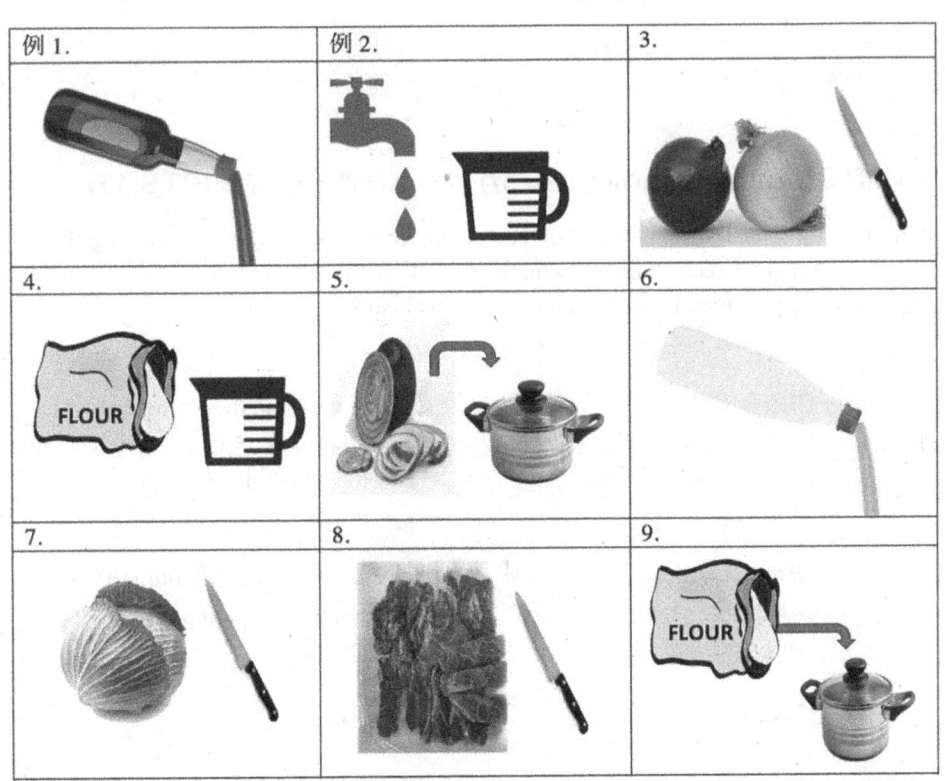

14-5-2P Suggesting a sense of imminent disaster
危機感を表現する (BTS 16)

You are talking with Saori, a friend of yours. When she asks you a question or makes a comment, respond and tell her what you thought was going to happen, using a verb from the pool of options below. You will use each option only once.

例 1.
沙織　　あれ、すっごく痛いんじゃない？大丈夫だったの？　　That's really painful, isn't it? Were you all right?
あなた　いや、死ぬかと思った。　　No, I thought I was going to die.

例 2.
沙織　　いい大学に入ってよかったね。でも、入るのは無理だって言ってたんじゃない？　　That's great that you got into a good university. But didn't you say getting in would be impossible?
あなた　いや、ダメかと思った。　　Yeah, I thought I wouldn't be allowed (to get in).

| ない | 落ちる | ~~ダメ~~ | 壊れる |
| 倒れる | ~~死ぬ~~ | 負ける | 泣く |

 ### 14-5-3P Stating the obvious わかりきったことを言う (BTS 17)

You are talking with Ichiro, a friend of yours. Previously he had said something that now seems obviously incorrect. Point out what is now obvious, assuming he would agree, based on the situations provided below. Then listen to his response.

例 1.
あなた　勝ったじゃない。　　And you said they wouldn't win.
一郎　　いや、今度は絶対負けるかと思ったんだけどさ。　　No, I thought for sure they were going to lose this time, you know.

例 2.
あなた　やったじゃない。　　And you said you wouldn't do it.
一郎　　無理かと思ったんだけど、よかった！　　I thought it was impossible, but I'm relieved.

1. Ichiro told you he didn't think they would win, but then they won.
2. Ichiro told you he didn't think he could do it, but then he did it.
3. Ichiro told you he wouldn't get it done, but then he got it done.
4. Ichiro said it was dirty, but it's actually clean.
5. Ichiro said he wouldn't give up, but then he gave up.
6. Ichiro said he wouldn't eat it, but then he ate it.
7. Ichiro said the package wouldn't come, but then it came.
8. Ichiro said it wasn't very impressive, but then it was impressive.
9. Ichiro said he had some energy, but he really doesn't have any energy.

14-5 腕試し

1. Find out if your Japanese associates or acquaintances have any experience with a competitive sport that you may be interested in. Discuss their experience.
2. Talk to your Japanese friend about an experience you had that was difficult because it was exhausting, scary, etc.

◆ シーン 14-6 練習

 14-6-1C Necessity or prohibition? 必要？禁止？ (BTS 18)

Listen to each conversation. If a speaker says something that must be done, mark "necessity"; or if something must not be done, mark "prohibition." Then write what either must or must not be done, choosing from the options provided.

~~Throw away~~   Show   Say   Get delivered
Take a day off   Attend   ~~Study~~   Do one's best
Go see a doctor   Be late   Begin   Be the division manager

		Necessity	Prohibition
例 1.	Study	○	
例 2.	Throw away		○
3.			
4.			
5.			
6.			
7.			
8.			
9.			
10.			

 14-6-2C What's going on? 何があったの？

Listen to statements about things going wrong. For each statement, select from the illustrations what is wrong, and indicate whether the speaker is taking responsibility for the outcome (i.e., by stating that they are the one that did the action) or not.

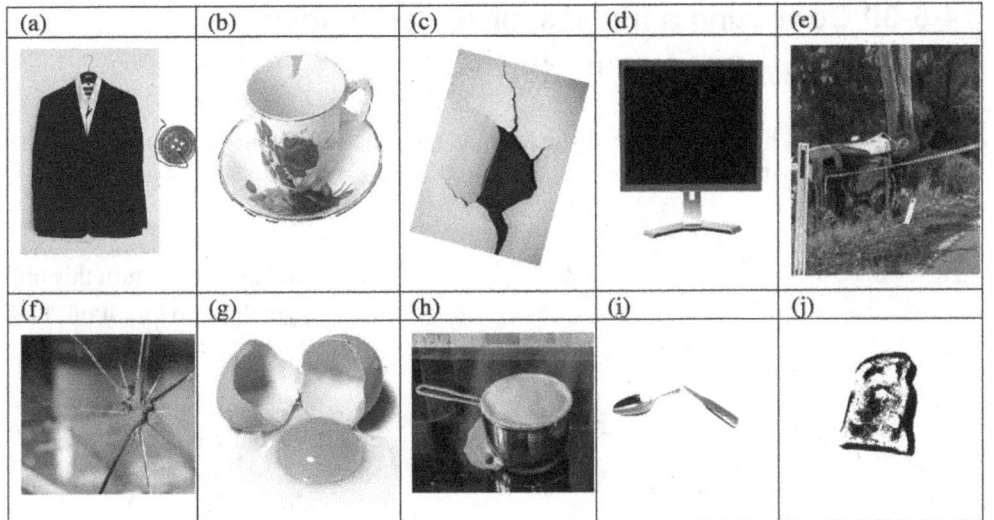

	Taking responsibility	Not taking responsibility
例 1. (c)	○	
例 2. (i)		○
3.		
4.		
5.		
6.		
7.		
8.		
9.		
10.		

14-6 一緒にお好み焼きを作ろう！

14-6-3P Correcting a friend's misunderstanding
思い違いを指摘する (BTS 18, 19)

Your friend, Yuya, has completely misunderstood the situation. Respond by telling him that the opposite of what he said is true.

例 1.
裕也　　消しちゃいけないの？　　　　　　So I'm not allowed to turn this off?
あなた　違う違う。消さなくちゃいけな　　No, no, you have to turn it off, I tell
　　　　いんだって。　　　　　　　　　　you.

例 2.
裕也　　使わなくちゃいけないの？　　　　So I have to use this?
あなた　違う違う。使っちゃいけないん　　No, no, you're not allowed to use
　　　　だって。　　　　　　　　　　　　this, I tell you.

 14-6-4P Reminding a friend about what the teacher said
先生の言葉を思い出させる (BTS 17, 18)

When your friend, Nobuko, wonders if it's okay not to do something, remind her that the teacher told her it needs to be done by tomorrow.

例 1.
信子　　調査、しなくてもいいかな？　　　I wonder if it's okay if I don't do the
　　　　　　　　　　　　　　　　　　　　survey.
あなた　え？明日までにしなくちゃいけな　What? The teacher told you it has to
　　　　いって先生が言ってたじゃない。　be done by tomorrow, right?

例 2.
信子　　デザイン、作らなくてもいいかな？　　I wonder if it's okay if I don't make the design.
あなた　　え？明日までに作らなくちゃいけないって先生が言ってたじゃない。　　What? The teacher told you it has to be made by tomorrow, right?

14-6-5P Suggesting a course of action
すべきか否かを言う (BTS 18)

Your office became the scene of a crime (theft)! When Yamane-kun, a part-timer, states what he is going to do, consider the situation illustrated and either encourage him that it needs to be done, or strongly discourage him from proceeding.

例 1.
山根くん　　集めますよ。　　I'm going to collect them.
あなた　　そうですね。集めなくちゃいけませんね。　　Right. we should collect them, don't we.

例 2.
山根くん　　食べますよ。　　I'm going to eat it.
あなた　　あ、食べちゃダメです。　　Oh, no, you can't eat that.

例 1.	例 2.	3.	4.
Statements from office people	Evidence	Evidence	A witness
5.	6.	7.	8.
Evidence	Evidence		A suspect

14-6 腕試し

Can you recall a time when you broke something? Talk about it with a Japanese friend and see if your friend might disclose a similar experience.

◆ シーン 14-7R 練習

14-7-1R Transitive or intransitive?
対象のある行動？ない行動？

Determine which verb to use in the following sentences.

例1. ドアが(開けます・<u>開きます</u>)。
例2. この料理、お肉をもう少し(<u>入れて</u>・入って)召し上がってください。
3. ドアを (閉めよう・閉まろう) としたら、友だちが来たそうですよ。
4. コンピューターですか？もう全部 (つけて・ついて) ありますよ。
5. (見る・見える) ことは (見る・見える) けど、ちょっと小さいな。
6. 水が (出しません・出ません) よ。困りましたね。
7. 15分待ったから、またプールに (入れよう・入ろう) としたら、雨になっちゃって……。
8. あのイベント、本当は (出よう・出そう) かと思ってたんだけど、仕事が忙しくなっちゃって行かなかったんです。

14-7-2R Resulting state or action? 結果の状況？過程？

Read the following statements and determine whether the underlined verbs represent a resulting state or an action.

例1. 魚ですか？<u>入ってない</u>そうですよ。	☒ Resulting state	☐ Action
例2. 肉ですか？今全部<u>入れている</u>そうですよ。	☐ Resulting state	☒ Action
3. プリント、まだの人は、今<u>出す</u>ようにしてください。	☐ Resulting state	☐ Action
4. クーラーボックス、まだ閉めてないけど、<u>閉めて</u>おきましょうか。	☐ Resulting state	☐ Action
5. あのデパート、まだ開いてるかと思ったら、もう<u>閉まって</u>た。	☐ Resulting state	☐ Action
6. GOサイン、まだ<u>出てない</u>ですから、もう少し待たないとだめですね。	☐ Resulting state	☐ Action
7. 使ってない部屋の電気が<u>ついている</u>とつい気になってしまいますよね。	☐ Resulting state	☐ Action
8. お米料理、まだお出ししてませんでしたね。今<u>お出し</u>しますので、召しあがってください。	☐ Resulting state	☐ Action

14-7-3W Writing down what to buy 買い物リスト

Listen to your voicemail and write down what you need to buy. When specified, write down the requested amount.

例 1.	例 2.	3.
魚(マグロ)	とり肉 200 g	
4.	5.	6.

◆ シーン 14-8R 練習

14-8-1R Transitive or intransitive?
対象のある行動？ない行動？

Determine which verb to use in the following contexts.

例1. みんなが (集める・(集まる))前に練習しておきましょう。

例2. あの店の主人って、魚料理も ((出して)・出て) くれるの？

3. ドアが (閉めない・閉まらない) うちに早くここから出ないと！

4. 9時過ぎになって、リクエストが (集めて・集まって) きました。

5. 店長さんがお店を (開ける・開く) まで外で待ってます。

6. みんなが自分の持ち物を (集めている・集まっている) 間に、帰ってしまったそうです。

7. 今日は練習したあとで、みんなで (集めて・集まって) 飲みにでも行こうよ。

8. お皿を (出よう・出そう) かと思ったら、持ってきてないことに気がついた。

14-8-2R When? いつ？

Determine which form of the verb to use in the following contexts. Try to picture the scene.

例1. 練習((する)・した) 前にウォーミングアップをしておこうよ。

例2. みんなが (集まる・(集まった)) 後で話すそうですよ。

3. プールに (入る・入った) までに気をつけることがあります。

4. (飲み過ぎる・飲み過ぎた) 前に帰らないとやばいですよ。

5. 私が持ち物 (見ている・見ていた) 間に早く行ってきて。

6. お店が (閉まらない・閉まらなかった) うちに買っておきましょう。

7. 主人と (話す・話した) 後で電話するようにします。

8. 自分も前にこのお皿を (買う・買った) ことありますよ。

14-8-3W Adding a time frame タイミングを明らかにする

Add a time frame to the following notes.

例1. While you wait ＿待っている間に＿ 持ち物をチェックしておいてください。

例2. Before you cook ＿料理をする前に＿ お皿とかボールを出しておいてください。

3. While the store is open ＿＿＿＿＿＿＿＿＿＿ 店の主人に会いに来てください。

4. Before we practice today ＿＿＿＿＿＿＿＿＿＿ 先生から話を聞きます。

5. Before it gets past 8:00 ＿＿＿＿＿＿＿＿＿＿ ３１〜３５ページを勉強しておいてください。

6. After everyone is gathered ＿＿＿＿＿＿＿＿＿＿ お店に行くようにしましょう。

◆ シーン 14-9R 練習

14-9-1R Transitive or intransitive?
対象のある行動？ない行動？

Determine whether to use a transitive or an intransitive verb in the following sentences.

例1. みんなが来るまでにメニュー (**決めて**・決まって) おかなくちゃ。

例2. ゲームのセーブデータが (消して・**消えて**) しまいました。

3. この料理、野菜ってどのぐらい (入れる・入る) んだっけ？

4. お茶でも飲んで話しているうちに、いいアイディアが (出して・出て) くるよ。

5. メニューは和食なんだけど、何を作るかがまだ (決めて・決まって) ないんだ。

6. あの部屋、もう使わないかと思ったから電気 (消して・消えて) おいたんですけど……。

7. いいじゃない。ひさしぶりに (集めた・集まった) んだから、ちょっとぐらいお酒飲んだってさ。

8. 部屋を (出よう・出そう) かと思ったら、洋一くんがいてびっくりした。

14-9-2R Should or should not? するべきか否か

Determine whether you should or should not do the activities referred to by the underlined kanji.

例1. ２０才にならないとお酒は飲んじゃいけないんだよ。　☐ Should　☒ Should not
例2. 和食だから、お茶でも出した方がいいですよね？　☒ Should　☐ Should not
3. 野口さん、仕事のことは一人で決めちゃだめだよ。　☐ Should　☐ Should not
4. 部屋を出る前に電気はちゃんと消しておかなくちゃ。　☐ Should　☐ Should not
5. 大人が多く来るから、お酒も出すようにしないとね。　☐ Should　☐ Should not
6. 洋子ちゃんとはもう会わない方がいいのかと思ったよ。　☐ Should　☐ Should not
7. 緑色は少ないからあんまり使ってはいけないんだっけ？　☐ Should　☐ Should not
8. だめだめ！肉だけじゃなくて、野菜もしっかり食べなくちゃ！　☐ Should　☐ Should not

14-9-3W Writing names for a game 名前を書く

Takashi asks you to write down individual names on separate pieces of paper to be used for a game tomorrow.

例 1.	例 2.	3.	4.
洋一くん	緑ちゃん		
5.	6.	7.	8.

◆ Act 14 評価

聞いてみよう

Read the context, listen to the audio, and then answer the questions. If you hear something unfamiliar, rely on what you know to choose the correct answer.

1. Kanda-san and his wife are getting ready for a wedding party for a friend.

    a. How are they sending the present to their friend?
    b. What reasons do they give for doing it this way?
    c. What does Mrs. Kanda still need to do?
    d. When will she do it?
    e. What is Mrs. Kanda having a hard time remembering?

2. The Kandas are tidying up their house together.

    a. What does Mrs. Kanda want to do?
    b. Why does she want to do this?
    c. What type of box is Kanda-san looking for?

3. Kanda-san notices that a new intern looks concerned.

    a. Why is the intern concerned?
    b. What does Kanda-san say the intern should do?
    c. What does the intern normally do?
    d. Why did the intern do something different?

4. Mizuno-san is running late as she leaves home.

    a. Why does Mizuno-san's husband tell her to wait?
    b. What does Mizuno-san's husband decide to do when she refuses? When will he do this?
    c. What question does Mizuno-san ask him?

5. Kanda-san and Sasha are looking at some samples that just arrived.

    a. What does Kanda-san tell Sasha that she finds surprising?
    b. What did Sasha think of the item?
    c. What detail does Kanda-san point out?

6. Ichiro's *senpai*, Takeda-san, just won a race.

    a. How long was the race?
    b. What did Takeda-san think would happen?

    c. How many more races does Takeda-san have this year?
    d. What is she planning on doing between now and the next race?

7. Sasha notices that Kanda-san has a full schedule today.

    a. What does lunch time have to do with Kanda-san's schedule?
    b. How will Kanda-san get back to the office?
    c. When will Kanda-san visit the bank?

8. Kanda-san and Sasha are out to lunch together.

    a. What does Kanda-san ask Sasha to do?
    b. What question does Sasha ask Kanda-san about the flavor?
    c. What does Kanda-san think of the flavor?
    d. What does Sasha suggest Kanda-san do?
    e. Why did Sasha's suggestion work?

9. Sasha is looking at a clothing sample that just came in.

    a. What is Sasha's concern?
    b. How does Kanda-san respond to Sasha's concern?
    c. How does Kanda-san explain what レバーシブル means?

10. Ichiro and his Mother just came home.

    a. What comment do Ichiro and his Mother make when they get home?
    b. What did Ichiro think might happen?
    c. What does Ichiro's mother ask him to do?
    d. What is Ichiro having trouble remembering?
    e. Why does Ichiro's mother tell him to be careful?

11. Mizuno-san's husband just finished making dinner.

    a. What is Mizuno-san going to do?
    b. How does Mizuno-san's husband answer her question?
    c. What comment does Mizuno-san make about the food?
    d. What comment does Mizuno-san's husband make about the food?
    e. What does Mizuno-san suggest they do?

12. Kanda-san is trying to solve the mystery of the missing money for the new intern.

    a. What does Kanda-san ask the intern?
    b. How does she answer his question?
    c. What conclusion does Kanda-san draw from this information?

使ってみよう

For each of the following, listen to the audio, and respond to what was said based on the context. Then listen to the sample response.

1. You are talking to a *kohai* at work about an upcoming meeting. Tell your *kohai* that the time hasn't been decided yet, but you wonder if the meeting will end up happening tomorrow.
2. In response to your friend's question, tell him that you have to (a) go; (b) study; (c) take sociology; (d) turn off the light; (e) read the whole thing by tomorrow.
3. In response to your work *senpai*'s questions, tell her that you heard (a) Tomoda-san's father passed away last week; (b) the Giants won yesterday; (c) Murata-san cleaned the room while the division chief was speaking with the clients; (d) The person fixed the printer before going to China.
4. In response to a friend's question about how to get better at English, tell him that you try to use Japanese as much as possible (to get better at Japanese).
5. A *senpai* is concerned about how busy you are. Reassure him that you *are* busy, but you are still doing your best.
6. You just got out of the bath, and your homestay younger sister seems upset that you took so long. You knew someone was waiting but it felt nice, so you unintentionally . . .
7. A friend wants to look at a picture you're drawing. Tell him you'll show it to him after it's done.
8. A friend has invited you to go see kabuki. You love kabuki.
9. A friend complains about being too tired. Suggest that he try jogging or something.
10. When a friend asks if you remember the name of a certain study abroad student, confirm that it was the student wearing the blue sweater, and make a comment to yourself that shows you're trying to remember the name.
11. Assuming that your friend would surely agree, reassure your friend that (a) he knows a lot of people; (b) he can do it; (c) he's good at it.
12. You are making food with a friend. Tell him that you need (a) carrots, cabbage, and onion; (b) bread, tomato, and oil; (c) egg, flour, and salt.

Now it's your turn to start the conversation based on the given context. Listen to how the other person reacts to you. For some items, you may not get a verbal response. Don't be concerned if you hear things you have not yet learned.

13. Ask a friend to: (a) open the window; (b) turn off the light (and keep it off); (c) heat up the bentos (for later); (d) clean the large room on the second floor.
14. Tell a friend that: (a) this window is open; (b) the light is off; (c) the bentos are heated up; (d) the large room on the second floor is clean.

15. Tell a friend that you were in a hurry, and dropped the plate you had borrowed from Suzuki-san, and thought it was going to break, but it didn't.
16. Ask a work *senpai* what she would do if it were the case that she ended up going to New York on business.
17. Tell a friend that while you were studying at college in the U.S. you didn't have a car so you used the bus everyday.
18. Tell a work *kohai* to finish all of this by the time the bucho gets back from Fukuoka.
19. You are out taking care of some business with a work *senpai*. Comment that you've started to get a bit hungry.
20. Encourage an acquaintance to eat some food that you have served, saying that it should be eaten while it's hot.

読んでみよう

Consider the context provided and read the passage to answer the questions that follow.

1. You just got on the elevator. You see a co-worker in the distance who wants to get on the elevator.

    Which button do you press to hold the door open for that person? _____

    [パフォーマンス] A co-worker from another unit thanks you for holding the door. Ask the person what floor they are going to and press the button for them. Have a follow up short conversation as appropriate.
2. This is an ad from the elevator of a business hotel where you and your colleague are staying on a business trip.

a. Who is running this advertisement?
b. What two claims are made in the ad?
c. What invitation is made? Provide details.

[パフォーマンス] Suggest to the people you are traveling with that you have dinner at the place mentioned in the ad.

3. You saw the following reminder about a cooking class on your social media feed.

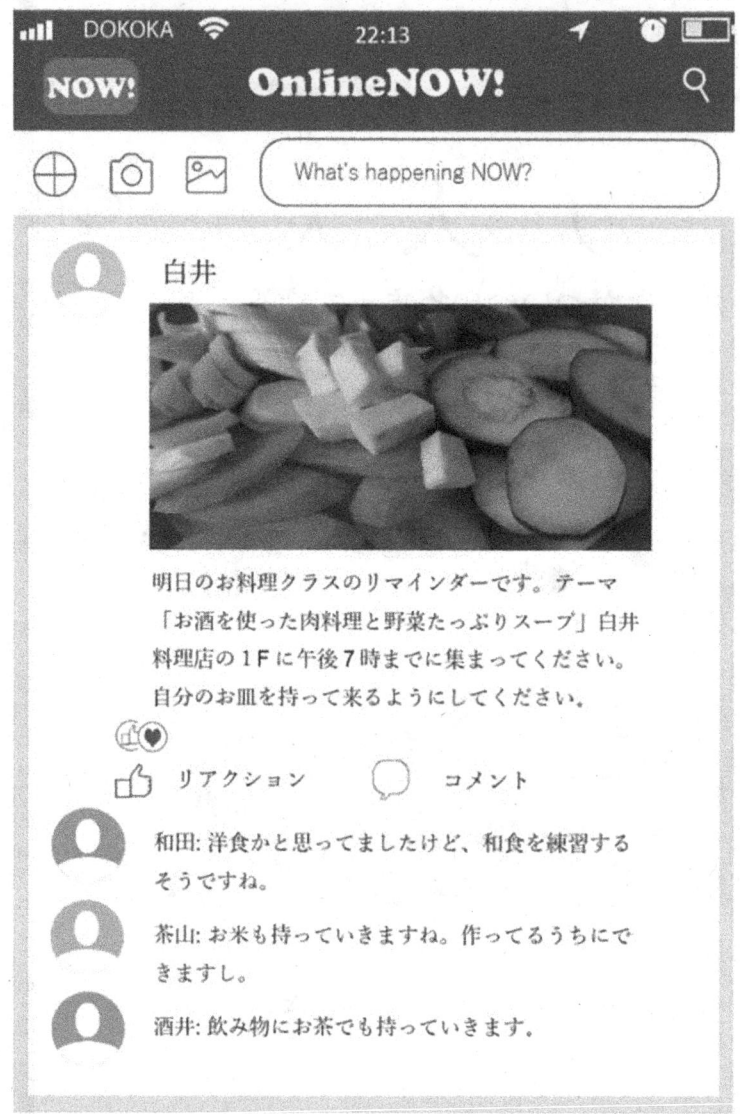

a. What is the cooking lesson theme? Can you guess what たっぷり means?
b. What two instructions are provided?
c. What did Wada-san hear about the event? What was he originally thinking?
d. Who is bringing rice? What reason does she give for doing this?
e. Who is going to bring tea?

[パフォーマンス] You are also participating in the foregoing activity. Add a message. Tell them what you are bringing.

4. Midori and Nana, fellow group members on social media, are talking about tomorrow's cooking class.

a. Is the relationship between Midori and Nana formal or casual? How do you know?
b. What happened to Nana's schedule? How?
c. What is preventing Nana from going?
d. What will Midori do for Nana? In what time frame?
e. What is Nana going to do? When?

[パフォーマンス] You are going to the above event. Call Midori and ask if there is something you can do to help during the cooking class.

書き取り

Listen to the audio, repeat silently what you hear, then write it down. What do you think the context is?

1. _____。
2. _____。
3. _____。
4. _____。
5. _____。
6. _____。
7. _____。
8. _____。

書いてみよう

Consider the context provided and compose a text according to the directions.

1. Create a small poster that reminds people to close the door after they open it.

2. Make a list of things to bring: rice (1 cup), dish, meat (100g per person), vegetables, sake.

3. Write a post on social media about cooking that says, "In college, I have to cook by myself, but as I practice (cooking) I am starting to get better at it (able to cook well)."

知ってる？

Select the most appropriate option and write the letter on your answer sheet.

1. You tell your roommate you haven't decided your major yet.
   専攻はまだ＿＿＿＿＿＿＿＿＿＿いない。(BTS 1)
   a. 決めて
   b. 決まって

2. You're wondering if the bookshelf was already delivered.
   あの本棚、もう＿＿＿＿＿＿＿＿＿でしょうか。(BTS 1)
   a. 届けた
   b. 届いた

3. You ask your assistant to clean up the conference room.
   会議室を＿＿＿＿＿＿＿＿＿＿＿ください。(BTS 1)
   a. 片付けて
   b. 片付いて

4. You notice that the windows are all open.
   ここの窓、みんな＿＿＿＿＿＿＿いますね。(BTS 1)
   a. 開けて
   b. 開いて

5. You trust that all the toys will fit in the box, but you have some doubt.
   このおもちゃ、全部＿＿＿＿＿＿＿が……。(BTS 1, 2)
   a. 入れると思います
   b. 入るかと思います
   c. 入っていないと思います

6. You ask your friend what she would do if, hypothetically speaking, the room hasn't been cleaned up when the guests arrive.
   片付いていない＿＿＿＿＿＿＿＿＿＿＿＿どうするの？(BTS 3)
   a. としたら
   b. だったら
   c. ということにして

7. You've heard that your co-worker Tanaka-san really likes *okonomiyaki*.
   田中さんはお好み焼きが大好き＿＿＿＿＿＿そうです。(BTS 4)

   a. な
   b. だ
   c. Ø

8. You tell your friend that you've heard that the time of the meeting hasn't been decided yet.
   会議の時間はまだ決まっていない＿＿＿＿＿＿＿です。(BTS 4)

   a. こと
   b. よう
   c. そう

9. You know it's true that dining out every night is more convenient, but you think it's better to cook for oneself.
   外食するのは便利＿＿＿＿＿＿は便利だけど、自炊した方がいいと思わない？
   (BTS 5)

   a. こと
   b. なこと
   c. だったこと

10. You tell your friend that as recently as just last week there was a strong earthquake where you live.
    ＿＿＿＿＿＿＿＿＿＿強い地震があったよ。(BTS 6)

    a. つい先週
    b. 先週だけ
    c. ただ先週

11. Since you're trying your best not to eat meat, you turn down an invitation to a barbeque.
    せっかくですが、実はお肉を食べない＿＿＿＿＿＿んです。(BTS 7)

    a. 方がいい
    b. ことにした
    c. ようにしている

12. You tell your assistant to mix it well so that it doesn't brown right away.
    すぐ焼けない＿＿＿＿＿＿によく混ぜてください。(BTS 7)

    a. よう
    b. こと
    c. の

13. Japanese cuisine is _____. (BTS 8)
    a. mostly vegetarian
    b. relatively inexpensive
    c. often seasonal

14. You've been complimented on your Japanese. You explain that you studied Japanese for two years before you came to Japan.
    日本に_____前に、2年ぐらい勉強したんです。 (BTS 9)
    a. 来る
    b. 来た
    c. 来ている

15. You want to cook for yourself as much as possible while you're studying abroad.
    留学_____間は、できるだけ自炊したいんですが……。 (BTS 10)
    a. した
    b. していた
    c. している

16. You've been asked how long you lived in a certain apartment.
    大学を卒業_____まであのアパートに住んでいました。 (BTS 11)
    a. する
    b. した
    c. しちゃった

17. You want to clean the apartment thoroughly by the time your roommate gets home.
    ルームメイトが帰ってくる_____しっかり片付けたいんです。 (BTS 11)
    a. まで
    b. までに

18. You tell your co-worker that you won't know until you consult with Yagi-bucho.
    八木部長と相談する_____分からないんです。 (BTS 11)
    a. まで
    b. までに
    c. 前に

19. You noticed that the pasta started to cool down as soon as you added the sauce.
    ソースを乗せたらすぐ_____きた。 (BTS 12)
    a. 冷まして
    b. 冷やして
    c. 冷えて

20. You suggest that the team decides after everyone has gathered.
    みんなが＿＿＿＿＿＿後で、決めましょう。 (BTS 13)

    a. 集まっていた
    b. 集めた
    c. 集まった

21. You'd like to go to Europe while the airfares are still low.
    安い＿＿＿＿＿＿にヨーロッパへ行きたいと思う。 (BTS 14)

    a. うち
    b. まで
    c. まだ

22. You explained the situation to the client while the division chief wasn't back in the office.
    部長が戻って＿＿＿＿＿＿うちに、お客さんに説明したんです。 (BTS 14)

    a. いらっしゃらなかった
    b. いらっしゃらない
    c. いなかった

23. You are trying to remember the name of the new exchange student.
    新しい留学生の名前は何＿＿＿＿＿＿。 (BTS 15)

    a. かと思った
    b. っけ
    c. だっけ

24. You really thought you were going to lose the game (but you didn't).
    ＿＿＿＿＿＿と思ったけど……。 (BTS 16)

    a. 負けたじゃない
    b. 負けるか
    c. 負けたっけ

25. A sentence followed by じゃない with falling intonation indicates that you ＿＿＿＿＿＿. (BTS 17)

    a. expect the other person to agree
    b. can't remember something
    c. are making a negative assumption

26. You tell your friend that you have to wait about five more minutes before you can leave for home.
    あと５分ぐらい＿＿＿＿＿＿いけないよ。 (BTS 18)

    a. 待たなくても
    b. 待たなくちゃ
    c. 待たないで

27. You're wondering if you have to rewrite the proposal.
    企画書＿＿＿＿＿＿＿＿＿＿でしょうか。(BTS 18)
    a. 書きなさなくてもいい
    b. 書きなおさなくてはいけない
    c. 書きなおしちゃならない

28. Words are sometimes repeated to ＿＿＿＿＿＿. (BTS 19)
    a. emphasize a point
    b. confirm an assumption
    c. seek a response

29. You're wondering about adding something like soy sauce to the dipping sauce you've made.
    お醤油＿＿＿＿＿＿入れようかなあ。(BTS 20)
    a. にも
    b. って
    c. でも

第15幕
Act 15

教(おし)えてもらえますか?
Can I have you explain it to me?

百(ひゃく)聞(ぶん)は一(いっ)見(けん)にしかず。
Seeing is believing.

◆ シーン 15-1 練習

15-1-1C Can you do it? できますか？ (BTS 1)

Listen to each statement and select from the two English options the one that corresponds to what the speaker says.

例 1. __b__   例 2. __a__   3. _____   4. _____   5. _____
6. _____   7. _____   8. _____   9. _____   10. _____
11. _____   12. _____   13. _____   14. _____   15. _____

Ex. 1. a. I don't think I will go tomorrow.
         b. I don't think I can go tomorrow.

Ex. 2. a. I think Suzuki-san will write it cleanly.
         b. I think Suzuki-san can write it cleanly.

3. a. If it's next week, Sato-san won't come, right?
    b. If it's next week, Sato-san can't come, right?

4. a. Murata-san said he wasn't going to swim.
    b. Murata-san said he couldn't swim.

5. a. Is there anyone who won't be riding?
    b. Is there anyone who can't ride?

6. a. If it's that far, I don't think they'll walk.
    b. If it's that far, I don't think they can walk.

7. a. I doubt that we'll make a decision right now.
    b. I doubt that we can make a decision right now.

8. a. How many kanji are you going to write?
    b. How many kanji can you write?

9. a. Yes, I'll be speaking in English.
    b. Yes, I can speak English.

10. a. If you don't study more, you won't graduate.
    b. If you don't study more, you won't be able to graduate.

11. a. She said she definitely wouldn't forget.
    b. She said she definitely wouldn't be able to forget.

12. a. If it's that long, I will read it.
    b. If it's that long, I can read it.

13. a. He said he wouldn't attend the next meeting.
    b. He said he can't attend the next meeting.

14. a. Yes, I think I'll be back by next week.
    b. Yes, I think I can be back by next week.

15. a. I am going to use everything in this room.
    b. I can use everything in this room.

15-1-2P Reassuring Nozaki-san that it'll work out!
大丈夫と力づける (BTS 1)

Reassure your associate Nozaki-san that she can do what she wants to do.

例 1.
| 野崎さん | できたら2時までに帰りたいんだけど、難しいかな。 | If possible, I'd like to return by two o'clock, but is it difficult, would you suppose? |
| あなた | 大丈夫ですよ。帰れますよ、きっと。 | It'll work out. You'll be able to return by then, I'm sure. |

例 2.
| 野崎さん | 必要だから買いたいんだけど、やっぱり無理ですかね。 | It's necessary, so I want to buy it, but I wonder if it's impossible after all. |
| あなた | 大丈夫ですよ。買えますよ、きっと。 | It'll work out. You'll be able to buy it, I'm sure. |

15-1-3P Asking if Asano-san can do it?
できるかどうか確認する (BTS 1)

You are working together with a colleague, Asano-san, on a project. Ask her if she can do the things illustrated below. Then listen to her response.

例 1.
| あなた | 割れますか？ | Can you break it? |
| 浅野さん | はい。細くですか？ | Yes. Into thin slices? |

例 2.
| あなた | 混ぜられますか？ | Can you mix it? |
| 浅野さん | 了解です。どのぐらいですか？ | Got it. How much? |

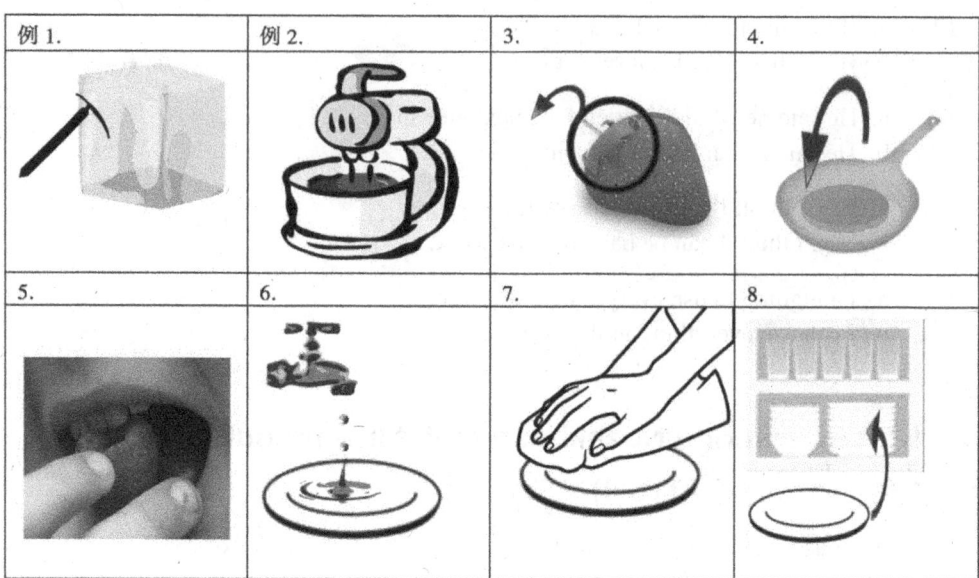

15-1 腕試し

Go through some procedures with a Japanese associate, checking to ensure that either you or your associate can do each step.

◆ シーン 15-2 練習

15-2-1P Talking about a weekend trip
旅行の予定について話す (BTS 2)

Today is Friday. When a colleague asks about a weekend trip you are planning, answer his questions based on the plan you have written for yourself.

例 1.

| 村田さん | 週末はどこか行くんですか。 | Are you going somewhere over the weekend? |
| あなた | 草津に行くつもりです。 | I'm planning on going to Kusatsu. |

例 2.

| 村田さん | へえ。明日行くんですか。 | Wow. Are you going tomorrow? |
| あなた | そのつもりです。 | That's the plan. |

Saturday (tomorrow):

To Kusatsu (Stay at Ryokan Yamamura)

8:18 train (Arr. 12:23)

Relax in onsen

Sunday:

Hiking (8:30–11:30)

Lunch at Soba "Kihachi" in Kusatsu

Lv. 13:04 train (Arr. 16:13)

15-2-2P Compass directions 方向を正す

An acquaintance is considering moving to a town that you're familiar with and is interested in where things are located generally. Answer his questions based on the illustration provided.

例 1.

| 石川さん | 病院は南の方ですか。 | Is the hospital on the south side? |
| あなた | いえ、北の方ですけど……。 | No, it's on the north side. |

例2.

| 石川さん | 図書館は西の方ですか。 | Is the library on the west side? |
| あなた | はい、そうですね。 | Yes, that's right. |

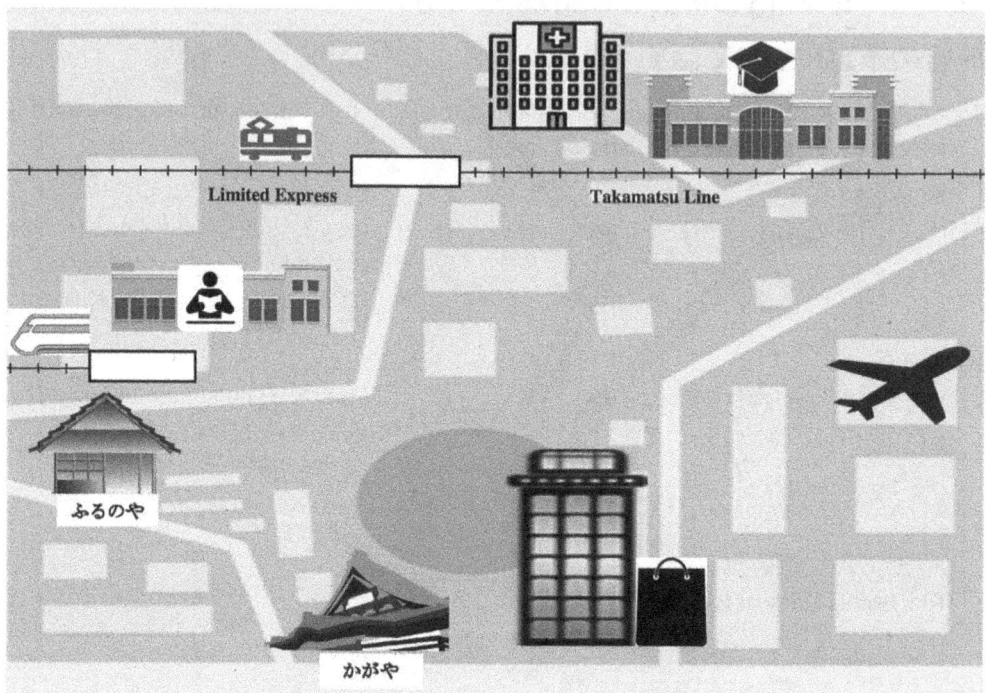

15-2 腕試し

Find out what your Japanese associates/friends are planning to do for their next vacation. Get some details without making your conversation sound like an interrogation. Providing reactions to the information offered is a good conversational strategy to that end.

◆ シーン 15-3 練習

15-3-1C Hearsay or not? 伝言か否か (BTS 5)

Listen to the conversation. If one of the speakers is reporting information they heard from someone else, mark "hearsay"; if not, mark "not hearsay."

	Hearsay	Not hearsay
例 1.	○	
例 2.		○
3.		
4.		
5.		
6.		
7.		
8.		
9.		
10.		
11.		
12.		
13.		
14.		

15-3-2P Confirming an arrival time 到着(とうちゃく)時間を確認(かくにん)する (BTS 5, 6)

You and your work colleague Yoshida-san are studying a train schedule between Omiya and Jujo. When Yoshida-san suggests taking a particular train by its departure time, indicate what that means in terms of the arrival time.

例１．
吉田さん　　７時４１分発に乗ったら？

あなた　　　特急ですね。７時４１分発ということは、十条着は８時３分ですね。

What if I took the one departing at 7:41?

That's a limited express. 7:41 departure means arrival in Jujo at 8:03, doesn't it.

例２．
吉田さん　　１３時２５分発に乗ったら？

あなた　　　普通ですね。１３時２５分発ということは、十条着は１４時３０分ですね。

What if I took the one departing at 13:25?

That's a local. 13:25 departure means arrival in Jujo at 14:30, doesn't it.

Departs: Omiya	Arrives: Jujo	Departs: Omiya	Arrives: Jujo
7:15 (Local)	8:20	11:17 (Local)	12:22
7:41 (Limited Express)	8:03	11:38 (Limited Express)	12:00
7:57 (Local)	9:02	11:56 (Local)	13:01
8:23 (Local)	9:28	12:18 (Local)	13:23
8:50 (Limited Express)	9:12	12:41 (Limited Express)	13:03
9:02 (Local)	10:07	13:00 (Local)	14:05
9:27 (Local)	10:32	13:25 (Local)	14:30
9:48 (Limited Express)	10:10	13:47 (Limited Express)	14:09
9:59 (Local)	11:04	13:53 (Local)	14:58
10:26 (Local)	11:31	14:02 (Local)	15:07
10:44 (Limited Express)	11:06	14:27 (Limited Express)	14:49
10:52 (Local)	11:57	14:54 (Local)	15:59

15-3-3P Reporting a train issue 延着（えんちゃく）の伝言（でんごん）を伝（つた）える (BTS 5, 6)[1]

Yoshida-san, a work colleague, is coming from Omiya to Jujo by train, but she left a voice message to tell you about an issue she was having with the train she was planning to take. Listen to the message and relay the pertinent information to your supervisor, using the train schedule in the previous practice as a reference.

例1.

吉田さん	すみません！１４時２７分の特急に乗るつもりだったんですが、乗れなかったので、１４時５４分発の普通で行きます。よろしくお願いします。	Sorry! I was planning to take the 14:27 special express, but I couldn't, so I'm going by the local that leaves at 14:54. I appreciate your handling things there.
あなた (上司へ)	乗る予定だった特急に乗れなかったので、着くのは１６時ちょっと前とのことです。	She says that she couldn't get on the special express that she planned to, so she'll arrive a little before 16:00.

例2.

吉田さん	すみません！７時４１分の特急に乗るつもりだったんですが、乗れなかったので、７時５７分発の普通で行きます。よろしくお願いします。	Sorry! I was going to take the 7:41 special express but I couldn't, so I'm taking the local that leaves at 7:57. I appreciate your handling things there.
あなた (上司へ)	乗る予定だった特急に乗れなかったので、着くのは９時すぎとのことです。	She says that she couldn't get on the special express that she planned to, so she'll arrive after nine o'clock.

15-3 腕試し

1. If you live in a city where there are some metro or train lines, discuss with your Japanese associates and friends which line certain stations service.
2. Discuss with your Japanese associates/friends about their upcoming air travel. Find out what time the flight they are planning to take leaves and their scheduled arrival time at their destination.
3. Find out if your Japanese associates/friends have had the experience of a long delay when traveling by train, bus, or plane. Try to get some details of their experience. Remember to give appropriate *aizuchi* as you listen.

---

1. Ambient noises courtesy of OtoLogic (otologic.jp).

◆ シーン 15-4 練習

 15-4-1C Follow the procedures 指示に従う (BTS 7, 8)

For this activity, you need to be sitting in front of a device with word-processing capability. You are working with an online tutor to practice writing and editing a Japanese document. Follow the instructions you hear.

　　例１：来月の会は「銀屋」でします。来れるか来れないか、決まりましたか。それをベンさんにテキストしてください。銀屋は魚がおいしい店です。ご家族も友だちもどうぞごいっしょに。

 15-4-2P Adding deadlines to a request
締め切り情報を加えて依頼する (BTS 7)

Your *kohai*, Erika, offers to do a task. Confirm the request, adding the specific time frame indicated in the illustrations.

例 1.
恵里香　集まる店、選んでおきますから。　　　　I'll select the place (restaurant) to get together.
あなた　あ、どうも。悪いけど、８日ま　　　　　Oh thanks. Sorry, but could you select it by
　　　　でに選んどいてもらえます？　　　　　　the 8th (so that we'll be ready)?

例 2.
恵里香　集まる人、登録しておきます　　　　　　I'll register in advance the people who'll
　　　　から。　　　　　　　　　　　　　　　　be gathering.
あなた　あ、どうも。悪いけど、１４日　　　　　Oh thanks. Sorry, but could you register them
　　　　までに登録しといてもらえます？　　　　by the 14th (so that we'll be ready)?

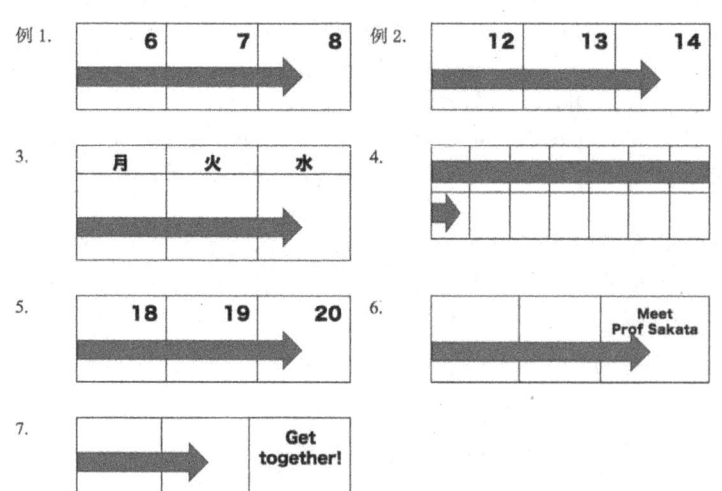

15-4-3P Making a request 依頼(いらい)する (BTS 7)

Your *senpai,* Okuda-san, has offered to help you on a project. Request that she do the things illustrated below. Listen to how Okuda-san responds.

例1.
| あなた | 搭乗口で待っていていただけますか？ | Could you please be waiting at the boarding area? |
| 奥田さん | いいですよ。何時発の便ですか？ | Sure. What time is the departure for this flight? |

例2.
| あなた | バス停に来ていただけますか？ | Could you please come to the bus station? |
| 奥田さん | いいですよ。えっと、駅の南口の方のバス停ですよね？ | Sure. Um, it's the bus station on the south exit side of the station, right? |

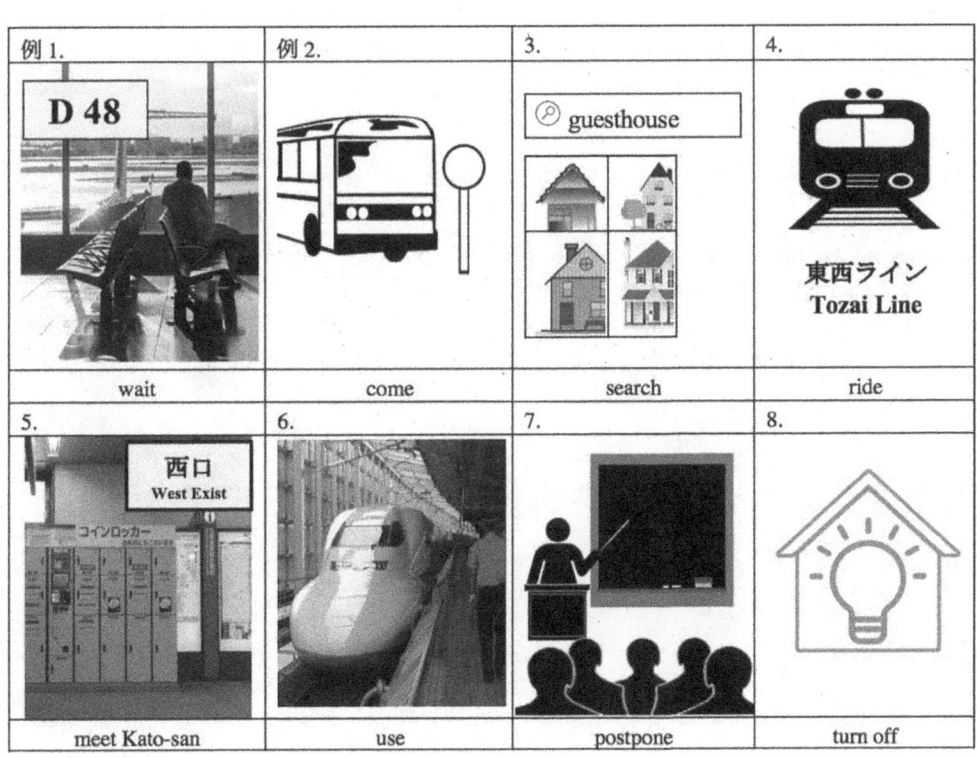

15-4-4P Being modest about your abilities 謙遜(けんそん)する (BTS 1, 9)

Your supervisor Mitani-san is impressed by what she witnessed of your performance. Reply that you've become able to do it finally, but that there is still room for improvement.

例1.
三谷さん	お客さんと日本語で話しているの、聞きましたよ。すばらしいですね。	I heard you speaking Japanese with a client. It's wonderful!
あなた	いえいえ、やっと少し話せるようになりましたけど、まだまだです。	No, no. I've somehow reached the point where I can speak a little, but it's hardly enough.

例2.
三谷さん	新しいコンピュータ使っているの、見ましたよ。すばらしいですね。	I saw you using the new computer. It's wonderful!
あなた	いえいえ、やっと少し使えるようになりましたけど、まだまだです。	No, no. I've somehow reached the point where I can use it a little, but it's hardly enough.

15-4 腕試し

1. Ask your Japanese associate/friend to perform some tasks for you. If a task has several steps, be sure to use appropriate transitional words.
2. Be complementary to *kohai* associates and friends by noting how they have become able to do something that they have been putting their effort into doing.

◆ シーン 15-5 練習

15-5-1C Intention or assumption? 意図？思い込み？
(BTS 2, 11)

Listen to the audio and mark whether the sentence preceding つもり refers to (a) the speaker's own plan, or (b) what the speaker assumed about someone or something.

	Intention	Assumption
例 1.		○
例 2.	○	
3.		
4.		
5.		
6.		
7.		
8.		
9.		
10.		

15-5-2P Describing a fictitious situation
仮定に基づいて話してもらう (BTS 2)

You are leading a role play practice as part of a training for new employees. When a trainee asks about a particular element of the role-play context, confirm that she should assume that to be the case.

例 1.

| 吉田さん | ここ、会議室なんですね。 | So, it's the conference room, here, right? |
| あなた | そう。ここが会議室のつもりで話してください。 | Right. Assume that it's the conference room here and speak. |

例 2.

| 吉田さん | リストに野崎さんの名前が書いてあるんですね。 | Nozaki-san's name is on the list of people that are coming, right? |
| あなた | そう。リストに野崎さんの名前が書いてあるつもりで話してください。 | Right. Assume that Nozaki-san's name is written there and speak. |

15-5-3P Dealing with a gap in preparation
しそびれたことをすぐする (BTS 11)

Your *kohai* is concerned about the chaotic state of preparation for an upcoming event. For each thing that he says hasn't been done yet, tell him that you thought you'd done it already, then reassure him that you'll get it done.

例 1.

| 友田さん | まだ片付いてないんですけど……、例の問題。 | It's not resolved yet . . . the issue you know about. |
| あなた | へ？本当に？もう片付けたつもりだったけど。大丈夫。すぐやるから。 | What? Really? I thought I'd resolved it. Don't worry. I'll do it right away. |

例2.

| 友田さん | まだ開いてないですけど……、会場の鍵。 | It's not open yet . . . the lock to the event hall. |
| あなた | へ？本当に？もう開けたつもりだったけど。大丈夫。すぐやるから。 | What? Really? I thought I'd opened it. Don't worry. I'll do it right away. |

15-5 腕試し

Tell a friend about an experience you had where things didn't go as planned.

◆ シーン 15-6 練習

15-6-1P Making a suggestion with *enryo*
遠慮がちに意見を述べる (BTS 12)

You are with a group of co-workers, considering restaurants to go out to eat at. When you express your opinion that one of the restaurants looks good, add a follow-up comment that shows 遠慮, based on the illustration. Then listen to how one of your co-workers responds.

例 1.
あなた	ここ、美味しそうですけど、座れないですかね。	Here, it looks good, but perhaps we can't be seated, do you suppose?
吉田さん	ん……。そうですね……。ちょっと狭すぎるかもしれませんね。	Hmm. . . . Yeah. . . . It's maybe a little too small, isn't it.

例 2.
あなた	ここ、美味しそうですけど、歩いて行けないですかね。	Here, it looks good, but perhaps we can't walk to it, do you suppose?
八木部長	あ、それは大丈夫。田中さんが車持ってるから。	Oh, that's fine. Tanaka-san has a car.

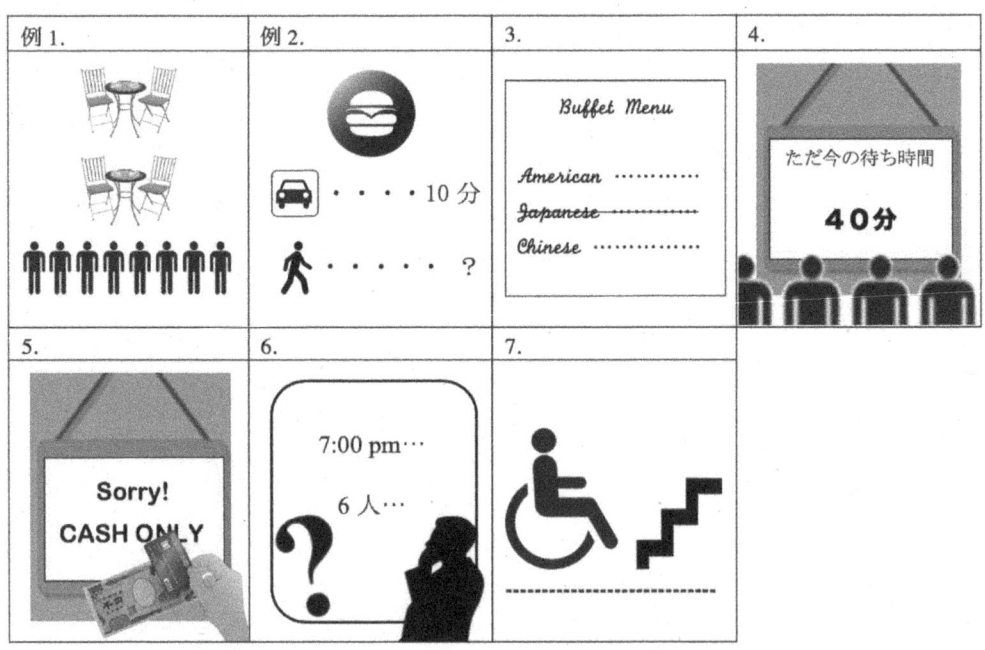

15-6-2P Being prepared for mishaps 予定の変更に備える (BTS 12)

Accept an invitation from a friend, adding that you'll contact him if your situation changes.

例1.
裕也　　土曜日、どこか食べに行かない？　　How about going somewhere to eat on Saturday?

あなた　いいね。行こう、行こう。もし行けなくなったら早めに連絡するようにするから。　　Great! Let's go! I'll be sure to contact you if I end up not being able to go (then).

例2.
裕也　　週末、２階のラウンジでお好み焼き作らない？　　How about making *okonomiyaki* in the second-floor lounge this weekend?

あなた　いいね。作ろう、作ろう。もし作れなくなったら早めに連絡するようにするから。　　Great! Let's make it! I'll be sure to contact you if we end up not being able to make it (there).

15-6 腕試し

Go do something with a group of friends. When deciding what to do, be careful to use 遠慮 when making suggestions or sharing your opinion.

◆ シーン 15-7R 練習

15-7-1R Potential or honorific passive? 可能？尊敬の受け身？

How are the underlined verbs to be interpreted? Can they be interpreted either way?

例1.	お酒は<u>飲めます</u>か？	☒ potential ☐ honorific passive ☐ either
例2.	社長さんもそう<u>言われた</u>そうですよ。	☐ potential ☒ honorific passive ☐ either
例3.	明日は<u>来られます</u>か？	☐ potential ☐ honorific passive ☒ either
4.	その時間でも電車に<u>乗れる</u>んですか？	☐ potential ☐ honorific passive ☐ either
5.	先生がいらっしゃるまで少し<u>練習でき</u>ますか。	☐ potential ☐ honorific passive ☐ either
6.	ドア、少し開いてますけど、<u>閉められ</u>ますか？	☐ potential ☐ honorific passive ☐ either
7.	ご主人は今週は出張で名古屋まで<u>行か</u>れているそうです。	☐ potential ☐ honorific passive ☐ either
8.	消すことは消したんですけど、全部は<u>消せません</u>でした。	☐ potential ☐ honorific passive ☐ either
9.	来年のイベントの場所、いつまでに<u>決められます</u>か？	☐ potential ☐ honorific passive ☐ either
10.	このスーツ、部長は<u>着られない</u>と思いますよ。	☐ potential ☐ honorific passive ☐ either
11.	図書館でもう少し<u>待たれた</u>方がいいと思いますけど……。	☐ potential ☐ honorific passive ☐ either
12.	旅館を出る前に持ち物はチェック<u>され</u>ましたか？	☐ potential ☐ honorific passive ☐ either

15-7-2R Potential or intransitive? 可能系？自動詞？

Read the following statements by paying special attention to the underlined verbs and determine whether it is the speaker or another entity that is assumed to be at fault.

例1.	全部入れるつもりでしたが、<u>入りません</u>でした。	☐ speaker ☒ another entity
例2.	図書室のドアが<u>閉められなくて</u>困っているんです。	☒ speaker ☐ another entity
3.	本当は全部決めるつもりだったのですが、場所がなかなか<u>決まらなかった</u>とのことです。	☐ speaker ☐ another entity
4.	ごめんね。言われた通りに人が<u>集められなくて</u>……。	☐ speaker ☐ another entity
5.	みんなが来る前に開けておくつもりだったんだけど、<u>開かなかった</u>んだ。	☐ speaker ☐ another entity

6. 出しておくつもりだったんだけど、一人じゃ<u>出せ</u> ☐ speaker ☐ another entity
   <u>なくて</u>……。
7. あのフォルダー、消そうかと思って消してみたん ☐ speaker ☐ another entity
   だけど、<u>消えなかった</u>の。
8. 出張のスケジュール、時間がなくてまだあんまり ☐ speaker ☐ another entity
   <u>見れてない</u>とのことです。

15-7-3W Filling out a schedule 予定表（よていひょう）に書き込む（かきこむ）

Add the following memos to the schedule in Japanese.

例1. (Mon) Departing Office at 9:00, arriving at the bank at 9:30
例2. (Tue) Event location (~~Shirai Restaurant~~ → Aoki Restaurant)
3. (Wed) Director Sakai at 3 o'clock
4. (Thu) Business Trip (Departing Tokyo at 8, arriving Nagoya at 10 o'clock)
5. (Fri) Practice Location (~~302~~ → 201)
6. (Sat) Study Group (Library at 4 o'clock)
7. (Sun) Travel (Bus boarding area at 10 o'clock)

9/30	月	例1. 会社9時発、銀行9時半着
10/1	火	例2. イベントの場所 (白井料理店 → 青木料理店)
10/2	水	
10/3	木	
10/4	金	
10/5	土	
10/6	日	

◆ **シーン 15-8R 練習**

15-8-1RW Organizing explanations 手順(てじゅん)を示(しめ)す

Put the following explanations in the appropriate order.

例 1.
- ベーコンを半分にします
- 電子レンジで３分、チンするだけだから、だれにでもできますよ
- 半分にしたベーコンにアスパラガスを乗せて

まず、ベーコンを半分にします。
次に、半分にしたベーコンにアスパラガスを乗せて
最後(さいご)に、電子レンジで３分、チンするだけだから、だれにでもできますよ。

例 2.
- プレゼンを書くようにしてみたら、書きやすいと思いますよ。
- 自分の好きなトピックを決めなくてはいいプレゼンができません。
- 決めたトピックについて色々とアウトラインを書いて

最初(さいしょ)に、自分の好きなトピックを決めなくてはいいプレゼンができません。
それから、決めたトピックについて色々とアウトラインを書いて
次に、プレゼンを書くようにしてみたら、書きやすいと思いますよ。

3.
- その上にチーズと好きな野菜を乗せて
- トースター（２００°C）に入れて１０分〜１２分待ったらできるよ。
- パンの上にケチャップをつけて

最初(さいしょ)に、_____
で、_____
最後(さいご)に、_____

4.
- 空港に着いてからチェックインしなくちゃいけません。
- セキュリティーチェックです。
- ゲートに行って、フライトに乗りますので、パスポートは出しやすいところに持っていた方がいいですよ。

まず、_____
次に、_____
それから、_____

5.
- 作る料理が決まったら買い物かな、私だったら。
- どちらかに決まったら、好きなレシピの本を見て、自分が作れる料理を見つける。
- 和食にするか洋食にするか決める。

最初（さいしょ）に、_____
次に、_____
で、_____

6.
- みんなで集まって不便なことをリストアップしていきます。
- どうやったら「不便」なことを「便利」にできるかアイディアを出していきます。
- どうして不便なのかをブレーンストーミングして。

まず、_____
それから、_____
で、_____

15-8-2R する？なる？

Read the following statements and determine whether the change is intentional (する) or not intentional (なる).

例1. 宅急便で送れなくなったので、不便に(し・<u>なり</u>)ました。
例2. 遅れて不便だから、アメリカではバスはあまり使わないように(<u>して</u>・なって)います。

3. スマホのアプリを使って勉強するように (して・なって) いたら、本を使って勉強しなくなりました。
4. オンラインで買い物をするようになってから、キャッシュを使わなく (し・なり) ました。
5. 飲み過ぎるとよくないから、お酒はあまり飲まないように(して・なって)います。
6. 空港まで電車で行けるように (して・なって)、便利になりました。
7. リモコンが使えなくなったから、だれもテレビを見なく (し・なり) ました。
8. だれにでも分かっちゃうから、もう少し分かりにくいパスワードに (しよう・なろう) と思っています。
9. 日本語だけで話すようにしていたら、日本語だけで話せるように(し・なり)ました。
10. コンビニで宅急便のサービスが使えるように (した・なった) こと、知ってますか？

15-8-3W Convenient? Inconvenient? 便利か不便か

Write down the opinion and justifications regarding the following topics in Japanese.

例 1.	You think the college library is convenient because you can read a variety of books.	大学の図書館は色々な本が読めるから便利だと思います。
例 2.	You think the bus you ride is inconvenient because it is often late.	私が乗るバスはよく遅れるから不便だと思います。
3.	You think the airport that you often use is inconvenient because it is hard to find the gate locations.	
4.	You think the shop where you do your shopping is convenient because you can buy things inexpensively that can be eaten right away.	
5.	You think the delivery service you use is convenient because you can have them deliver (things) to your home on the day after you place the order.	

◆ シーン 15-9R 練習

15-9-1R Intention or mistaken assumption?
意図？思い違い？

Read the following and determine whether the writer is expressing an intention or a mistaken assumption.

例1. おいしい料理を (作る・<u>作った</u>) つもりでしたけど、だれも食べてくれませんでした。

例2. 社員旅行に (<u>行く</u>・行った) つもりだったけど、出張に行かなくてはいけなくなった。

3. 西田君、お客様とはいつ (会う・会った) つもりなの？明日までに来月のスケジュールを全部決めなくちゃいけないんだけど。

4. ちょっと失礼なんじゃない？「おはよう」って言っただけで (話す・話した) つもりなの？

5. お父さんとは (会わない・会わなかった) つもりなの？せっかく近くまで来たんだから、会った方がいいって。

6. 失礼しました。メールを昨日 (送る・送った) つもりだったのですが、送れていなかったことにさっき気がつきました。

7. 3時発の電車に (乗る・乗った) つもりなんだけど、5時までに着くかなあ？やっぱり3時発じゃ遅過ぎると思う？

8. 南口で (待つ・待った) つもりでしたが、人が多過ぎるので、北口で待つことにしました。

15-9-2R Whose opinion matters? 誰の意見？

Whose option fits better with the following statements and questions?

例1. わざわざ名古屋から来てくださっているのだから (社員・<u>お客さん</u>) に決めてもらいましょう。

例2. まだ大人じゃないし、やっぱり (<u>学生</u>・先生) だけじゃ決められないと思うんですけど……。

3. お金のことは (会社員・部長) に決めていただいた方がいいんじゃないですか？

4. (店員さん・お客さん)に聞かなくちゃ、トイレのドアを開けてもらえない所もあるそうですよ。

5. 北田君、プロジェクトをやるかどうかはやっぱり (上・下) が決めるんだよね？

6. 忙しくて話を聞く時間があまりないかもしれないけど、やっぱり (社長・社員) と話をしてからじゃないと失礼になりますよ。
7. 小さなお子様がたくさん来るイベントなんだから、まずは (子ども・部長) がしたいことを聞いてみた方がいいと思いませんか？
8. ウェディングセレモニーだけど、(家族・お客さん)だけでもいいんじゃない？人がたくさん来ると色々とあるからね〜。
9. 近いうちに家族で旅行に行きたいと思ってるんだけど、会社を２、３日休まなくちゃいけなくなるから、まず (部長・父) に話をしてみます。
10. よくお店で思うんだけど、(客・店員) としてお礼って言った方がいいと思う？

15-9-3W Filling out a schedule 予定表に書き込む

Add the following memos to the schedule in Japanese.

例1. (Mon) Kitada-san appointment (4:30)
例2. (Tue) Buy a gift of gratitude for clients
3. (Wed) Send the gift of gratitude (to clients) (from a nearby convenience store)
4. (Thu) Practice with Shirai-kun (7:00)
5. (Fri) Nishida-san appointment (9:30)
6. (Sat) Company Trip (Tokyo Station South Gate, 8 a.m.)
7. (Sun) Company Trip

4/7	月	例1. 北田さんアポ(４時半)
4/8	火	例2. お客様にお礼を買う
4/9	水	
4/10	木	
4/11	金	
4/12	土	
4/13	日	

◆ Act 15 評価

 聞いてみよう

Read the context, listen to the audio, and then answer the questions. If you hear something unfamiliar, rely on what you know to choose the correct answer.

1. Amy is working with another club member, packing some materials for an upcoming school event.

    a. What does Amy want the club member to do?
    b. Why does Amy want him to do this?
    c. What does Amy think he should use?

2. Kanda-san's co-worker appears to be unhappy about the way a document has been prepared.

    a. What does Kanda-san's co-worker claim she can't do?
    b. What does Kanda-san's co-worker want him to do to address the issue?

3. Kanda-san is about to finish his monthly meeting with a client and needs to set up a time for the next meeting.

    a. What is Kanda-san's initial question?
    b. Which day is preferable for the client?
    c. What time will the next meeting be?

4. The company outing is about to be over, and Yagi-bucho approaches Kanda-san.

    a. What does Yagi-bucho ask Kanda-san?
    b. What was Kanda-san able to do?
    c. What was difficult?
    d. What does Yagi-bucho think was good?

5. Sasha and Kanda-san are on their way to a meeting. Kanda-san just received a text message from Yagi-bucho, who is already there.

    a. What did Yagi-bucho's message say?
    b. What does Sasha suggest they do?
    c. What does Kanda-san notice?

6. Kanda-san is at home and is trying to turn on the TV. His wife notices that the TV isn't turning on.

    a. What does Kanda-san's wife tell him?
    b. What does Kanda-san's wife intend to do?

c. What does Kanda-san offer to do?
d. What does Kanda-san's wife think of this offer?

7. Mizuno-san is taking a client to the airport so he can go home, but the road is congested.

   a. What seems to be the reason for the congestion?
   b. Why is 20:20 mentioned?
   c. Why is 18:00 mentioned?
   d. What is Mizuno-san's suggestion?
   e. How does the client respond to this suggestion?
   f. What does the client say regarding today?

8. A new intern forgot to do something and Mizuno-san is not happy.

   a. Why does the intern mention the morning?
   b. How does Mizuno-san respond to this comment?
   c. What does the intern say he did so that he wouldn't forget?
   d. What does Mizuno-san think actually happened?
   e. What actually happened, according to the intern?
   f. What does the intern say he will do?

9. Yagi-bucho and Kanda-san are talking over lunch.

   a. What does Yagi-bucho want to know?
   b. What did Sasha do that benefitted the company?
   c. What other comment does Kanda-san make about Sasha?
   d. What does Yagi-bucho suggest they do?
   e. What does Kanda-san say he will do?

10. Takashi notices that one of the members of the club has a nice-looking notebook.

    a. What positive qualities are mentioned about the notebook?
    b. What kinds of things does the club member use the notebook for?
    c. Why is Takashi surprised?
    d. What does the club member also have on her phone?
    e. Why does the club member use a notebook?
    f. What is the club member unable to stop doing?

使ってみよう

For each of the following, listen to the audio, and respond to what was said based on the context. Then listen to the sample response.

1. Tell a friend that you were intending to buy a new suitcase, but it's expensive (among other things).

2. Tell a work *senpai* that you intend to take the rapid train that leaves at 15:43.
3. You are looking at an email with information regarding who will be coming tomorrow. Tell a work *senpai* that Ikegami-san and Nozaki-san (both company clients) are coming.
4. Tell a friend that you thought you had made the deadline.
5. Tell a work *kohai* you don't care who starts.
6. Respond to compliments with some humor: (a) first tell a fellow presenter that this kind of thing is simple, then add that that's what you wish you could say; (b) agree with your teacher that it was good, then add that it's because the teacher is fabulous; (c) tell your tutor that it'd be regrettable if you couldn't do it since you practiced it so much; (d) question your friend's use of the word "unexpectedly" by asking what his intention is; (e) indicate to a project team member that it'd be a disaster if you didn't make it in time; (f) underscore what the interviewer says and state that it's hard to make it appear as if it were simple.

Now it's your turn to start the conversation based on the given context. Listen to how the other person reacts to you. For some items, you may not get a verbal response. Don't be concerned if you hear things you have not yet learned.

7. Ask a *senpai* if he is able to (a) go; (b) speak English; (c) come at around 7 p.m.; (d) see the person over there; (e) clean this room in less than 1 hour.
8. Ask Tomoda-san, a work *kohai*, to (a) stay in the office; (b) delete what's left; (c) look up Nakatani-san's phone number; (d) save that file on his computer as well.
9. Explain to a friend how to order a meal at the cafeteria by explaining that you (a) first, choose what you want to eat from the menu; (b) then put the money in here; (c) next, press the button of the thing you chose; (d) then take the ticket from here; (e) lastly show the ticket to the person at the window over there and they will make it for you.
10. Tell a friend that you want to (a) get to the point where you can run a marathon; (b) speak Japanese better; (c) be able to read over 500 kanji; (d) be able to write even complicated kanji.
11. Tell a friend that you've gotten to the point where you (a) cook *okonomiyaki* every week; (b) don't study at the library anymore; (c) take a nap almost every day; (d) don't stay up all night anymore.

読んでみよう

Consider the context provided and read the passage to answer the questions that follow.

1. Kanda-san received a wrapped gift box with the following note attached.

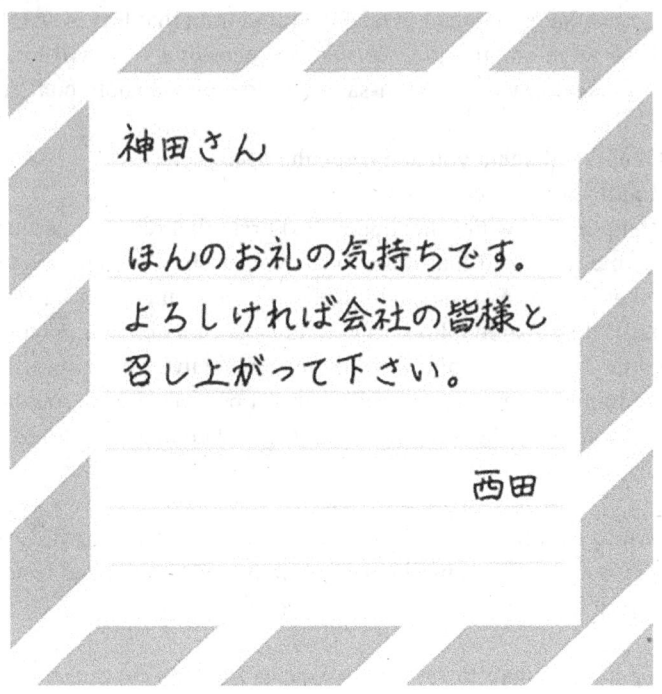

a. Who is the gift from?
b. What kind of gift is inside? What does the writer tell Kanda-san to do?
c. Can you guess what ほんの means?

[パフォーマンス] Assume the role of Kanda-san and call and thank Nishida-san for the gift.

2. Kitada-san, one of the secretaries at Ogaki Trading, sent the following email to Kanda-san.

件名：Re: 旅館の場所
神田さん 出張の旅館の場所ですけど、こちらになります。 www.mapnow.com/search/2-10-5+fuji,+takamatsu/ 近くに図書館があるので分かりやすいかと思います。 電車は午後4時発の電車に乗るつもりとのことでしたが、その電車だと9時過ぎ着となってしまいます。1時間早いですが、午後3時発のに乗れますか？ 北田

a. What does the map indicate? What factor makes it easy to understand?
b. What was Kanda's original schedule? What problem is associated with the original schedule?
c. What alternative suggestion is provided? Can you guess why Kanda-san used 乗れますか rather than 乗られますか?

[パフォーマンス] Assume the role of Kanda-san and call Kitada-san and confirm the schedule.

3. Kanda-san asks Kitada-san a favor via email.

> 件名: 西田さん
>
> 北田君
>
> いつもお世話になっています。
>
> 一つお願いしたいことがあるのですが、お客様の西田さんとの次のアポを８月１８日(火)ではなく、８月１７日(月)にすることはできますか？その週の水曜日から休みをとって家族旅行に行こうと思っているのですが、その日は朝８時発のフライトに乗るので、空港に６時には着いていないといけなくて、自宅４時半発なんです。それで前日の火曜日は、パスポートをとりに行ったり、宅急便に電話したりで、バタバタ忙しくなるので、お客様に失礼になってしまうのではないかと思って……。
>
> 忙しいと思うんですけど、西田さんに電話を入れて話をしてもらえますか？
>
> 神田

a. Who is Nishida-san? What favor does Kanda-san ask Kitada-san with regard to Nishida-san?
b. What is Kanda-san's schedule on Wednesday?
c. What concerns does Kanda-san have about his schedule on Tuesday? Can you guess what バタバタ means?
d. What does Kanda-san ask Kitada-san to do at the end of the email?

[パフォーマンス] Assume the role of Kitada-san and reach out to Nishida-san about the upcoming appointment.

書き取り

Listen to the audio, repeat silently what you hear, then write it down. What do you think the context is?

1. _____。
2. _____。
3. _____。
4. _____。
5. _____。
6. _____。
7. _____。
8. _____。

書いてみよう

Consider the context provided and compose a text according to the directions.

1. You brought something for your client, Nishida-san, but he was not in his office. Leave a note by addressing Nishida-san with an apology for not being able to meet the other day. Conclude your memo by inviting him to eat it with his family if it suits them. Be polite.

   _____
   _____
   _____
   _____

2. You are going to the airport tomorrow, but you have no choice but to leave one of the heavy suitcases in your office. Leave a note to your assistant, Kitada-kun, and ask if you can have him send it via delivery service.

   _____
   _____
   _____
   _____

3. You bought and placed a train ticket in an envelope for Minami-san. On a sticky note attached to the envelope, tell Minami-san that it leaves Tokyo at 3:00 and arrives in Nagoya at 5:15. Tell her to take care of herself on her business trip.

4. (Typing) Text your colleague who is stuck at the train station because she is not sure how to get to the inn. Provide directions.

First, go to "Toshokan Mae" (the bus stop named "in front of library") via bus. Next, there is a convenience store if she walks towards the nearby school, so take a right there. The inn will be there if she keeps on going straight.

知ってる？

Select the most appropriate option and write the letter on your answer sheet.

1. All potential Verbs are _____. (BTS 1)

    a. passive
    b. transitive
    c. intransitive

2. You tell your roommate that you don't think you'll be able to go home until late.
   遅くまで_____と思う。 (BTS 1)
    a. 帰らない
    b. 帰られない
    c. 帰れない

3. You ask your co-worker if she is able to see all of the entries in the online database on her computer.

   全部＿＿＿＿＿＿でしょうか。(BTS 1)

   a. 見れる
   b. 見せる
   c. 見る

4. You tell your friend that you don't plan to take the express train.

   急行に乗るつもり＿＿＿＿＿ないけど……。(BTS 2)

   a. が
   b. は
   c. で

5. You assumed that the company trip would be postponed, so you bought tickets for a different trip.

   社員旅行が延期になるつもり＿＿＿、別の切符買っちゃったんだ。(BTS 2)

   a. と
   b. で
   c. に

6. It is customary to ＿＿＿＿＿. (BTS 3, 4, 6)

   a. start a meeting before superiors arrive
   b. take a shower after soaking in an *onsen* bath
   c. buy a lunchbox before a long-distance trip

7. You hang up the phone and report that the guests will arrive at 9 p.m.

   9時に着く＿＿＿＿＿＿です。(BTS 5)

   a. とのこと
   b. つもり
   c. だそう

8. You ask a *kohai* in the calligraphy club to register by the deadline for the upcoming conference.

   締め切りまでに登録して＿＿＿＿＿＿か。(BTS 7)

   a. もらわないです
   b. もらえません
   c. もらいません

9. You ask your homestay father to help you with your homework.

   宿題を手伝って＿＿＿＿＿＿＿か。(BTS 7)

   a. いただけません

b. いただきません
c. いただかないです

10. You've reached the point where you can write an email all in Japanese.
    メール、日本語で書ける_____になった。 (BTS 9)
    a. の
    b. こと
    c. よう

11. Tell your friend that you don't cook for yourself anymore.
    もう自炊_____なった。 (BTS 9)
    a. しなく
    b. しなくて
    c. しないよう

12. You're willing to go anywhere on vacation.
    どこ_____行きますよ。 (BTS 10)
    a. も
    b. へも
    c. へでも

13. You tell the interviewer that you can be ready to start the new part-time job at any time.
    いつから_____始められます。 (BTS 10)
    a. も
    b. でも
    c. にも

14. You assumed that you put your cellphone on the bookshelf, but it's not there.
    本棚に_____つもりだけど、ないんです。 (BTS 11)
    a. 置いた
    b. 置く
    c. 置いてた

15. When the symbol 々 is used to repeat the sound of the preceding kanji, often the meaning of the first kanji is _____. (BTL 1)
    a. indefinite
    b. emphasized
    c. pluralized

第 16 幕
Act 16

呼(よ)んでくれれば行ったのに……。

**If only you had called me
I would have gone . . .**

郷(ごう)に入(い)っては郷(ごう)に従(したが)え。

When in Rome, do as the Romans do.

◆ シーン 16-1 練習

16-1-1C Declining invitations 誘いを断る (BTS 2)

In each conversation one of the participants will decline an invitation. Listen to each refusal and mark all of the elements that are present: (a) ちょっと; (b) an apology expression; (c) postponing giving an answer; (d) vague reference to another commitment; (e) intention to accept next time.

	ちょっと	an apology expression	postponing giving an answer	vague reference to another commitment	intention to accept next time
例1.	○	○			○
例2.	○	○		○	
3.					
4.					
5.					
6.					

16-1-2C A reflection session 反省会 (BTS 1)

You are attending a reflection meeting after a campus event. Listen to various people and write down what each person is pointing out.

例1.	青木さん	Should have made more posters
例2.	金田さん	Should have worked harder on the posters
3.	川上さん	
4.	高木さん	
5.	安田さん	

6. 古田さん _____

7. 北川さん _____

8. 西野さん _____

16-1-3P Saying what should be done in a certain situation するべきことをアドバイスする (BTS 1)

You are supervising Ikebe-san, an intern. When she shows some hesitation about doing something, assure her that in this situation she should do it.

例 1.
池辺さん (インターン)	やっぱり、何か部長に言ったほうがいいでしょうか。	Is it better to tell the division manager something, all things considered?
あなた	いや、もちろん、言うべきですよ、こういう時は。	Why, of course, you should tell her under these circumstances.

例 2.
池辺さん (インターン)	やっぱりちゃんとお詫びしたほうがいいでしょうか。	Is it maybe better to apologize properly, all things considered?
あなた	いや、もちろん、お詫びするべきですよ、こういう時は。	Why, of course, you should apologize under these circumstances.

16-1-4CP Acknowledging a thoughtful act 意外（いがい）な手助（てだす）け (BTS 3)

You are supervising Tomoda-san, an intern. When he informs you of something that Nozaki-san, a client of your company, did, comment that she didn't need to do that. As you practice, consider what your conversation with Tomoda-san may be about and write it down. There is no one correct answer for this part.

例 1.
友田さん (インターン)	これ、野崎さんがしてくださいました。	Nozaki-san did this for us.
あなた	本当に？何もしなくても良かったのに……。申し訳なかったですね。	Really? She didn't need to do anything. We are indebted to her, aren't we.

例2.
友田さん（インターン）　この新しいの、野崎さんが作ってくださいました。　Nozaki-san made this new one for us.
あなた　本当に？何も作らなくても良かったのに……。申し訳なかったですね。　Really? She didn't need to make anything. We are indebted to her, aren't we.

例1.　Translation _____

例2.　Planning document _____

　　3.　_____

　　4.　_____

　　5.　_____

　　6.　_____

16-1 腕試し

Invite someone to do something. If they decline, respond graciously to their refusal.

◆ シーン 16-2 練習

16-2-1C Enlisting help to continue
話(はなし)を続(つづ)けるための助(たす)けを求(もと)める (BTS 6)

In each of the conversations you hear, Teressa only has a vague memory of the expression she wants to use and gets her Japanese associate to help her recall it. Write down the approximation Teressa uses in katakana and the correct expression she successfully elicits in hiragana.

	Approximation	The correct version
例1.	メタメタ	めちゃめちゃ
例2.	センニャク	せんやく
3.		
4.		
5.		
6.		
7.		

16-2-2P I'm about to do it するところ (BTS 5)

You just received a phone call from Ikebe-san, one of the interns. Answer her question based on the current date and time and the information given below regarding when you will do various activities.

例1.	11/20 12:59		
池辺さん(インターン)	親睦会のこと、部長に相談しに行きましょうか。		Shall we go consult with the division chief about the meet-and-greet?
あなた	今しに行くところですけど。		I'm just about to go do that.

例 2.	11/20 1:14	
池辺さん (インターン)	親睦会のこと、もう部長と相談しました？	Have you consulted with the division chief about the meet-and-greet?
あなた	今相談しているところですけど。	I'm in the middle of consulting with her.
例 3.	11/20 1:28	
池辺さん (インターン)	報告書はいつ部長に出しますか。	When will you submit the report to the division chief?
あなた	明後日出しますけど。	I'll send it the day after tomorrow.

11/20	11/21	11/22
1:00–1:20 Consult with the division manager about the meet-and-greet	11:00–12:00 Go see the location of the welcome party	9:30–9:45 Send Ikegami-san's luggage to the airport
2:25–2:30 Send Ikegami-san the new schedule	12:30–2:00 Go pick up Ikegami-san from the airport	10:00–11:30 Take Ikegami-san to the airport
2:50–3:10 Register for the academic conference	2:15–2:45 Show the proposal draft to Kanda-san	1:00–2:00 Write a report for the division manager
	4:00 Go home early	3:00 Send the report to the division manager

4. 11/20 2:28
5. 11/20 2:48
6. 11/20 2:59
7. 11/21 10:58
8. 11/21 12:29
9. 11/22 9:29

16-2-3P 〜たら or 〜えば？ (BTS 4)

You are talking to Tomoda-san, an intern. Listen to what Tomoda-san says, and then respond based on the context provided.

例 1.	You are going to go when Nozaki-san gets here (and you know she's coming).	
友田さん (インターン)	行きますか。	Are you going?
あなた	野崎さんが来たら行きます。	I'll go when Nozaki-san gets here.

例 2. You are going to go if Nozaki-san comes (but you'll stay if she doesn't show up).

| 友田さん (インターン) | 行きますか。 | Are you going? |
| あなた | 野崎さんが来れば行きます。 | If Nozaki-san comes, I'll go. |

3. If Kanisawa-san quits you will quit too (but if he doesn't quit you won't quit).
4. You will submit the proposal if the division chief says it's okay (and you expect her to say yes soon).
5. You want to go too if the weather clears up (but you don't want to go if the weather is bad).
6. You will go if you can go.
7. If you can, you want to turn it in by 4 p.m.

16-2-4P Stating a regret 後悔(こうかい)する (BTS 4)

You are talking to your friend, Saori. Respond to what she says by saying that you should have done something using one of the verbs from the pool of options below. You will use each verb only once.

例 1.

| さおり (友人) | ここ、間違ってるよ。もう印刷しちゃったの？私知ってたら言ったのに。 | This is a mistake. Did you print it already? If I had known, I would have told you. |
| あなた | そっか。見せておけばよかったな。 | Oh, really? I should have showed you. |

例 2.

| さおり (友人) | 今朝のメールまだ見てないの？スケジュールが変わったんだよ。 | Have you not looked at your email from this morning yet? The schedule's been changed. |
| あなた | そっか。読んでおけばよかったな。 | Oh, really? I should have read it. |

| 言う | 見(み)る | 読(よ)む | 聞(き)く |
| ~~見(み)せる~~ | 勉強(べんきょう)する | 調(しら)べる | 頼(たの)む |

16-2 腕試し

1. Tell someone a story about something you did that didn't go very well.
2. Tell someone about something that you should have done but didn't do.

◆ シーン 16-3 練習

 16-3-1C Just happened or about to happen? どんなところ? (BTS 5, 7)

Listen to the audio and mark whether the sentence preceding ところ refers to (a) something that is/was about to happen, or (b) something that just happened. Then write what it was that just happened or was about to happen in the space provided.

	About to . . .	Just . . .	
例 1.	○		Go
例 2.		○	Rewrote
3.			
4.			
5.			
6.			
7.			
8.			
9.			
10.			
11.			

 16-3-2C Like what? たとえて言うと (BTS 8)

In each of the conversations, identify the entity being described with a metaphor and provide an explanation of how this entity is described.

例 1.	Section chief	Slow reactions, like a broken remote control.
例 2.	President's room	A mess, like failed *okonomiyaki* that has become messy when it's flipped over.
3.		
4.		
5.		
6.		

16-3-3P It seems as if . . . はっきりとは言えないですが…… (BTS 8)

You are talking with your associate, Ogawa-san, who is concerned about a task that had been assigned to another person. Give her some reassurance saying that the person seems to have been able to do it.

例 1.

| 小川さん (同僚) | 掃除、すぐする、すぐするって言ってたけど、どうなったんでしょうかね。 | He was saying repeatedly that he'd clean up right away, but I wonder what happened. |
| あなた | あ、できたようですよ、ちゃんと。 | Oh, it seems that he actually was able to do it, you know. |

例 2.

| 小川さん (同僚) | 相手の都合、聞く聞くって言ってたけど、聞かなかったんだったらどうしましょうね。 | He was saying repeatedly that he'd ask the other side, but what shall we do if he in fact hasn't? |
| あなた | あ、聞けたようですよ、ちゃんと。 | Oh, it seems that he actually was able to ask, you know. |

16-3-4CP Expressing envy うらやましさ (BTS 8)

You and your associate Kurita-san are talking about various people. Follow his description of the person by saying how you wish you could do things the way that person can. Write down what is so amazing about each person mentioned.

例1.
栗田さん (同僚)	木下さんってすごいですよね。編集が素晴らしく上手で、木下さんが見てくれたら、すっごくいい文書になるんだからね。	Kinoshita-san is amazing, don't you think? She is wonderfully good at editing, so, if Kinoshita-san looks at it, documents become really good, right?
あなた	ああ、私も木下さんのように編集が上手にできたらいいのに。	Oh, how I wish I could edit as well as Kinoshita-san!

例2.
栗田さん (同僚)	清水さんってすごいですよね。いろいろなところでボランティアしてるんだって。	Shimizu-san is amazing, don't you think? He is volunteering at various places, I hear.
あなた	ああ、私も清水さんのようにいろいろなところでボランティアできたらいいのに。	Oh, how I wish I could volunteer at as many places as Shimizu-san!

Person	Amazing feature
Kinoshita-san	Edits well.
Shimizu-san	Volunteers at various places.
Kato-san	
Mori-san	
Sasaki-san	
Kobayashi-san	
Yamaguchi-san	
Minamida-san	

Now repeat this practice, assuming that the setting for the conversation is more casual.

◆ シーン 16-4 練習

16-4-1C Just happened or about to happen?
今あったこと？これから？ (BTS 5, 7, 9)

Listen to the audio and mark whether the sentence preceding ところ refers to (a) something that just happened, or (b) something that is/was about to happen. Then write what it is/was that just happened or is/was about to happen in the space provided.

	Just . . .	About to . . .	
例 1.		○	Submit
例 2.		○	Call
3.			
4.			
5.			
6.			
7.			
8.			
9.			

16-4-2P If I put my mind to it . . . 機会を逃して後悔する (BTS 3, 4)

Your colleague, Tabata-san, is incredulous about something you didn't do. Respond to her indicating your regret, since you could have done it if you had been determined to do so.

例1.
| 田端さん (同僚) | え？今回も行かなかったんですか？社員旅行。 | What? You didn't go this time, either? I mean to the company trip. |
| あなた | 残念ながら。今回も行こうと思えば行けたのにね。 | Unfortunately. I could have gone this time, too, if I was determined to, but, you know. |

例2.
| 田端さん (同僚) | え？食べなかったんですか？山田さんが作ってくれたケーキ。 | What? You didn't eat it? I mean the cake that Yamada-san made for us. |
| あなた | 残念ながら。食べようと思えば食べられたのにね。 | Unfortunately. I could have eaten it, if I was determined to, but, you know. |

16-4-3P Just as I was about to . . . ちょうどしようとしたところに…… (BTS 9)

Another colleague, Kitayama-san, expresses his incredulity about something you didn't do. Explain to him that something unexpected came up just as you were about to begin the activity.

例1.
| 栗山さん (同僚) | ええ？また行かなかったんですか？社員旅行。 | What? You didn't go again? I mean to the company trip. |
| あなた | そうなんです。あり得ないでしょう？ちょうど行こうとしたところに邪魔が入っちゃって……。 | That's what happened. No way, right? Just as I was about to go, something troublesome came up unexpectedly, and . . . |

例2.
| 栗山さん (同僚) | ええ？全然食べなかったんですか？山田さんがせっかく作ってくれたケーキ。 | What? You didn't eat it at all? I mean the cake that Yamada-san went through the trouble of making for us. |
| あなた | そうなんです。あり得ないでしょう？ちょうど食べようとしたところに邪魔が入っちゃって……。 | That's what happened. No way, right? Just as I was about to eat it, something troublesome came up unexpectedly, and . . . |

16-4-4P Presenting observation as evidence
見たことを証拠として出す (BTS 5)

Persuade a skeptical friend, Shino, by stating that you saw with your own eyes your mutual friend, Matsuura-kun, engage in various activities.

例1.

| 志乃 (友人) | 松浦君が料理するって？まさか？うそでしょ？全然しないと思ってた。 | Matsuura-kun cooks? No way! That's not true, is it? I've been thinking that he doesn't cook at all. |
| あなた | いやいや、本当。松浦君が料理しているところをこの目で見たもの。 | No, no, it's true. I saw with my very own eyes Matsuura-kun in the middle of cooking. |

例2.

| 志乃 (友人) | 嘘みたいだけど、松浦君ってマラソンに出るトレーニングしてるんだって。 | It's as if it's a lie, but I heard that Matsuura-kun is training to enter a marathon. |
| あなた | いやいや、本当。松浦君がトレーニングしているところをこの目で見たもの。 | No, no, it's true. I saw with my very own eyes Matsuura-kun in the middle of training. |

◆ シーン 16-5 練習

 16-5-1C Reason or purpose? 理由？目的？ (BTS 10)

Listen to the audio and mark whether the sentence preceding ため refers to (a) a reason for something, or (b) the purpose for which something is or was done.

	Reason	Purpose
例 1.		○
例 2.	○	
3.		
4.		
5.		
6.		
7.		
8.		
9.		
10.		
11.		

 **16-5-2C Doing something for a purpose
目的を持って行動する (BTS 10)**

There are a number of ways to express purpose. What purposes are mentioned in each of the conversations? Write down the purposes mentioned.

例 1.　　To study Japanese

例 2.　　To pass the test

　3.　　_____

　4.　　_____

　5.　　_____

　6.　　_____

　7.　　_____

16-5-3P Explaining the purpose of an item
使用目的を説明する (BTS 10)

When your friend, Ai, asks if you will do something, respond affirmatively and explain that the item you have is for that purpose.

例 1.
藍 (友人)　文学を勉強するの？　　　　　　　　Are you going TO study literature?
あなた　　そう。これは文学を勉強するためのノー　Yeah. This notebook is for
　　　　　トなんだ。　　　　　　　　　　　　　studying literature.

例 2.
藍 (友人)　プリンターを直すの？　　　　　　　Are you going to fix the printer?
あなた　　そう。これはプリンターを直すための道　Yeah. This tool is for fixing the
　　　　　具なんだ。　　　　　　　　　　　　　printer.

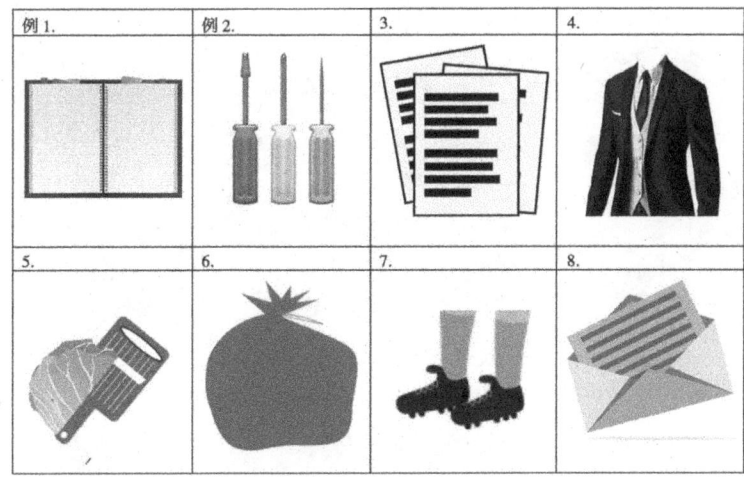

16-5-4P Approaching a task collaboratively
一緒に取り組む

You are working with a group of colleagues on a team project. When one makes a suggestion, accept it and invite others to weigh in on how to go about taking the suggested course.

例1.
チームメンバー	これを取ってみましょうか。	Shall we try and take this off?
あなた	いいですね。じゃあ、どのように取ればいいか、皆さんの考えを聞かせてください。	That's good. Then, let us hear everyone's thoughts about good ways to take it off.

例2.
チームメンバー	このページを書き直すっていうのはどうでしょう。	Suppose we rewrite this page?
あなた	いいですね。じゃあ、どのように書き直せばいいか、皆さんの考えを聞かせてください。	That's good. Then, let us hear everyone's thoughts about good ways to rewrite it.

◆ シーン 16-6 練習

16-6-1C Listening to opinions and taking notes
意見を書き取る (BTS 11)

In each of the following you will hear someone express an opinion at a meeting. Listen to the opinion, and write (a) what the positive feature is, (b) what the concern is, and (c) what justification is provided for the concern.

例 1. Positive   The content of the event seems good.

       Concern   The time is too early.

       Justification   There are many people not done with work at this time.

例 2. Positive   It seems that there were many people who said it was an interesting theme.

       Concern   The content was too difficult.

       Justification   There seem to have been many people who specialized in something different.

3. Positive   _____

    Concern   _____

    Justification   _____

4. Positive   _____

    Concern   _____

    Justification   _____

5. Positive   _____

    Concern   _____

    Justification   _____

6. Positive   _____

    Concern   _____

    Justification   _____

16-6-2C Writing down opinions that you hear
意見を聞いて書きとめる (BTS 11)

Listen to various people expressing their opinions about a report your project team drafted and write down each person's point succinctly.

例 1.	Masuda-san	Overall message isn't coming through.
例 2.	Mizuno-san	Should look for a better photo for page two.
3.	Takeshita-san	
4.	Suzuki-san	
5.	Hayashi-san	
6.	Ono-san	
7.	Miki-san	

16-6-3P Summarizing an opinion 意見をまとめる

You are running a meeting. As various members of the project team state their opinion, restate it as a critical question.

例 1.

チームメンバー	細かいところはできていますよね。ただ、全体として話が通じていないような気がします。	The details are done, right? Yet, overall, the message doesn't come through, it seems.
あなた	全体として、話が通じているかということですね。	You are asking if overall, the message is coming through, right?

例 2.

チームメンバー	増田さんは細かいところができているっておしゃいましたけど、2ページの写真、これ、もっといいのがあるんじゃないかと……。	Masuda-san said that the details are done, but I wonder if there isn't a better one than the photo on page two.
あなた	2ページ目の写真よりいいのがないかということですね。	You are asking if there isn't a better one than the photo on page two, right?

16-6-4P Expressing an opinion 意見を言う (BTS 11)

You are discussing how an event went with a group of colleagues. When asked about a particular part of the event, respond based on the prompt. When your response relates to the same topic as the previous response, use an appropriate transitional phrase.

例 1.		The pamphlet was made too late.	
八木部長	パンフレットについて何かありますか。はい、どうぞ。		Does anyone have anything regarding the pamphlets? Yes, go ahead.
あなた	はい。作るのが遅すぎたように思います。		Yes. It seems to me that it was made too late.
例 2.		The pamphlet's font was too small.	
八木部長	確かに。他にありますか。はい、どうぞ。		Absolutely. Anything else? Yes, go ahead.
あなた	少し違うのですが、フォントが小さすぎたように思います。		This is a little different, but it seemed to me that the font was too small.

3. The pamphlet's content was difficult to understand.
4. That location was a little too small.
5. The location had too few chairs.
6. The location was too far away.
7. The content was not that interesting.
8. The content was a little difficult to understand at the beginning.

16-6 腕試し

When you see a brain-storming conversation in Japanese, observe how ideas and observations are posited and are restated and see if you can make a suggestion or respond to an opinion as well.

◆ シーン 16-7R 練習

16-7-1R Contrast or reason? 逆接？理由？

Read the following statements and determine whether to use the first sentence as a contrast (に) or a reason (で).

例 1.　せっかく招待してもらったの (<u>に</u>・で)、家族で行くべきですよ。
例 2.　開けないつもりだったの (<u>に</u>・で) つい中が見たくなってしまって……。
　 3.　せっかく覚えたの (に・で) 全部忘れるところだったよ。
　 4.　時間に気を付けていたの (に・で)、電車に遅れないで乗れました。
　 5.　伝言、2、3回伝えておいたの (に・で) 覚えてるだろうと思いますよ。
　 6.　せっかく呼んでくれたの (に・で)、週末忙しくて行けなそうです。
　 7.　料理、せっかく作ってもらったの (に・で) 食べていきましょう。
　 8.　せっかく紙買っておいたの (に・で)、家に忘れてきてしまったよ。

16-7-2RW Things that I should do or should have done . . . やるべきこと、後悔してること。

Determine which verb from the selection fits appropriately in the statements that follow.

| 気をつけて | 招待する | 覚えて | 呼んだ |
| 使って | <u>伝える</u> | <u>送れば</u> | やめた |

例 1.　仕事に遅れていかなければならない事はちゃんと部長に＿＿＿<u>伝える</u>＿＿＿べきだ。
例 2.　急いでいたのなら宅急便で＿＿＿<u>送れば</u>＿＿＿よかったのに……。
　 3.　この漢字、練習してちゃんと＿＿＿＿＿＿おけばよかった……。
　 4.　家族ならウェディングセレモニーにはちゃんと＿＿＿＿＿＿べきだ。
　 5.　あ、また忘れるところだった！＿＿＿＿＿＿おかないとすぐ忘れちゃうなあ。
　 6.　もう回すの＿＿＿＿＿＿方がいいんじゃない？目が回りそう……。
　 7.　酒田君、次回からはこっちにある紙は＿＿＿＿＿＿はいけないそうだよ。
　 8.　週末のパーティーだけど、せっかくだから弟や妹も＿＿＿＿＿＿方がいいよね。

16-7-3W Writing down reminders 忘(わす)れないよう記録(きろく)する

Write down the following reminders in Japanese.

例 1. Buy red paper　　　　　　　　　　　　赤い紙を買う

例 2. Write a memo in order to　　　　　忘れないようにメモする
not forget

3. Memorize kanji (write　　　　　_____
10 times each)

4. Invite Sakata-san　　　　　　　　　_____

5. A pen that can write on　　　　　　_____
black paper

6. Be careful not to forget　　　　　　_____
the umbrella

7. Send an invitation mail　　　　　　_____

8. Tell the *bucho* about the　　　　　_____
schedule for the weekend

◆ シーン 16-8R 練習

16-8-1R Provisional expressions 仮(かり)の表現(ひょうげん)

Determine which of the provisional expressions in the selection fits appropriately in the statements that follow.

直せば	覚えなければ	聞けば	合えば
話し合えば	来週なら	社長なら	話してあげれば

例1. 明日ミーティングがあるみたいなんだけど、どんなことを＿＿話し合えば＿＿いいんだろう。

例2. 週末は都合が合わないようなんだけど、＿＿来週なら＿＿どうかな。

3. 5時からなら出られるよ。都合が＿＿＿＿＿＿＿＿＿出たいと思ってるんだけど……。

4. 内容を書き直そうと思ってたところなんだけど、どこから＿＿＿＿＿＿＿＿＿いいか分からなくて……。

5. さっき電話番号を聞いたところなのにもう忘れてしまって……。もう一回どう＿＿＿＿＿＿＿＿＿失礼じゃないかな。

6. ブライアンはまだ強気みたいなんだけど、白井君はかなり弱気になってるみたいで……。白井君にどう＿＿＿＿＿＿＿＿＿いいかな？

7. 部長はあまり乗り気じゃないようなんだけど、＿＿＿＿＿＿＿＿＿どうかな。

8. プレゼンの内容、全部＿＿＿＿＿＿＿＿＿ならないんだけど、ちょっと長過ぎて……。自分の番がもうすぐ回って来ちゃうんだけど。

16-8-2R Explaining what happened 何(なに)が起(お)こったか説明(せつめい)する

Determine what likely happened in the following situations.

仕事の付き合いが入って	番号が消えて
みんなびっくりして	部長が部屋に入って来て
プログラムがフリーズして	雨がふってきて
~~Wi-Fi が使えなくなって~~	会社から連絡が入って

例1. 家に電話しようとしたところに
　　　会社から連絡が入って＿＿＿＿＿＿＿＿＿＿＿＿＿＿＿＿＿＿＿＿しまって……。

例2. ファイルを送ろうとしたところで、
　　　Wi-Fiが使えなくなって＿＿＿＿＿＿＿＿＿＿＿＿＿＿＿＿＿＿＿しまって……。

3. ちょうど会社を出ようとしたところに
　　＿＿＿＿＿＿＿＿＿＿＿＿＿＿＿＿＿＿＿＿＿＿＿＿＿＿＿＿＿＿＿しまって……。

4. お客様を外に案内しようとしたところに
　　＿＿＿＿＿＿＿＿＿＿＿＿＿＿＿＿＿＿＿＿＿＿＿＿＿＿＿＿＿＿＿しまって……。

5. プレゼンの内容を直そうとしたところで、
　　＿＿＿＿＿＿＿＿＿＿＿＿＿＿＿＿＿＿＿＿＿＿＿＿＿＿＿＿＿＿＿しまって……。

6. すみません、書こうとしていたところで、
　　＿＿＿＿＿＿＿＿＿＿＿＿＿＿＿＿＿＿＿＿＿＿＿＿＿＿＿＿＿＿＿しまって……。

7. 部長のサプライズパーティーについて話し合おうとしたところに
　　＿＿＿＿＿＿＿＿＿＿＿＿＿＿＿＿＿＿＿＿＿＿＿＿＿＿＿＿＿＿＿しまって……。

8. 部長が部屋に入って来たところを見て、
　　＿＿＿＿＿＿＿＿＿＿＿＿＿＿＿＿＿＿＿＿＿＿＿＿＿＿＿＿＿＿＿しまって……。

16-8-3W Asking a favor by leaving a note お願いをメモする

Leave the following notes to people you associate with.

例1.　　　Kitada (friend)　　　rewrite (it)
北田君、よかったら書き直してもらえますか。

例2.　　　Sakai (guest)　　　discuss it with family
酒井様、よろしければ家族と話し合っていただけますか。

3.　　　Noguchi (guest)　　　pass along (lit. 'tell') the contents of the presentation as well
＿＿

4.　　　Yoko (friend)　　　(e)mail the contact information
＿＿

5.　　　Midori (friend)　　　tell (lit. 'teach') me the phone number
＿＿

6.　　　Yagi-bucho　　　give guests a tour around the company
＿＿

◆ シーン 16-9R 練習

16-9-1R Expressing cause, reason, and purpose
原因、理由、目的の表現
げんいん　りゆう　もくてき　ひょうげん

Select an appropriate cause, reason, or purpose for the following statements.

招待する	物を売る	出張	部屋が広い	細くなる
売り切れ	考える	変える	太った	約束

例1. 今日の「ためになる話」では「自分のキャリアについて＿＿考える＿＿ために大切なこと」について話し合っていきたいと思っています。

例2. 社長は＿＿出張＿＿のため会社にはおりませんが、電話で連絡することはできますよ。

3. 友人との＿＿＿＿＿＿＿＿＿のために今まで言わないようにしてたんだけど、今なら話してもいいように思う。

4. 考子さんのように＿＿＿＿＿＿＿＿＿ためにはどんなダイエットをすればいいんですか。

5. 今日はフリーマーケットサービスで＿＿＿＿＿＿＿＿＿ためにできるテクニックを３つ、細川さんが教えてくれます。

6. ＿＿＿＿＿＿＿＿＿ために話が聞こえにくいんですけど、マイクのボリュームをもう少し上げてもらえますか。

7. パン・デザート全部＿＿＿＿＿＿＿＿＿のため今日は早目に店を閉めました。

8. この１ヶ月だけで約２０キロ＿＿＿＿＿＿＿＿＿ためにプロレスラーみたいになってしまった。

9. 次回の「ためになる話」では「自分を＿＿＿＿＿＿＿＿＿ために知っておくべき５つこと」について話し合っていくつもりです。

10. 広明さん、チャットのグループに新しいメンバーを＿＿＿＿＿＿＿＿＿ためにはどうすればいいですか。

16-9-2R Which statement is softer? より柔らかい表現は？

Determine which statement sounds relatively softer.

例1. ⓐ もっと考えるべきだよ。　　　　　b. もっと考えなくてはいけないよ。

例2. a. 細川さん、ちょっと変わったと思うんだけど。　　ⓑ 細川さん、ちょっと変わったように思うんだけど。

3. a. 考え方を変えなくちゃいけないんだよ。　　b. 考え方を変えなければいけないそうだよ。

4. a. 約束には間に合うようにした方がいいよ。　　b. 約束には間に合うようにするべきだよ。

5. a. ちょっと太り過ぎのようにも思えるんだけど……。　　b. ちょっと太り過ぎのように思うんだけど……。

6. a. 大変だけど、今日中に全部売っておかなければ……。　　b. 大変だけど、今日中に全部売っておいた方が……。

7. a. あと5分で野菜を全部切らないといけないんだって。　　b. あと5分で野菜を全部切らなくちゃならないんだって。

8. a. キャンパス広いから、案内してあげればいいじゃない。　　b. キャンパス広いから、案内でもしてあげればいいじゃない。

16-9-3RW Softening your statements and opinions
供述・意見を和らげる

Rewrite the following statements and opinions by using roundabout expressions as indicated in the models.

例1.　細くした方がいいと思います。
　　　もう少し細くした方がいいように(いいかと)思いますけど……。＿＿＿＿

例2.　安いのも売ってるよ。
　　　ちょっと安いのも売ってるみたい(よう)だよ。
＿＿＿＿＿＿＿＿＿＿＿＿＿＿＿＿＿＿＿＿＿＿＿＿＿＿＿＿

例3.　広明君、今日は大切な約束があるから……。
　　　広明君、今日はちょっと大切な約束があるみたい(よう)だから……。＿＿＿

4.　この案、変えた方がいいと思います。
＿＿＿＿＿＿＿＿＿＿＿＿＿＿＿＿＿＿＿＿＿＿＿＿＿＿＿＿

5. 考え過ぎだと思います。
   _____

6. 太いのは売り切れだよ。
   _____

7. 細川さん、考えてみるって言ってたよ。
   _____

8. 雪の天気で大変なので……。
   _____

◆ Act 16 評価

 聞いてみよう

Read the context, listen to the audio, and then answer the questions. If you hear something unfamiliar, rely on what you know to choose the correct answer.

1. Yagi-bucho and Kanda-san are looking at something that a new employee produced.

    a. What does Yagi-bucho think of what was produced?
    b. What does Kanda-san feel he should have done?

2. Mizuno-san seems to need help from her colleague Kanda-san.

    a. What does Mizuno-san want Kanda-san to do?
    b. What is expected to happen at this appointment?
    c. What happened last week?
    d. How does Kanda-san feel about what happened last week?

3. Kanda-san catches one of the interns looking at her cell phone.

    a. How does Kanda-san describe the intern?
    b. What is the intern doing?
    c. What does the intern ask Kanda-san to do?
    d. How does Kanda-san respond to this request?
    e. How does Kanda-san describe what the intern is doing?

4. Takashi is trying to give a fellow member of the Japanese Language Club some encouragement.

    a. What is the meaning of what Takashi said, according to the club member?
    b. What connection does the phrase have to English?
    c. Which of the two versions of the phrase is most commonly heard, the first or the second?
    d. What does もと mean in this phrase?

5. A member of the JLC and Takashi are having a discussion about the Japanese language during their weekly meeting.

    a. What is the club member's issue?
    b. What does Takashi say about Japanese people?
    c. What question does the club member ask Takashi?
    d. How does Takashi answer the question?

6. Kanda-san is concerned about Ikebe-san, an intern.

   a. What does Kanda-san ask Sasha to do?
   b. Why does Kanda-san want Sasha to do this?
   c. What does Sasha think is the reason for Ikebe-san's mood?
   d. How does Kanda-san feel about Ikebe-san's abilities?

7. Sasha reports back to Kanda-san about Ikebe-san.

   a. What was apparently the reason for Ikebe-san's mood?
   b. What does Ikebe-san intend to do? What does she not intend to do?
   c. How has Ikebe-san's mood been recently?
   d. How does Sasha' respond to Kanda-san's expression of gratitude? How does she qualify her statement?

8. Sasha and Kanda-san are about to give a presentation together.

   a. What request does Kanda-san make of Sasha?
   b. What will Sasha do? What will Kanda-san do?
   c. What does Kanda-san check on?
   d. What did Sasha just do?

9. Kanda-san and Sasha exchange some updates about Ikebe-san.

   a. How is Ikebe-san doing?
   b. What did Sasha see?

10. Yagi-bucho and Kanda-san are talking about a product that they promoted.

    a. What comment does Yagi-bucho make about the product?
    b. Why did Kanda-san say 結果から言えば when talking about the success of the product?
    c. What does Kanda-san intend to do at next week's meeting?

11. Brian's classmate and Brian are talking about a gathering the previous week.

    a. What did Brian's classmate think of the gathering?
    b. What did Brian think was funny?
    c. What does Brian's classmate admire about Sakamoto-sensei?
    d. What has Brian never seen?
    e. What happens to Brian when he's with Sakamoto-sensei?

使ってみよう

For each of the following, listen to the audio, and respond to what was said based on the context. Then listen to the sample response.

1. When a colleague expresses an opinion, provide the following supporting evidence: Just recently there was a similar project, and it also had only 5 people, and even though everyone was working late every day they didn't make the deadline.

2. You are at a meeting, and a colleague expresses an opinion. Restate what you hear.
3. A friend invites you to do something tomorrow, but you are planning on seeing a movie with Suzuki-san. Decline the invitation appropriately.
4. You have just declined an invitation from a friend because you are planning on seeing a movie with Suzuki-san. Respond appropriately to your friend's inquiry.
5. You have just declined an invitation from a friend. Express appreciation for the invitation.
6. You have just declined an invitation from a friend. Express your hope that you can accept next time.
7. In response to your friend's inquiry, tell her that (a) it seems you can't get through; (b) it seems Ichiro-kun knows a lot; (c) it seems Yuya-kun already rewrote his paper 5 times; (d) it seems that Akiko has a cold.
8. When a *kohai* at work apologizes for not coming at the right time, respond that you should have told him that the schedule had changed.
9. Tell a *senpai* that you don't know why, but Murata-san said he had to go home.
10. Respond to a friend's question by telling him they're (a) clothes for a trip to Hokkaido; (b) materials (ingredients) for rewriting your thesis; (c) stationery for writing letters.
11. Respond to an acquaintance's question by telling her that because you've known Sato-san since you were young, he's like family (lit. 'he's a person like family').
12. Tell a friend that you are just about to (a) go; (b) start; (c) rewrite it; (d) ride; (e) turn it off.
13. Tell a work *senpai* that you just saw the division chief about to leave.
14. Tell a friend that you (a) just finished; (b) just completed it; (c) just arrived; (d) just got home.

Now it's your turn to start the conversation based on the given context. Listen to how the other person reacts to you. For some items, you may not get a verbal response. Don't be concerned if you hear things you have not yet learned.

15. At a business meeting, express your opinion that the content of the event is excellent, and there seem to be many people who are interested, but you think the registration process is too complicated.
16. At a business meeting, express your opinion that the content of the proposal was excellent, but because the way it is written is difficult to understand, what we want to do may not have been understood.
17. Tell a friend that it would have been better if you didn't take sociology.
18. Tell a friend that if she doesn't worry so much, she will be able to do splendidly in her interpretation.
19. Tell a co-worker that you're a bit busy this week, but you can do it if it's tomorrow.
20. Tell a friend that if she sees it, she'll understand.
21. Tell a *senpai* at work that you need more information on yesterday's meeting with Mima-san in order to write a report, then ask your *senpai* who you should ask.
22. Tell a friend that you (a) almost got in an accident; (b) almost forgot your homework; (c) almost gave up.
23. Tell a work *senpai* that this morning, just as you were about to leave home, your mom called.

読んでみよう

Consider the context provided and read the passage to answer the questions that follow.

1. Brian is texting Ichiro about an issue that he is having at home.

   a. What is the issue? What does Brian have to do?
   b. How does Ichiro respond?

   [パフォーマンス] Assume the role of Brian and ask another host family member for help.

2. Suzuki-san is texting one of her *kohai* about Brian.

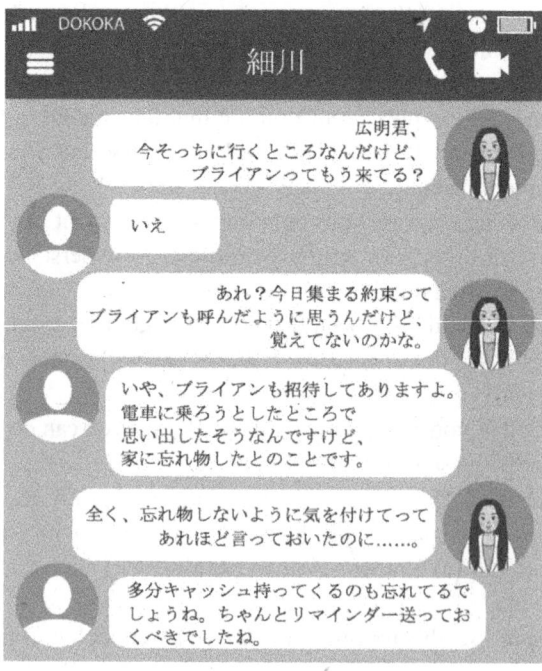

a. Who is Suzuki-san texting? Provide the first and last name.
b. What does Suzuki-san vaguely remember about Brian?
c. What is Brian likely doing? Provide details.
d. What comment does Suzuki-san say with regards to Brian? How does the other person resonate with Suzuki-san's comment?

[パフォーマンス] Assume the role of Suzuki-san and call Brian. Ask him where he is and if he has everything he needs.

3. Brian is texting his friend, Hiroaki.

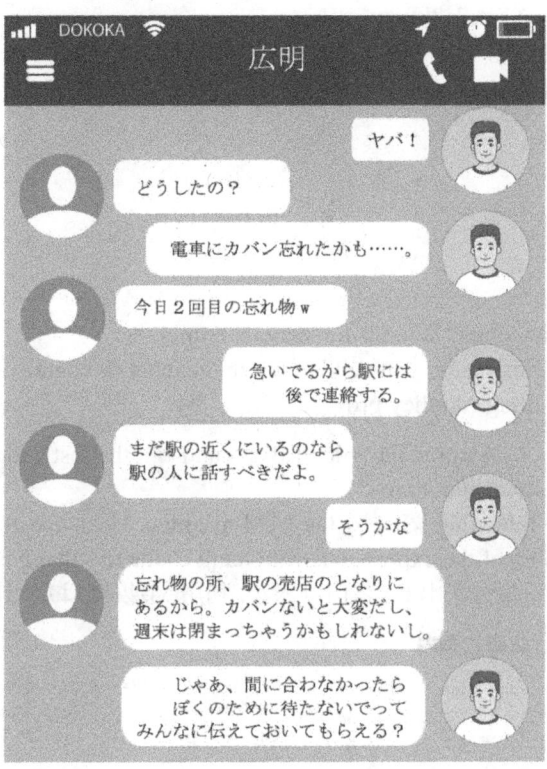

a. The w symbol represents the initial letter of *warai* 'laughter.' What does Hiroaki find laughable about Brian?
b. What does Brian propose to do initially?
c. How does Hiroaki respond to Brian's initial proposal?
d. Where does Hiroaki tell Brian to go? Why?
e. What does Brian request the other person to do?

[パフォーマンス] Assume the role of Hiroaki and tell others in the group about Brian's situation.

4. Brian found the following 案内 posted at the lost and found. Make use of contextualized cues to work around some of the expressions with kanji characters that have not been introduced so far (i.e., 受付, 際に, 以下, 事柄, 特徴, 等, 物品, and 携帯).

お忘れ物のご案内

受付時間: 月〜金　9:00~17:00
電話番号: 050-5555-3920

ご連絡の際に、以下の事柄を教えていただけますとスムーズにご案内できます。

- お忘れ物の内容
- お忘れ物をされた時の日時
- お忘れ物をしたと思われる場所
- お忘れ物の特徴（色、サイズ、ブランド、メーカー等）

お忘れ物の多い物品の例

- 携帯電話・スマートフォン
- カバン
- パスケース
- 紙ぶくろ
- サイフ

a. When are they open? What is the contact number?
b. What kind of things do you need to tell them about the item when contacting them?
c. What list of things do they provide?

[パフォーマンス] Assume the role of Brian and call the lost and found. Tell them what you lost and describe the item.

5. Brian found the following 案内 by the ATM machine. Make use of contextualized cues to work around some of the expressions with kanji characters that have not been introduced so far (i.e., 現金, お引き出し, お預け入れ, 利用, 手数料, お取引き, and その他).

◉ ATMサービスのご案内

キャッシュを使わなければならないのに現金がない！キャッシュを持って来ればよかった……。そんなお困りのあなたを365日、便利さフルタイムでサポート！２４時間いつでもお引き出しやお預け入れができて、おサイフ気分でご利用いただけます。

		ATM利用手数料				
		月曜〜金曜日			土曜・日曜日・休日	
銀行カード	お取引き	8:45〜18:00	18:00〜21:00	その他の時間 21:00〜8:45	8:45〜21:00	その他の時間 21:00〜8:45
ナウ銀行カード	お引き出し	0円	100円		0円	120円
	お預け入れ					
その他の銀行カード	お引き出し	150円	240円			
	お預け入れ	120円				

a. What kind of trouble is そんなお困りのあなた described to have? Can you guess what 現金 means?
b. What kind of support is being described? Can you guess what お引き出し, お預け入れ, and 利用 mean?
c. It is Saturday at 9:30 a.m. What is the fee associated with withdrawing money with ナウカード?
d. It is Tuesday at 5:00 p.m. What is the fee associated with depositing money without ナウカード?

[パフォーマンス] Check the current time in Japan and determine how much it would cost to make a withdrawal using your credit card. Compare it with the NOW Bank card.

書き取り

Listen to the audio, repeat silently what you hear, then write it down. What do you think the context is?

1. _____ 。
2. _____ 。
3. _____ 。
4. _____ 。
5. _____ 。
6. _____ 。
7. _____ 。
8. _____ 。

書いてみよう

Consider the context provided and compose a text according to the directions.

1. You brought a textbook that your classmate forgot in class, but they weren't there. Leave a note by telling them to be careful about forgetting things.

2. You are asked to collect the contact information of new club members for the Japanese Language Club. Provide the Japanese equivalent of the following list by hand.

   English:

JLC members Contact information		
Name	Telephone number	Email address
Ex. Hosokawa Hiroaki	614-555-2918	h.hosokawa@fukuzawadaigaku.edu

   Japanese:

3. You and others are planning a Christmas party to reach out to those who are going to spend Christmas alone at Fukuzawa University. Draft a simple invitation by typing the following information in Japanese.

> Information with regard to Christmas party
>
> It's Christmas, but you don't have family or significant others (lit. 'important people') close by.
>
> A party for someone like us (lit. 'everyone')!
>
> Date and time: December 23rd, Sat 19:00 ~ 21:30
>
> Location: Friend Hall 201
>
> Contents: Game, dessert, presents!
>
> Contact: Your name (your email address)

4. Draft the following journal entry in Japanese as if you were Brian. Make use of emoji to convey relevant feelings.

I had an appointment to get together with everyone today, but as I was getting on the train, I realized that I forgot my bag, so I had to go home (surprised face). Then, I went in a hurry after that, but I forgot that (same) bag on the train because I was in a hurry. . . . (sad face) It was nice for them to invite me, but I didn't make it in time (disappointed).

_____
_____
_____
_____
_____

知ってる？

Select the most appropriate option and write the letter on your answer sheet.

1. You tell your roommates that they shouldn't have gone out after 10 p.m.

    10 時過ぎ_____べき_____よ。(BTS 1)

    a. 出かける　　　　じゃなかった
    b. 出かけない　　　だった
    c. 出かけなかった　だ

2. You tell your friends that they should have said the truth.

   本当のこと____べき_____よ. (BTS 1)

   a. 言った　　　　　だ
   b. 言う　　　　　　だった
   c. 言った　　　　　だった

3. When you turn down an invitation in Japanese, it is customary to _____. (BTS 2)

   a. give a detailed reason for refusing
   b. express your appreciation
   c. refuse two or three times

4. You wish you had studied harder for the test.

   もっと勉強_____。 (BTS 3, 4)

   a. するべきです
   b. しなければならない
   c. すればよかったのに

5. You tell your friend that unless he takes his medication, he won't get better.

   薬_____治らないよ。 (BTS 4)

   a. のまなければ
   b. のまなくて
   c. のんでいないのに

6. You tell a team member that you're just about to practice the new routine.

   これから練習_____ところです。 (BTS 5, 7)

   a. する
   b. している
   c. した

7. You tell your roommate that your mother phoned just when you were taking a shower.

   シャワーを浴びているところ_____母から電話がかかってきた。 (BTS 5, 7)

   a. を
   b. に
   c. で

8. You comment that your drink tastes like medicine.

   薬_____味ですよ。 (BTS 8)

   a. のよう
   b. ような
   c. みたいな

9. You're wondering if you'll ever be able to play a game as well as Brian.
   ブライン_____できるようになるでしょうか。(BTS 8)
   a. みたいに
   b. ように
   c. のような

10. You complain that the guest arrived just when you were about to eat lunch.
    お昼を_____ お客さんが来ちゃって……。(BTS 5, 9)
    a. 食べたところに
    b. 食べるところに
    c. 食べているところを

11. You tell the caller that Mizuno-san just got back.
    水野さんはちょうど今_____ところです。(BTS 5, 9)
    a. 帰ってくる
    b. 帰っていた
    c. 帰ってきた

12. You show your classmate a new app for looking up kanji.
    漢字を調べるため_____アプリだよ。(BTS 10)
    a. の
    b. に
    c. な

13. You tell the passport control agent that you've come to Japan to teach English.
    英語を教える_____来ました。(BTS 10)
    a. ように
    b. ところに
    c. ために

14. You think that the plans are quite complicated.
    かなり複雑_____に思います。(BTS 11)
    a. のよう
    b. なよう
    c. みたい

15. You're of the opinion that the schedule is too detailed.
    ちょっと細かすぎる_____に思います。(BTS 11)
    a. よう
    b. のよう
    c. みたい

第 17 幕
Act 17

この記事（きじ）によると……
According to this article . . .

一石二鳥（いっせきにちょう）
Two birds with one stone.

◆ シーン 17-1 練習

17-1-1C Meanings of ながら (BTS 1)

Listen to the conversations and determine whether the ながら expression is used to express a contradiction (i.e., similar to "although" in English) or simply the occurrence of simultaneous activities and check the option accordingly.

	Contradiction	Simultaneous activities
例 1.	○	
例 2.		○
3.		
4.		
5.		
6.		
7.		
8.		
9.		
10.		

17-1-2P Stating that you are multi-tasking
同時にしていると伝える (BTS 1)

Your teammate seems to think that you were doing something instead of what you said you'd do. Correct him and say that you were doing what you said you'd do while doing the other thing.

例 1.
| チームメンバー | 論文のこと考えるって言ってたけど、今寝てなかった？ | You said you'd think about the research paper, but weren't you sleeping now? |
| あなた | いや、いや。寝ながら考えてたんですよ。 | No, no. I was thinking as I was laying down. |

例 2.
チームメンバー	山田さんに相談するって言ってたけど、ただ食事してたみたい。	You said you'd consult with Yamada-san, but it appears that you were just having a meal.
あなた	いや、いや。食事しながら相談してたんですよ。	No, no. I was consulting with her as we were having a meal.

17-1-3P Apologizing for not being prompt
遅れていることを謝罪する (BTS 1)

When a staff member, Yamakawa-san, asks if you've done something, apologize for being delayed, even though you'd said you'd do it right away. Assure her that you'll do it speedily.

例 1.
山川さん (スタッフ)	すみません。新しい情報、共有していただけました？	Excuse me. Did you share (on the cloud, for example) the new information for us?
あなた	あ、すみません。すぐ共有するといいながら遅くなってしまいました。急いで共有するようにします。	Oh, I'm sorry. Here I said I'd share it right away, and I'm delayed. I'll be sure to share it right away.

例 2.
山川さん (スタッフ)	すみません。あの基本の部分、書き直していただけました？	Excuse me. Did you rewrite that basic portion for us?
あなた	あ、すみません。すぐ書き直すといいながら遅くなってしまいました。急いで書き直すようにします。	Oh, I'm sorry. Here I said I'd rewrite it right away, and I'm delayed. I'll be sure to rewrite it right away.

17-1-4P Affirming solidarity 仲間意識を高める (BTS 2)

When Ito-san, an associate, observes how several others are like you and her, agree and say that you are all that way.

例 1.
伊東さん (知人)	山田さんも松浦君もながら世代ですよね。	Yamada-san and Matsuura-san are both also the multi-tasking generation, aren't they?
あなた	本当に。私たちみんな「ながら世代」ですね。	Indeed. We are all the multi-tasking generation, aren't we.

例2.
伊東さん (知人)	浜田さんも松浦君もよく食べますよね。	Hamada-san and Matsuura-san both also eat heartily, don't they?
あなた	本当に。僕たちみんなよく食べますね。	Indeed. We all eat heartily, don't we.

17-1 腕試し

1. Have a discussion with your Japanese associate/friend as to what name you might give your generation.
2. Talk to a Japanese friend about simultaneous activities they do. For example, you could ask if they ever study and listen to music at the same time or check their smartphone while walking.

◆ シーン 17-2 練習

17-2-1C What's the expectation? 予想されていること (BTS 3)

Listen to the audio and write what is expected in the space provided.

例 1.　Family paid the tuition for this term.

例 2.　Yuya will be present.

　　3. _____
　　4. _____
　　5. _____
　　6. _____
　　7. _____
　　8. _____

17-2-2P Giving assurance 確信を伝える (BTS 3)

Your associate, Shoji-san, seems unsure about various things. Assure her that everything should be in order and provide justification for your belief using the information provided.

例 1.
| 庄司さん (知人) | 山田さん、見えませんね。来ないんでしょうか。 | I don't see Yamada-san. I wonder if she isn't coming. |
| あなた | 来るはずですよ。全員出席だから。 | She should be coming, you know. Since everybody is attending. |

例 2.
| 庄司さん (知人) | 飲み物代、ちょっと足りませんね。全員、払わなかったんでしょうか。 | There isn't quite enough beverage money. I wonder if not everybody paid. |
| あなた | 払ったはずですよ。全員に払うように言いましたから。 | Everybody should have paid, you know. Since I told everybody to pay. |

Example 1.　Everybody attends.
Example 2.　You told everybody to pay.
　　　　3.　You sent an email to Mizutani-san, too.

4. Wang-san said he also studied Japanese for three years in China.
5. It was Matsumoto-san's major in college.
6. The research shows results that it is effective.
7. Everybody likes this kind of stuff.

17-2-3P Stating that it's unlikely 可能性が低いことを伝える (BTS 3)

Your team member Fujita-san suggests something that's not likely about various other members. Show your disbelief.

例1.

| 藤田さん (チームメンバー) | 高野さんが会費を払ってくれなかったみたいです。 | It appears that Takano-san didn't pay the membership fee. |
| あなた | ええ？まさか。高野さんが払ってくれないはずはないでしょう。 | What? You're kidding. There's no way that Takano-san wouldn't pay. |

例2.

| 藤田さん (チームメンバー) | 石川さんがなぜかとても弱気なんだそうです。 | I hear that Ishikawa-san, for some reason, is being rather timid. |
| あなた | ええ？まさか。石川さんが弱気なはずはないでしょう。 | What? You're kidding. There's no way that Ishikawa-san is being timid. |

17-2-4P Disagreeing partially 一部を否定する (BTS 3)

You and your team member are making plans for various events. When Sasaki-san makes statements about a potential option, gently disagree with one of the statements.

例1.

| チームメンバー | あのホテルの部屋は、広いし、高いし、親睦会にはどうでしょうかねえ。 | The room in that hotel is big and expensive. I wonder if it's really suitable for an informal meet-and-great. |
| あなた | う〜ん、確かにちょっと広いかもしれないけれど、高くはないはずです。 | Hmm, certainly it may be big, but it shouldn't be expensive. |

例2.

チームメンバー	このあいだの人は行儀が悪いし、話が下手だし、大切なプレゼンを頼むのはどうでしょうかねえ。	The person from the other day has bad manners and is not a good speaker. I wonder if it's really a good idea to request that she do an important presentation.
あなた	う〜ん、確かにちょっと行儀は悪いかもしれないけれど、話は下手ではないはずですよ。	Hmmm, certainly she may have bad manners, but her speech shouldn't be bad.

17-2 腕試し

Find out what sort of costs are included in 交際費(こうさいひ) or 教育費(きょういくひ) by discussing these items with your Japanese friends or associates.

◆ シーン 17-3 練習

 17-3-1C Who did it? したのは誰？ (BTS 5)

Write the name of who did the action and the action that was done. For this activity, if the verb is causative, the one who did the action is the one who was made to do it, not the one who made them do it.

	Who did it	What they did
例 1.	Tanaka-san	Wrapped
例 2.	Yamaguchi-san	Painted
3.	_____	_____
4.	_____	_____
5.	_____	_____
6.	_____	_____
7.	_____	_____
8.	_____	_____
9.	_____	_____
10.	_____	_____
11.	_____	_____
12.	_____	_____

 17-3-2P Suggesting that someone else do it 他の人にさせる (BTS 5)

When an associate asks if he and you will do a task, suggest that you have someone else do it.

例 1.		
知人	私たちがします？	Are we going to do it?
あなた	いや、いや、誰か他の人にさせましょう。	No, no, let's have someone else do it.
例 2.		
知人	私たちが払います？	Are we going to pay?
あなた	いや、いや、誰か他の人に払わせましょう。	No, no, let's have someone else pay.

17-3-3P Volunteering an expert できる人を勧める (BTS 5)

Your client, Okamoto-san, is looking for a person with a particular expertise. Volunteer someone from your group by stating you'll have that person do what Okamoto-san wants.

例1.
岡本さん (顧客)	どなたか、経済関係のことに詳しい方に教えていただけるとありがたいのですが。	We'd be grateful if we could get someone who is well-informed about economic matters to teach.
あなた	お任せください。経済関係のことに詳しいものがおりますので、教えさせますから。	Please leave it to us. There is someone who is well-informed about economic matters, and we'll have that person teach.

例2.
岡本さん (顧客)	どなたか、こう言うところを飾るのが得意な方に飾っていただけるとありがたいのですが。	We'd be grateful if we could get someone who is good at decorating a place like this to decorate it.
あなた	お任せください。こう言うところを飾るのが得意なものがおりますので、飾らせますから。	Please leave it to us. There is someone who is good at decorating a place like this, and we'll have that person decorate it.

17-3-4P Committing to get it done right away
すぐ行うよう約束する (BTS 6)

When a colleague suggests that you ask someone to perform various tasks tell him that you'll convey the request to the person he mentions.

例1.
同僚	この荷物、全部上に運ばなくちゃね。アルバイトさんに頼んでくれます？	We need to carry all of these pieces of luggage upstairs, don't we. Will you ask the part-timers?
あなた	了解です。すぐ運ぶように言っておきますから。	Sure. I'll tell them to carry them right away, so don't worry.

例2.
同僚	この箱、今日中にきれいに包まなくちゃね。上手な人に頼んでくれます？	We need to wrap these boxes nicely today, don't we. Will you ask someone who is skillful?
あなた	了解です。すぐ包むように言っておきますから。	Sure. I'll tell them to wrap them right away, so don't worry.

◆ シーン 17-4 練習

17-4-1C Who did it? したのは誰? (BTS 7)

Mark whether the action was done by the speaker or someone else. Then write the action that was done. For this activity, if the verb is causative, the one who did the action is the one who was made to do it, not the one who made them do it.

	The speaker	Someone else	
例 1.	○		Scan
例 2.	○		Ask
3.			
4.			
5.			
6.			
7.			
8.			
9.			
10.			
11.			
12.			
13.			

17-4-2C According to what? 何によると? (BTS 7)

In each of the following, the second speaker reports some second-hand information. Write the information that is second hand, and the source of the information.

	Second-hand information	Source
例 1.	It's now next week	Email from the division chief
例 2.	Tuition is going to be higher next year	What I heard from Yoshida-san

3. _____   _____
4. _____   _____
5. _____   _____
6. _____   _____
7. _____   _____

17-4-3P Accepting an invitation 促されたことをする (BTS 7)

Your teacher, Hayashi-sensei, urges you to do various things. Accept the invitation gracefully.

例 1.
| 林先生 | どうぞ、どうぞ。ノートに写してください。 | Go right ahead. Please copy it to your notebook. |
| あなた | では、ちょっと写させていただきます。ありがとうございます。 | Then, I'll (have you let me) copy it. Thank you. |

例 2.
| 林先生 | どうぞ、どうぞ。ゆっくり読んでください。 | Go right ahead. Please take your time and read it. |
| あなた | では、ちょっと読ませていただきます。ありがとうございます。 | Then, I'll (have you let me) read it. Thank you. |

17-4-4P Making a conjecture from a graph
グラフを読み取る (BTS 8)

You and your *senpai* are looking at various graphs related to a recent survey. Report the most prominent feature of each graph. Then listen to your *senpai*'s reaction.

例 1.
| あなた | このグラフによると、２０代の人はテレビのニュースをあまり信じないようですね。 | According to this graph, it appears that people in their 20s don't believe TV news very much. |
| 先輩 | へえ、そう。まあ、ソーシャルネットワークの方が本当だと思いやすいかもしれませんね。 | Oh, is that right? Well, perhaps it's easier for them to think that what's on social media is true. |

例 2.
| あなた | このグラフによると、このグループは３０代の男性に人気があるようですね。 | According to this graph, it appears that this group is popular among men in their 30s. |
| 先輩 | へえ、そう。ちょっと意外ですね。もっと若い人が好きなグループかと思いした。 | Oh, is that right? That's a bit surprising, isn't it. I thought that it's a group that younger people like. |

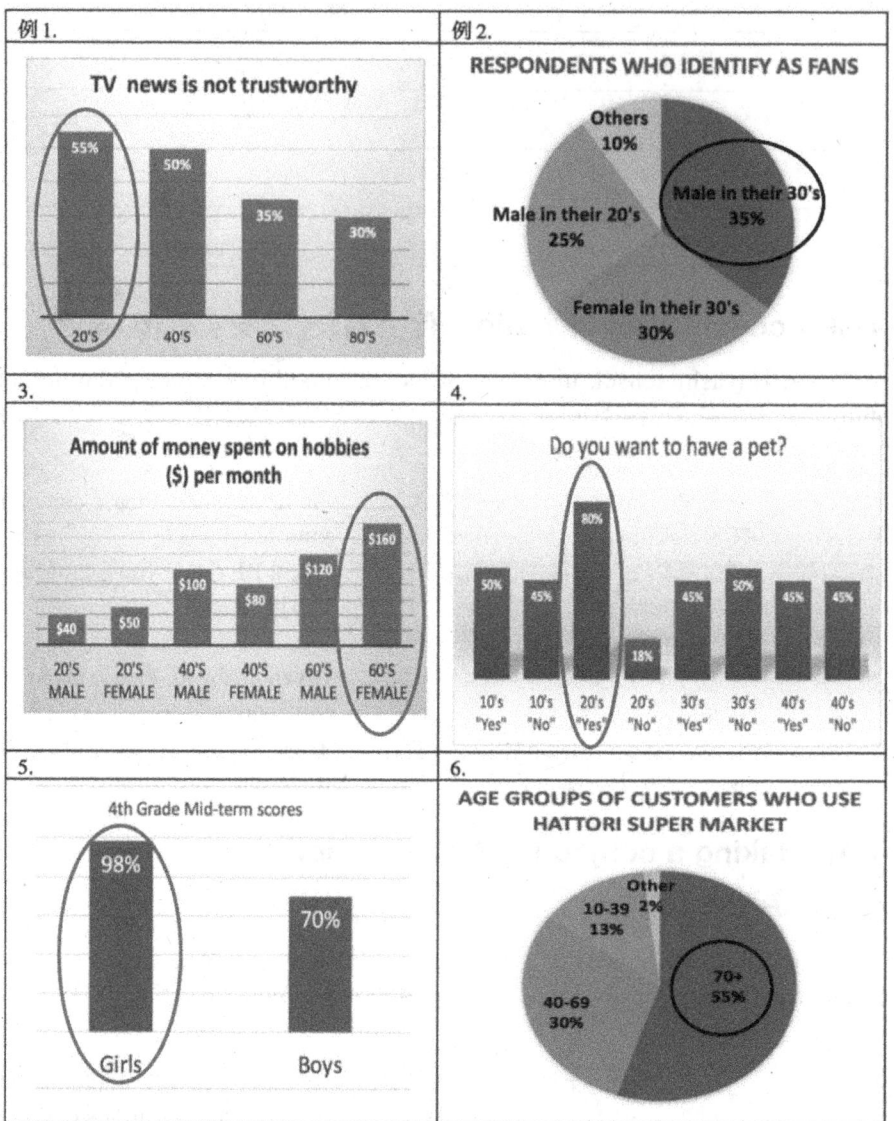

17-4 腕試し

1. Offer to your associate/friend your interpretation of a graph, a chart, or an illustration as a way to start a conversation.
2. Convey some second-hand information to your associate/friend, identifying the source of the information.

◆ シーン 17-5 練習

17-5-1C Qualified responses 〜次第？ 情報源？ (BTS 8, 11)

In each of the following, you will hear the male speaker qualify his response. Mark whether the speaker states that the answer depends on something or that the answer comes from second-hand information. Then write either what the answer depends on or the source of the information.

	It depends on . . .	According to . . .	
例 1.	_____	○	Kanda-san
例 2.	○	_____	The place
3.	_____	_____	_____
4.	_____	_____	_____
5.	_____	_____	_____
6.	_____	_____	_____
7.	_____	_____	_____
8.	_____	_____	_____

17-5-2P Predicting a gradual change
緩やかな変化を予測する (BTS 10)

You and your colleague, Sato-san, are watching someone who just keeps doing the same thing. When Sato-san wonders if nothing will happen, make a prediction that there will be a gradual change.

例 1.
佐藤さん (同僚) さっきからずっと言い合ってるけど、疲れないのかな。 They have been quarreling for a while now; I wonder if they aren't getting tired.

あなた しばらく言い合っているうちに、疲れてきますよ、きっと。 They'll start to get tired as they continue to quarrel, I'm sure.

例 2.
佐藤さん (同僚) あの子たち、さっきからずっとあの辺走ってるけど、おとなしくならないのかな。 Those kids have been running over there for a while now; I wonder if they're going to calm down.

あなた しばらく走っているうちに、おとなしくなってきますよ、きっと。 They'll start to calm down as they continue to run, I'm sure.

17-5-3P Describing a collaborative effort
協働したことを伝える (BTS 9)

Your *senpai* in a project team notices that other members are helping out. Tell him that the two of you did the task by helping each other.

例 1.
先輩　　水野さんにもノート見せてくれたんだね。　　You also showed your notes to Mizuno-san, right?
あなた　はい。二人で見せ合ってやったんです。　　Yes. The two of us worked by showing them to each other.

例 2.
先輩　　武田君も支えてくれたんだね。　　You also supported Takeda-kun, right?
あなた　はい。二人で支え合ってやったんです。　　Yes. The two of us worked by supporting each other.

 17-5-4P Saying that it depends 状況によることを指摘する (BTS 11)

People at the school you work at got food poisoning! It is suspected that the curry dish was the cause. Respond to the investigator's questions by stating that the situation mentioned doesn't apply equally to everyone involved.

例 1.
調査員　みんなひどい下痢になったんですか？　　Did everybody suffer severe diarrhea?
あなた　いえ、それは人によります。ひどくなかった人もいます。　　No, that depends on the person. There are people who didn't have it that bad.

例 2.
調査員　いつもここのキッチンで作るんですか？　　Do you always make it in the kitchen here?
あなた　いえ、それは時によります。このキッチンで作らないこともあります。　　No, that depends on the time (of day). There are times when it's not made here.

17-5 腕試し

When appropriate, make an observation about a change that is beginning to occur, such as the weather warming up or cooling down, work becoming busier, absences increasing, etc. Use it as a starter for a conversation.

◆ シーン 17-6 練習

17-6-1C When? いつ? (BTS 13)

Listen to two people discussing business plans and write down what item(s) is(are) being discussed and when action will be taken.

例 1.	Software	Purchase new software once the editing for the currently written document is complete.
例 2.	Yellow ink cartridges	Order more once the ones in this box are used up.
3.	_____	
4.	_____	
5.	_____	

17-6-2P Encouraging to do as much as possible
出来(でき)るだけするようアドバイスする (BTS 12)

Your friend is not being optimistic about something. Encourage him by urging him to try and do just as much as he can.

例 1.
友だち	これ、覚えなきゃいけないの？全部覚えられるかなあ。	You mean I have to memorize this? I wonder if I can memorize it all.
あなた	まあ、覚えられるだけ覚えてみたら？	Well, why not try and memorize what you can?

例 2.
友だち	わあ、言いたいことこんなにあるの？全部言えるかなあ。	You mean there are this many things we want to say? I wonder if I can say them all.
あなた	まあ、言えるだけ言ってみたら？	Well, why not try and say what you can?

17-6-3P Suggesting that the situation is limited
状況(じょうきょう)が限(かぎ)られていると示唆(しさ)する (BTS 12)

Your associate seems to have an exaggerated understanding of the situation. Gently correct her by saying that the situation is limited to only part of what she suggests.

例 1.
知人	安いし、味もいいんでしょ？大学の食堂。	It's cheap and things taste good, right? I mean the college cafeteria.

あなた	そうならいいんだけど、安いだけで味があまり良くはないですね。	I wish it were like that, but it's just cheap; it doesn't taste very good.

例2.

知人	みんなで話し合って、決めているんでしょ？	You're all talking to each other and making a decision, right?
あなた	そうならいいんだけど、みんなで話し合うだけで、決めてはいませんね。	I wish it were like that, but we just talk to each other; we haven't made a decision.

17-6-4P Defending the blamed person 弁護する (BTS 14)

You are dealing with the head of an institute who is blaming others for an undesirable outcome. Defend the person being attacked by negating his claim.

例1.

所長	あなたがよく考えないから、こういう残念な結果になったんじゃないですか？	It's because you don't think carefully that we have this kind of unfortunate result, isn't it?
あなた	私だって、考えてます。それは所長だってご存知じゃないですか。	But I am thinking. You know that too, don't you?

例2.

所長	水野さんがめちゃくちゃだから、こういうひどい結果になったんじゃないですか？	It's because Mizuno-san is all over the place that we have this kind of miserable result, isn't it?
あなた	水野さんだって、めちゃくちゃじゃないです。それは所長だってご存知じゃないですか。	But Mizuno-san isn't all over the place. You know that too, don't you?

◆ シーン 17-7R 練習

17-7-1R "Time" or "notwithstanding"? 並行か矛盾か

Determine which sense of 〜ながら is intended in each of the following statements.

例 1. このアパート、駅から<u>近いながら</u>なかなか広くていいですね。 ☐ time ☒ notwithstanding

例 2. <u>歩きながら</u>考えればいいんですよ。 ☒ time ☐ notwithstanding

3. 昨日物を運ぶのを<u>助けながら</u>色々と話したみたいですよ。 ☐ time ☐ notwithstanding

4. ミーティングに<u>出席しながら</u>、話を全く聞いてなかったみたいですよ。 ☐ time ☐ notwithstanding

5. あのお店って、駅から<u>遠いながら</u>よく売れるんですよね。 ☐ time ☐ notwithstanding

6. 以前から思ってたんだけど、あの社長、<u>若いながら</u>しっかりとしたビジョンを持っていますね。 ☐ time ☐ notwithstanding

7. 僕、<u>旅行しながら</u>できる仕事があればいいのになって時々思うんだ。 ☐ time ☐ notwithstanding

8. 出費を1万円以下にしたいかどうかは<u>話し合いながら</u>決めましょうよ。 ☐ time ☐ notwithstanding

17-7-2R Reasonable expectations 妥当な予想

Determine which of the expectations is more reasonable in each statement.

例 1. 駅から近いって言ってたから (遠い・⦅遠くはない⦆) はずだけど……。

例 2. 出席 (⦅する⦆・しない) はずですよ。昨日は来られるって言ってましたから……。

3. うちのネコ、(助かる・助からない) はずだったのに、助かったんです。

4. 以前会ったことあるから、(知ってる・知らない) はずはないんだけど……。

5. 会費、(安かった・安くなかった) はずなんだけど、思ったより高くなっててびっくりしたよ。

6. そんなにないから、僕たちだけでも (運べる・運べない) はずだけど……。

7. 学費、安くはないけど、4年間で300万円以上には (なる・ならない) はずだよ。

8. まだ若いけど、料理学校に行ってたそうだから、(上手な・下手な) はずはないんだけど……。

17-7-3RW Responding ambiguously 曖昧(あいまい)に答(こた)える

Write up ambiguous responses to the following inquiries.

例1. 出席できませんか。
　　　僕(私)ですか。いえ、できなくはないですよ。
　　　_____

例2. 食費って高いですか。
　　　食費ですか。まあ、高くはないけど、安くもないですよ。
　　　_____

3. 料理、上手ですか。
　　　_____

4. あの場所って便利ですか。
　　　_____

5. あの席って遠いですか。
　　　_____

6. 運べませんか。
　　　_____

7. 遠野先生って若いですか。
　　　_____

8. 助けられませんか。
　　　_____

9. 白井君、強気ですか。
　　　_____

◆ シーン 17-8R 練習

17-8-1R Making requests 依頼の内容

Determine whether the following requests are affirmative or negative.

例1. 急がないとできないから、うちの者にも (**させる**・させない) ようにお願いしてあります。

例2. 失礼なことを (言う・**言わない**) ようにあれほど言っておいたのに……。

3. お客様を (待たせる・待たせない) ように頼んでおいたんだけど、やっぱり遅いなあ。

4. スマホには (頼り過ぎる・頼り過ぎない) ようにって先生がおっしゃってましたよ。

5. あんな話 (信じる・信じない) ように言っておいたのに、信じちゃったようですね。

6. 先約のため出席できないので、代わりに弟に (出る・出ない) ようにお願いしておきました。

7. ２０代のころの写真はあんまり好きじゃないみたいだから、みんなに (見せる・見せない) ように言ってましたけど……。

8. 宿題多いからちゃんと助けて (あげる・あげない) ように頼んでおいたのに……。

17-8-2R Identifying the source 情報源は？

Identify the most probable source of each fact being shared in the following statements. You may use each option only once.

| 昨日読んだ本 | 神田さん | 若者の話 |
| 新聞 | スケジュール | このグラフ |

例1. ＿＿スケジュール＿＿によると明日の宿題は２５ページから２７ページまでのようです。

例2. ＿＿このグラフ＿＿によるとアメリカには日系人はハーフも入れると１２０万人近くいるそうだよ。

3. ＿＿＿＿＿＿＿＿＿によると午後から雨になるってあったから、外見てみたけど、雨にはならなそうな天気だね。

4. ＿＿＿＿＿＿＿＿＿によると写真の右の人が２０年前の八木部長で、となりにいるのがお子さんみたいですね。

5. ＿＿＿＿＿＿＿＿＿によると日本人は電車に乗る時にあまり話さないって書いてあるんだけど、これって本当？

6. ＿＿＿＿＿＿＿＿＿によるとこのエリアで食事代、エアコン付きで３０００円は信じられないぐらい安いんだって。

17-8-3RW Using causatives 使役表現(しえきひょうげん)

Change the verbs that are provided below to causative forms that are appropriate in the context. Determine what particle should be associated with the specified nouns.

例1.　入る　　　　　ドアが開いていたので、＿＿＿入らせて＿＿＿もらいました。

例2.　広明；決める　だれからも連絡がなかったので、＿＿＿広明に決めさせ＿＿＿ました。

3.　宿題；持つ　　お子様が忘れないように＿＿＿＿＿＿＿＿＿＿＿＿＿＿＿あげてください。

4.　勉強する　　　理系が好きならこの大学で＿＿＿＿＿＿＿＿＿＿＿＿＿＿＿あげたいですね。

5.　１０代の子；飲む　お酒は＿＿＿＿＿＿＿＿＿＿＿＿＿＿＿はいけませんよ。

6.　来る　　　　　今日は本当にいい時間を過ごせました。また次回も＿＿＿＿＿＿＿＿＿＿＿＿＿＿＿ください。

7.　子ども；乗る　このライドは小さい＿＿＿＿＿＿＿＿＿＿＿＿＿＿＿はいけないようです。

8.　漢字；覚える　学生にこのリストにある＿＿＿＿＿＿＿＿＿＿＿＿＿＿＿たいと思っているんだけど……。

9.　だれか；頼る　＿＿＿＿＿＿＿＿＿＿＿＿＿＿＿ほしいところだけど、自分でがんばらなくちゃ。

17-8-4RW Thank you messages 感謝(かんしゃ)のことば

Change the verbs that are provided below to causative forms that are appropriate in the context. Determine what particle should be associated with the specified nouns.

例1.　私；考える　　次のイベントの事、＿＿＿私に考えさせて＿＿＿くれてありがとう。

例2. 日本語のクラス；教える　　先日は教室で＿＿＿＿＿＿＿＿日本語のクラスを教えさせて＿＿＿＿＿＿＿＿くださり、とてもいい練習になりました。ありがとうございました。

3. 宿題；やり直す　　本田先生、＿＿＿＿＿＿＿＿＿＿＿＿＿＿くださってありがとうございました。

4. IT系の仕事の話；聞く　　先日は＿＿＿＿＿＿＿＿＿＿＿＿＿＿＿＿＿＿もらい、とても勉強になりました。大切なお時間、本当にありがとうございました。

5. 弟；待つ　　昨日は雨の中車で＿＿＿＿＿＿＿＿＿＿＿＿＿いただき、本当に助かりました。ありがとうございました。

6. ２０代のころの事；思い出す　　アルバムを見て＿＿＿＿＿＿＿＿＿＿＿＿＿＿＿＿＿もらいました。ありがとうございました。

7. 僕；出席する　　先日のレセプション、姉だけではなく、＿＿＿＿＿＿＿＿＿＿＿＿＿＿＿＿＿くださってありがとうございました。

8. 妹；聞く　　この間の話、弟だけではなく、＿＿＿＿＿＿＿＿＿＿＿＿＿＿くれてありがとうございました。

9. 写真；使う　　いつも＿＿＿＿＿＿＿＿＿＿＿＿＿＿くれてありがとう。これからもよろしくね。

◆ シーン 17-9R 練習

17-9-1R To or with each other? 〜合（あ）う

Select an appropriate verb for each statement below. You may use each option only once.

話し	分かり	言い	付き
呼び	出し	連絡し	通じ

例1. アメリカでは会社の人とファーストネームで＿＿呼び＿＿合ってますけど、日本ではやっぱり変ですよね。

例2. どのキャラが一番強いかを＿＿話し＿＿合うためにわざわざ集まるそうですよ。

3. 家族だけで、一緒に時間も過ごさないし、気持ちはあまり＿＿＿＿＿＿合わないんだよね……。

4. 暑かったり寒かったりする時は外での＿＿＿＿＿＿合いが大変し、人が多いと名前が覚えきれないんだ。

5. 場所と時間はできるだけ＿＿＿＿＿＿合ってから一緒に決めた方がいいと思う。

6. 本当の気持ちを伝えたいと思っているのに、つい＿＿＿＿＿＿合いになってしまうことってありませんか。

7. みんなで意見を＿＿＿＿＿＿合うのは少し考える時間を持ってからにしませんか。

8. ＿＿＿＿＿＿合える気がしないし、これ以上話しても意味がない気がするんだけど……。

17-9-2R Depending on what? 何によって？

For each statement below, determine which of the nouns that follow fits most suitably. You may use each option only once.

メニュー	先生	日	ライフスタイル
薬	スケジュール	天気	場合

例1. この店の料理、＿＿メニュー＿＿によっては大人だって食べきれないものもあるみたいだよ。

例2. 病院のレビューがいいっていうだけで、決めない方がいいと思うよ。＿＿先生＿＿によってはあんまりよくない人もいるみたいだし。

3. 「ごめんなさい」という意味もあれば、「失礼します」という意味もある「すみません」というフレーズは、＿＿＿＿＿＿＿＿＿＿＿＿＿＿によって意味が変わるフレーズのいい例ですね。

4. ＿＿＿＿＿＿＿＿＿＿＿＿＿＿によっては一緒に飲んではいけないものもあるので気を付けてください。

5. ＿＿＿＿＿＿＿＿＿＿＿＿＿＿によっては間に合わなくなるかもしれないけど、時間と場所が決まったら連絡ください。

6. 明日のハイキングは＿＿＿＿＿＿＿＿＿＿＿＿にもよるけど、暑くなるようであれば水をたくさん持っていかないときつくなると思います。

7. ＿＿＿＿＿＿＿＿＿＿＿＿＿＿によっては、０℃以下になって寒くなる場合もあるので、コートとかジャケットを持ってきておいたほうがいいですよ。

8. ＿＿＿＿＿＿＿＿＿＿＿＿＿によっては治る病気も治らなくなってしまうことがあるので、しっかり休む時間を持つようにしてください。

17-9-3RW Writing short memos メモを書(か)く

Fill in the blanks with kanji (and *okurigana* as needed) in the following memos.

例1. ＿＿会費(かいひ)＿＿は３０００円です。ここに入れておいてください。

例2. マフラー持ってきました。もし＿＿＿寒(さむ)かったら＿＿＿使ってください。

3. 昨日の＿＿＿＿＿(しゅくだい)＿＿＿＿＿です。遅くなってすみませんでした。

4. ＿＿＿＿＿(びょういん)＿＿＿＿＿の行き方です。分からなくなったらご連絡ください。

5. 来週のコンサートのチケット。＿＿＿＿＿(いっしょ)＿＿＿＿＿に行かない？

6. ＿＿＿＿(くすり)＿＿＿＿です。早く＿＿＿＿(なおる)＿＿＿＿といいですね。お大事に！

7. この＿＿＿＿＿(いみ)＿＿＿＿＿、分かりますか。

8. スポーツドリンクが入ってます。今日はすごく＿＿＿＿(あつく)＿＿＿＿なるそうなので、気を付けてください。

◆ Act 17 評価

 聞いてみよう

Read the context, listen to the audio, and then answer the questions. If you hear something unfamiliar, rely on what you know to choose the correct answer.

1. As Brian and his *senpai,* Haruka, are getting ready for a presentation, Haruka notices something.

   a. What does Haruka think of what Brian is doing?
   b. What did Haruka tell Brian previously?

2. Yagi-bucho seems happy as she talks with Kanda-san about a product.

   a. What does Yagi-bucho think is impressive?
   b. What does Kanda-san think the reason for this is?
   c. What evidence does Yagi-bucho give of their success?

3. Amy and Takashi are talking about a visitor.

   a. What does Amy want to know?
   b. What is Takashi's answer? How certain is he of this information?
   c. What conclusion does Amy draw from Takashi's answer?

4. Kanda-san and Sasha are attending a party. Their supervisor gives a short speech.

   a. What happened last week?
   b. What does the supervisor thank everyone for?
   c. What does the supervisor say he would like to do? Why does he want to do this?
   d. What does the supervisor tell everyone to do?
   e. What does the supervisor say will happen first?
   f. What does the supervisor say will happen later?

5. Sasha talks to her roommate, Eri, in the kitchen while Eri is using a package of herbs to prepare dinner.

   a. What does Sasha (the first speaker) initially claim?
   b. What does Sasha then try to confirm?
   c. What did Eri (the second speaker) apparently not realize?
   d. What does Eri plan to do now?

6. Amy talks to her *senpai*, who is a graduate student, at school.

   a. What is Amy's *senpai*'s plan for the conference?
   b. How does Amy respond when her *senpai* asks her about her plan? How does she explain her response?
   c. How does Amy's *senpai* attempt to address Amy's concern?
   d. What is Amy's plan after talking to her *senpai*?

7. A visitor is checking through a draft of an information packet with Sasha.

   a. What issue does the visitor raise?
   b. How does Sasha respond to the visitor?
   c. What is Sasha going to do about the issue?

8. Brian's homestay host mother notices there is something wrong with Brian.

   a. What does Brian initially say is the problem?
   b. What is the actual problem?
   c. How does Brian's host mother try to encourage Brian?
   d. How does Brian respond to his host mother's encouragement?

9. Sasha and Kanda-san are talking about something that Kanda-san is reading.

   a. What does Sasha want to know?
   b. What does Sasha learn from Kanda-san?
   c. What does Sasha say about the issue Kanda-san is reading about?

10. Sasha and Kanda-san continue to talk about the same topic.

    a. Give three examples of the issue Kanda-san is reading about.
    b. What clarification does Sasha make about senior citizens?
    c. How does Kanda-san respond to Sasha's comment? What is his opinion about senior citizens?

11. Professor Yamada has just given a lecture about studying English.

    a. What was Professor Yamada's lecture about?
    b. What is Professor Yamada asked to do?
    c. In clarifying the meaning of his lecture, what, according to Professor Yamada, is he not saying? What is he saying?

12. Kanda-san is visiting Ms. Ono at her office and he is at the reception desk.

    a. What information does Kanda-san initially provide the receptionist?
    b. What information does the receptionist attempt to elicit from Kanda-san?
    c. What does the receptionist ask Kanda-san to do?
    d. What does Kanda-san say he will do?

13. Ms. Ono just came out to greet Kanda-san.

   a. Why does Ms. Ono apologize?
   b. Why does Kanda-san apologize?
   c. What does Ms. Ono say will happen today?

 使ってみよう

For each of the following, listen to the audio, and respond to what was said based on the context. Then listen to the sample response.

1. Tell a work *senpai* that there is no expectation that (a) (he) wants to avoid this job; (b) (she) opposes it; (c) the number of hits went down; (d) the process is complicated; (e) it is difficult to use; (f) they will make Yamashita-san go.
2. Tell a work *kohai* that the item is neither cheap nor expensive.
3. Tell a work *senpai* that you're not well informed but heard a little from Yoshida-san.
4. Tell a friend that you heard that Mizuno-sensei made Ichiro-kun rewrite his thesis.
5. Tell a work client that because it might take time, you'll get Tomoda-san (a member of your firm) to assist.
6. A professor from Tokyo University has just showed you a useful website that he developed. Thank him and politely tell him that you will use the website.
7. A friend is wondering why you're home early, as you usually have a club activity at this time. Tell him that your *senpai* let you leave early.
8. In response to a friend's question, tell him that you think (a) it depends on the person; (b) it depends on the year; (c) it depends on the location; (d) it depends on the season.
9. Suggest to a work *senpai* that he try talking together with the people who are opposed.
10. In response to an acquaintance's question, tell him that you've started to get used to Japan a little.
11. You're not feeling well. In response to a friend's inquiry, tell him that all you did was eat sushi.
12. You and a friend are looking at an item in a store. In response to your friend's comment, tell him that all it is is pretty. It's difficult to use, and it's not useful at all.
13. Tell a friend that there are so many kanji you can't remember them all.

Now it's your turn to start the conversation based on the given context. Listen to how the other person reacts to you. For some items, you may not get a verbal response. Don't be concerned if you hear things you have not yet learned.

14. Suggest to a friend that you (a) talk while drinking tea or something; (b) walk (to a destination) while eating; (c) listen to music while studying.
15. Tell a work *senpai* that you expect that (a) Murata-san will arrive in about 10 minutes; (b) (she) already got someone to paint it; (c) you don't have to pay for it by yourself; (d) Yoshida-san won't be coming today; (e) the process is not difficult.

16. Ask if it is Yoshida-san that will be informing the professors at Tokyo University.
17. Ask a classmate if you can read her notes.
18. Very politely ask a superior if you can go home early.
19. You just went out to eat with a *senpai* from work. Request that she let you pay the check today.
20. Tell a work *senpai* that according to the information Tomoda-san gave you, this is the most popular.
21. Tell a work *kohai* to do it by the end of the week, if possible.
22. You are trying to encourage a friend to try something. Tell her it's easy, and that you were able to do it.

読んでみよう

Consider the context provided and read the passage to answer the questions that follow. Do your best to work around the expressions and *kanji* characters that have not been introduced.

1. You found the following sign at the train station.

   大雪による電車の運休により遅れが出ております。

   a. What does the sign tell you about the train schedule? Provide details.

   [パフォーマンス] Assume the role of Brian. Call your host family and explain why you might come late.
2. Brian wrote a journal entry in Japanese.

   だれにも頼らないで一人で日本の病院に行ってきた。僕だってやればできる！お医者さんの話によると薬を飲めばすぐ治るみたいだから早く飲んで治そうって！

   a. What is Brian so proud of? Why?
   b. What did the お医者さん tell Brian? What is he going to do?

   [パフォーマンス] Talk about something you've done recently that you are proud of with your conversation partner.
3. Brian wrote another journal entry in Japanese about his homework assignment.

   今日の宿題、先生ができるだけ一人でやるように言ってたけど、勉強してない漢字が多くてめちゃくちゃ大変だったし、テレビ見ながらやってたら4時間もかかった……。

a. What was Brian told by his teacher?
b. How long did it take him? Why?

[パフォーマンス] Talk with your conversation partner about how long it took you to complete your recent homework assignment. Briefly explain why.

4. Takashi posted something on his SNS account.

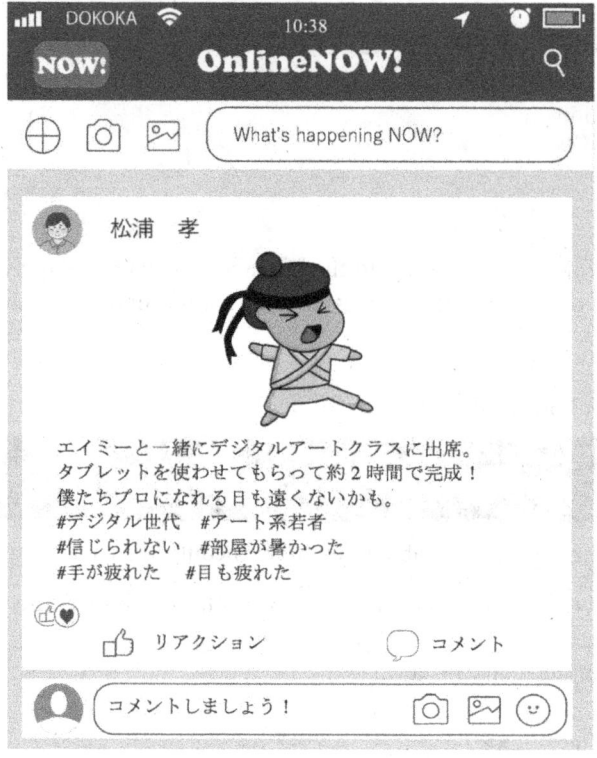

a. What did Takashi do?
b. Why is タブレット mentioned?
c. What is Takashi's aspiration for the future?
d. What do each of the expressions marked with the #s mean?

[パフォーマンス] Add a comment to the above post.

5. Takashi's budget for October.

１０月	金額	メモ
学費	７５０ドル	
食費	２００ドル	外食に５０ドル以上使わないように！
アパート代	３２０ドル	

電気代	２５ドル	家にいない時は電気を消す！
水代	１５ドル	シャワーは1日１回！
電話代	７０ドル	スマホのデータはできるだけ使い切らないように！
交通費	５０ドル	バス代・ライドサービス代
交際費	１００ドル	デート代・デジタルアートクラス参加料・写真クラス参加料・飲食代
オンラインストリーミング代	１０ドル	
その他	５０ドル	運送サービス代 洋服代(くつ下、Tシャツ)

a. How much tuition is he paying for October?
b. How much is rent, electricity, and water combined?
c. What special note is mentioned regarding the food cost?
d. What special note is mentioned regarding the phone cost?
e. Does Takashi have a car? How do you know?
f. What kind of entertainment activities and services are listed?
g. What additional cost is Takashi anticipating?

[パフォーマンス] Compare your monthly budget with that of Takashi. Talk about the differences and similarities with your conversation partner.

6. Professor Sakamoto sent out an email to her students about the homework assignment for tomorrow.

> 件名：明日の宿題
>
> 日本語２０１の学生の皆様
> 明日の宿題にはまだ勉強していない漢字もいくつか出てきます。読み方や意味の分からない漢字があっても、皆さんのレベルなら内容をフォローできるはずなので、頑張って読んでみてください。私としてはできるだけ一人でやってほしいと思っていますが、クラスメートと一緒に助け合ってやっても大丈夫です。
> それでは、寒い季節になってきましたが、風邪をひかないように気を付けてくださいね。
> 坂本

a. What kind of kanji characters appear in the assignment?
b. What promise does she make?

c. Why does she mention 一人で and クラスメートと in relation to the assignment?
d. What does she tell her students to be careful about at the end of her email? Why?

[パフォーマンス] Ask your classmates if they looked up any unfamiliar kanji characters in the email.

書き取り

Listen to the audio, repeat silently what you hear, then write it down. What do you think the context is?

1. _____。
2. _____。
3. _____。
4. _____。
5. _____。
6. _____。
7. _____。
8. _____。

書いてみよう

Consider the context provided and compose a text according to the directions.

1. You asked someone to take some medication to Tono-san (lit. 'far field'), your club mate, who is sick and did not make it to the club activity. Leave a short memo.

It's medicine that I got from the hospital. I expect you'll get better quickly if you take it and rest. Take care.

_____
_____
_____
_____

2. You missed a class. Write the following message in an email to your teacher, Nishida-sensei. You may use the following space to draft your email by hand.

Address your teacher. Apologize for not being able to attend class with an explanation that you are not fully recovered from your illness today. Explain that there are parts where you don't understand the meaning in the homework assignment and ask the teacher if you could have a little bit of time after class tomorrow. Finish your email with an appropriate concluding remark and your name.

件名：

3. You and your friends participated in a volunteer activity. Type up the following captions in Japanese to accompany the photo. You may use space that follows to draft your captions.

A volunteer (activity) that we, too, can do!

#helpeachotherwheninneed   #evenyoungpeopleworkhard   #letsstrivetogether
#goodpicture   #friendswhocanbelieveeachother

4. Write a blog entry about your volunteering experience.

Yesterday I had (an organization) let me help with the gardening work as a volunteer. I couldn't do it really well, but it allowed me to think about various things while I carried planters. The weather was pleasant – not too hot and not too cold.

_____
_____
_____
_____
_____

5. Plan your own budget in Japanese by either writing it down in the chart below or typing it up on your computer. Write down the month. Include food cost, rent, electricity, water, and phone, as well as other categories of expenses relevant to you. In the memo column, set a certain limit for food costs (don't spend more than X amount of money for things like eating out or alcohol) and phone fees (as much as possible, don't use up all your data). As needed, add other notes.

_____月	金額	メモ

知ってる？

Select the most appropriate option and write the letter on your answer sheet. (The symbol ∅ means that nothing is necessary in the blank above.)

1. You tell your friend that she mustn't use her cellphone while driving.
   携帯（けいたい）を_____ながら運転（うんてん）しちゃいけないよ。 (BTS 1)
   a. 使（つか）い
   b. 使う
   c. 使って

2. You're surprised that a certain child can do so much.
   子供＿＿＿＿＿何でもできるねぇ。(BTS 1)

   a. なんで
   b. だから
   c. ながら

3. What suffix can be used to pluralize 先生 politely? (BTS 2)

   a. 〜ら
   b. 〜たち
   c. 〜がた

4. What suffix is commonly used to pluralize 人? (BTS 2)

   a. 〜ら
   b. 〜たち
   c. 〜がた

5. Your friend thinks the membership fee will be high, but you don't expect it will be.
   ＿＿＿＿＿はずはないよ。 (BTS 3)

   a. 高い
   b. 高かった
   c. 高くない

6. Your colleague thinks that everyone can't attend the class, but you expect that they can.
   いや、みんな出席＿＿＿＿＿よ。(BTS 3)

   a. できないはずだ
   b. できるはずはない
   c. できないはずはない

7. You agree that the test is long, but you don't think it's difficult.
   長いですけど、難しく＿＿＿＿＿ないと思う。 (BTS 4)

   a. は
   b. も
   c. じゃ

8. You've been asked your opinion about a movie.
   よく＿＿＿＿＿悪く＿＿＿＿＿ない。(BTS 4)

   a. は　　は
   b. も　　も
   c. も　　は

9. You intend to have the part-timer clean up the conference room.
   会議室、アルバイトの学生＿＿＿＿＿片付けさせるつもりです。(BTS 5)

   a. を
   b. に
   c. が

10. You report that you told the guests to come a bit early.
    お客さまにちょっと早く来る＿＿＿＿＿言った。(BTS 6)

    a. と
    b. こと
    c. ように

11. You ask that you be allowed to pay for lunch.
    ＿＿＿＿＿ください。(BTS 7)

    a. 払って
    b. 払わせて
    c. 払ってもらって

12. You're grateful that the *bucho* let you go home early.
    早く＿＿＿＿＿いただきました。(BTS 7)

    a. 帰って
    b. 帰れて
    c. 帰らせて

13. You've read that it will be a really hot summer this year.
    記事に＿＿＿＿＿、今年の夏はすごく暑いそうです。(BTS 8)

    a. よって
    b. よると
    c. よったら

14. A Verb stem combined with 合う expresses an activity that you will ＿＿＿＿＿. (BTS 9)

    a. complete a year from now
    b. accomplish while you're away
    c. do together with someone

15. You realize that you've started to understand the situation.
    わかって＿＿＿＿＿。(BTS 10)

    a. きました
    b. なりました
    c. いきました

16. You suggest that you make a decision based on how many people will come.
    何人来るかに＿＿＿＿＿決めましょう。 (BTS 11)

    a. よって
    b. よると
    c. よったら

17. You've been asked about enrollments in Japanese classes at your school.
    学期に＿＿＿＿＿変わります。 (BTS 11)

    a. よる
    b. よると
    c. よって

18. You've been asked what you think of the new restaurant.
    きれい＿＿＿＿＿だけで、全然おいしくないよ。 (BTS 12)

    a. の
    b. な
    c. ∅

19. You tell your friend that you can't finish the whole pizza.
    ＿＿＿＿＿と思う。 (BTS 13)

    a. 食べられない
    b. 食べきれない
    c. 食べるはずはない

20. だって following a Noun X means ＿＿＿＿＿. (BTS 14)

    a. even X
    b. X also
    c. except X

21. Which of the following is true about Particle や? (BTL 1)

    a. It may appear between two Verbs.
    b. It can follow a single Noun.
    c. It appears only between Nouns.

22. だ is sometimes necessary before か in embedded questions in order to ＿＿＿＿＿. (BTL 2)

    a. reduce ambiguity
    b. add emphasis
    c. sound assertive

23. In spoken Japanese 和語(わご) are used more commonly than 漢語(かんご) because they make speech sound more _____. (BTL 3)

   a. polite
   b. friendly
   c. formal

24. When ぐらい follows a Noun it may indicate that the Noun is _____. (BTL 4)

   a. not very significant
   b. the maximum
   c. an approximation

第18幕
Act 18

怒(おこ)られた。
I got reprimanded.

以心伝心(いしんでんしん)
Meeting of the minds.

◆ **シーン 18-1 練習**

🎧 18-1-1C Who did it? 誰がした? (BTS 1)

For each of the following, indicate who performed the given action. If it was the speaker, mark "the speaker." If it was someone else, mark "other" and write in the person's name.

		The speaker	Other:	
例 1.	Showing	○		
例 2.	Laughing		○	Watanabe-san
3.	Sending			
4.	Crying			
5.	Writing			
6.	Refusing			
7.	Inviting			
8.	Requesting			
9.	Giving			
10.	Saying			
11.	Asking			
12.	Forgetting			

🎧 18-1-2C Listening to the weather forecast
天気予報を聞く (BTS 4)

Your friend Miyuki is checking the weather in various places on her weather app. What does she say the weather will be like tomorrow? Answer by writing the code of the illustration that best matches the description she gives. You may use each illustration only once.

例 1. h _____ 6. _____
例 2. d _____ 7. _____
3. _____ 8. _____
4. _____ 9. _____
5. _____ 10. _____

182

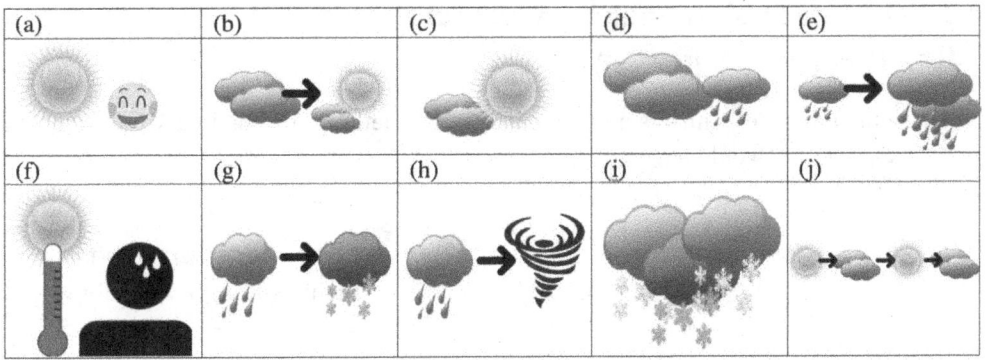

18-1-3P Describing a negative experience 嫌(いや)な経験(けいけん)を伝(つた)える (BTS 1)

You have been having a lot of negative experiences with Nakazawa-san, your work *senpai*. When your friend asks what happened, describe the negative experience based on the illustration.

例1.

友達　　どうしたの？　　　　　　　What happened?
あなた　中沢さんに泣かれたんだ。　　Nakazawa-san cried (and I was negatively affected).

例2.

友達　　どうしたの？　　　　　　　What happened?
あなた　中沢さんにお寿司食べられ　　Nakazawa-san ate the sushi (and I was negatively
　　　　たんだ。　　　　　　　　　　affected).

18-1-4P Describing based on expectations
期待と比べて伝える (BTS 2)

When your friend Yuya makes a comment about something, respond based on what the general expectation would be.

例 1.
裕也　　暖かいよね、この冬。　　　　　　　This winter is warm, isn't it?
あなた　そうね。冬にしては暖かいかも。　　Yeah, I guess it's warm for winter.

例 2.
裕也　　暑いよね、この夏。　　　　　　　　This summer is hot, isn't it?
あなた　そうね。夏にしても暑いよね。　　　Yeah, it's hot even for summer.

18-1 腕試し

1. Engage in some small talk with an associate or a friend, using a comment about the weather forecast to start the conversation. It may be based on your personal observation, or what you saw/heard on the media or from another person. If possible, make your comment relevant to a planned activity in the near future.
2. Discuss with an associate or a friend recent weather patterns in the area where you live. Remember to show sensitivity if your discussion includes references to natural disasters.
3. Discuss with an associate or a friend difficulties that the two of you (and perhaps others) have suffered due to weather.

◆ シーン 18-2 練習

18-2-1C What's going on? どういうこと? (BTS 6)

Even when one has a clear understanding of the situation, one may use みたい or らしい to soften the expression to be more indirect and therefore more polite. Listen to various statements that Mika makes and for each utterance identify which one of the two strategies Mika is using.

	Making a guess about the situation	Being polite by describing the situation in less certain terms
例 1.	○	
例 2.		○
3.		
4.		
5.		
6.		

18-2-2P Acknowledging lack of care
うっかりしていたことを認める (BTS 5)

Someone did something and has inadvertently failed to put things back the way they were. When a supervisor notices the situation, apologize and promise to remedy the situation.

例 1.
上司　　空調、消えてますよ。さっきから　　The heater is turned off. I've been
　　　　寒いと思ったら。　　　　　　　　　thinking it was cold.
あなた　あ、消しっぱなしになってました　　Oh, did someone leave it turned off?
　　　　か。すみません。すぐつけます。　　Sorry. I'll turn it on right away.
例 2.
上司　　色々机の上に出したままになって　　There is a lot of stuff left out on the
　　　　いて、ちょっと邪魔なんですけど。　　desk and it's in the way.
あなた　あ、出しっぱなしになってました　　Oh, did someone leave that stuff out?
　　　　か。すみません。すぐ片付けます。　　Sorry. I'll put it away right away.

18-2-3P Requesting to follow up
やりっぱなしにしないよう念を押す (BTS 5)

When your friend Keita volunteers to do something, tell him to do it, but ask him to follow-up afterwards.

例 1.
友人　ねえ、これからここで料理したいんだけど、いい？
あなた　してくれてもいいけど、しっぱなしにしないでよ。

Hey, I want to cook here now. Is that okay?
Yes, it's okay if you do that for us, but don't forget to follow up afterwards (e.g., clean up, serve the food), okay?

例 2.
友人　ねえ、この映画の感想、書きたいんだけど、いい？
あなた　書いてくれてもいいけど、書きっぱなしにしないでよ。

Hey, I want to write the critique of this movie. Is that okay?
Yes, it's okay if you do that for us, but don't forget to follow up (e.g., edit, take it to the reviewer), okay?

18-2-4CP Adding a conjecture 推測を加える (BTS 6)

Your host mother left the TV on when she stepped out. The reporter is interviewing Shimizu-san, a chef. Listen to the introduction and when your host mother returns and asks questions about him, answer the best you can by offering some related information you heard. If you find that you need to re-listen to the introduction, don't hesitate to do so!

例 1.
ホストマザー　清水さんって、何歳くらいでしょうね。
あなた　さあ、何歳かはわからないけど、若いらしいですよ。

I wonder about how old Shimizu-san is.
Hmm, I can't tell how old he is, but he is apparently young.

例 2.
ホストマザー　清水さんって、趣味は何かな。
あなた　さあ、趣味が何かはわからないけど、野菜を育てているらしいですよ。

I wonder what Shimizu-san's hobby is.
Hmm, I can't tell what his hobby is, but he apparently grows vegetables.

18-2 腕試し

1. With a friend that you feel comfortable confiding in, describe a difficult situation caused by someone else's action and seek advice.
2. Discuss with an associate or friend a person who has had a significant influence on you (or your associate/friend). What did that person do? Did you feel at the time of the action that you (or your associate/friend) benefited or that it caused you some discomfort? How do you (or your associate/friend) feel in retrospect?
3. When the opportunity presents itself, apologize to your Japanese associate/friend for having forgotten to do something you should have done.

◆ **シーン 18-3 練習**

18-3-1C Meanings of noun + らしい (BTS 6, 8)

Listen to the conversations and determine whether the Noun + らしい phrase is used to express an evidence-based conjecture or that something is typical of a certain class.

	Evidence-based conjecture	Typical of a class
例 1.	○	
例 2.		○
3.		
4.		
5.		
6.		
7.		
8.		

18-3-2P Doing things out of responsibility
責任上 仕方なく行う (BTS 7)
せきにんじょう し かた　　おこな

Your team member is surprised by something that you've proposed to do. Tell him that there is no other way, given that it's your responsibility.

例 1.

チームメンバー	え？今行くんですか？ザーザー降ってますよ。	What? You're going now? It's raining cats and dogs, you know.
あなた	行くしかないでしょう。責任ありますから。	There's nothing to do but go, is there? Since it's my responsibility.

例 2.

チームメンバー	え？これから書き変えるんですか？クタクタなんじゃないですか？	What? You're going to rewrite it now? You're exhausted, aren't you?
あなた	書き変えるしかないでしょう。責任ありますから。	There's nothing to do but rewrite it, is there? Since it's my responsibility.

18-3-3P Doing some damage control 失言から立ち直る (BTS 8, 9)

You apparently said something about Mizuno-san, your colleague, that she took the wrong way. Remedy the situation by saying that what you meant was that she was not acting like her normal self, using one of the descriptions provided below. Each description may be used only once.

例1.

| 水野さん | あの、私、素直じゃないですか？ | Um, am I not cooperative? |
| あなた | いえいえ、そうじゃなくて、いつも素直な水野さんらしくないというか、何というか……。 | Oh, no, nothing like that, but it's not like Mizuno-san, who is always cooperative, or what shall I say . . . |

例2.

| 水野さん | あの、私、自分勝手ですか？ | Um, am I selfish? |
| あなた | いえいえ、そうじゃなくて、いつも思いやりのある水野さんらしくないというか、何というか……。 | Oh, no, nothing like that, but it's not like Mizuno-san, who is always considerate of others, or what shall I say . . . |

```
素直           親切           責任感が強い      積極的
文句を言わない  思いやりのある  いろいろよく考える
```

18-3-4RP Giving mild correction 少し言い変える (BTS 9)

You are talking with Ai, a friend of yours, after work. When she asks a question about something, provide gentle correction to clarify what's really happening, based on what someone else said earlier, as indicated in the illustration.

例1.

| 愛 | 部長は褒めてたの？ | Did the *bucho* compliment you? |
| あなた | 褒めてたって言うか、もっと責任ある仕事をさせるってことだったんだけど。 | I don't know if you'd call it complimenting. She said she'd give me a bigger responsibility. |

例2.

| 愛 | 大村さんは反対してたの？ | Was Omura-san against it? |
| あなた | 反対してたって言うか、細かいところもっと考えた方がいいってことだったんだけど。 | I don't know if you'd say he was against it. He said I should think more about the details. |

例1. なるほど。これぐらいできるならもっと責任ある仕事をさせてもいいんだ。

例2. そうですね…悪い企画ではないんですけど、細かいところをもうちょっと考えた方がいいですね。

3. 行くけど、随分遅れて行くと思うよ。ごめんね。

4. 例の仕事ですか。池辺さんにさせるので、どうぞご心配なく。

5. 練習さえすればわかってきますよ、きっと。だからもっとがんばりましょう。

6. これじゃちょっと…明日までに書き直してください。

7. この本、あまり使わないから欲しい人にあげることにしました。

18-3 腕試し

1. During a conversation, use と言うか or って言うか to self-correct something you said that wasn't entirely accurate.
2. When a friend attempts to restate something you said, but doesn't quite have it right, use と言うか or って言うか to gently correct their understanding.
3. Ask your Japanese colleagues/friends what they consider to be characteristically Japanese places, foods, or behaviors. What makes them feel that way about these places, foods, or behaviors?
4. When you observe an atypical action by someone, or an atypical condition, describe it to your Japanese colleague/friend and comment about how unusual it is for that person, time, season, etc. See how your colleague/friend reacts.

◆ シーン 18-4 練習

18-4-1C Who is she talking about? 誰のこと? (BTS 10)

Mark whether the speaker is most likely talking about herself, or another person.

	The speaker	Another person
例 1.	○	
例 2.		○
3.		
4.		
5.		
6.		
7.		
8.		
9.		
10.		
11.		
12.		
13.		
14.		

18-4-2P Responding to unreasonable demands
無理な要求に対応する (BTS 1, 10)

You are working as an assistant to someone who is a bit impulsive. Respond to his demands by telling him he's being unreasonable.

例 1.
上司　　今食べたい！　　　　　　　　　I want to eat it now!
あなた　いや、今食べたがられても困り　　Well, no, even if you say you want to eat
　　　　ます。　　　　　　　　　　　　it now there's nothing I can do.

例 2.
上司　　全部一人で使いたい！　　　　　I want to use them all myself!
あなた　いや、全部一人で使いたがられ　　Well, no, even if you say you want to use
　　　　ても困ります。　　　　　　　　them all yourself there's nothing I can do.

18-4-3P Adding an observation about Kato-san
加藤さんについて気づいたことを加える (BTS 10)

Your *senpai* gives her impression about what happened. Agree and add your observation that Kato-san, another *senpai*, obviously felt the same way.

例 1.
先輩	講演会、楽しみにしてたのに行けなくて残念だったね。	Given that we were looking forward to the lecture, it was too bad that we ended up not being able to go, wasn't it?
あなた	はい。加藤さんも残念がってましたね。	Yes. Kato-san was also clearly sad about it, wasn't he?

例 2.
先輩	北風の中ですっごい寒さだったから、暖かいお茶がありがたかったね。	It was so awfully cold in the middle of that northern wind, so it was nice to have warm tea, wasn't it?
あなた	はい。加藤さんもありがたがってましたね。	Yes. Kato-san was also clearly grateful, wasn't he.

18-4-4P Modifying the description of the situation
状況が違うことを伝える (BTS 1, 9, 10)

Your *senpai* friend thinks that you did something in response to someone else's order. Modify his version of the story by indicating that you acted based on your observation of what appeared to be that person's desire.

例 1.
先輩	この書類、課長に調べるように言われて調べたんじゃないの？	Didn't you research these documents because you were told to by your section chief?
あなた	というか、課長が調べてもらいたがってるみたいだったので調べたんです。	Or rather, I researched them because it appeared that the section chief wanted to have them researched.

例 2.
先輩	この計画書、上司に書くように言われて書いたんじゃないの？	Didn't you write this proposal because you were told to by your superior?
あなた	というか、上司が書いてもらいたがってるみたいだったので書いたんです。	Or rather, I wrote it because it appeared that my superior wanted to have it written.

18-4 腕試し

1. When you see someone showing signs of feeling a certain way, report your observation to a third person.
2. Work together with your associate to prepare details for an upcoming visit to an organization or a location. Have you visited the place before? Are you going by an invitation?

◆ シーン 18-5 練習

18-5-1C What are they talking about? 話題は? (BTS 12)

In each of the following, you will hear a sentence followed by か used as a Noun. Write the content of the sentence followed by か.

例 1. <u>What to do</u>
例 2. <u>Where to get together</u>
3. _____
4. _____
5. _____
6. _____
7. _____
8. _____
9. _____
10. _____

18-5-2P Describing the type of place
どんなところを選んだか伝える (BTS 11)

You took your guest to see some places associated with various cultures from around the world. Your guest is impressed with what she sees. Indicate that you simply responded to her wishes.

例 1.
| 客 | わあ、おしゃれ！日本の旅館に来たみたいですね！ | Wow, it's so chic! It's as if we've come to a Japanese-style inn! |
| あなた | 日本風のところに行きたいと言うことでしたから。 | I figured that you wanted to go to a place with a Japanese feel to it, so . . . |

例 2.
| 客 | わあ、すごい！中国の公園に来たみたいですね！ | Wow, it's fantastic! It's as if we've come to a Chinese park! |
| あなた | 中国風のところに行きたいと言うことでしたから。 | I figured that you wanted to go to a place with a Chinese feel to it, so . . . |

18-5-3P Giving reassurance of satisfactory performance
満足度を示す (BTS 11)

Your associate seems unsure if what he did was all right. Give him the reassurance that what he did was exactly the way you wanted it done.

例 1.
同僚	例の記事、書くことは書きましたけど、あれでいいですか？	I did write that article, but was that acceptable?
あなた	バッチリですね。ちょうどあんな風に書いてもらいたかったんです。	It's perfect! That was exactly the way I wanted you to write it.

例 2.
同僚	あのグラフ、直すことは直しましたけど、あれでいいですか？	I did fix that graph, but was that acceptable?
あなた	バッチリですね。ちょうどあんな風に直してもらいたかったんです。	It's perfect! That was exactly the way I wanted you to fix it.

18-5-4P Identifying the issue 問題点を挙げる (BTS 12)

You are talking with your team about what to do next, and a team member is skeptical about an idea that you've mentioned. Agree with her that her concern is indeed the issue.

例 1.
チームメンバー	そんなこと言うんですか？気分を害さないでしょうか。	Are we going to say that sort of thing? Won't they feel offended?
あなた	そうですよね。こんなこと言って、気分を害されないかが問題ですよね。	You are right. The issue is whether our saying this sort of thing won't offend them (which would negatively affect us).

例 2.
チームメンバー	そんな時間に訪問するんですか？怒らないでしょうか。	Are we going to visit with them at such a time? Won't they become angry?
あなた	そうですよね。こんな時間に訪問して、怒られないかが問題ですよね。	You are right. The issue is whether our visiting at such a time won't make them angry (which would negatively affect us).

18-5 腕試し

Strategize with a Japanese colleague/friend about how to go about doing certain things. For example, how to get an opinion from someone who tends to be reticent, how to organize a workplace that tends to get cluttered, or how to approach someone when you want to ask that person to do something for you.

◆ シーン 18-6 練習

18-6-1C Even supposing that ... 条件の不足を指摘する (BTS 13)

In each of the following, you will hear the word たとえ combined with a 〜ても form. For each conversation, write the hypothetical situation that is brought up with the たとえ 〜ても phrase.

例 1.　Even a specialist _____
例 2.　Even if there were some _____
　　3.　_____
　　4.　_____
　　5.　_____
　　6.　_____
　　7.　_____

18-6-2P Being critical of others' behavior 言動を批判する (BTS 13)

When your friend uses someone's position as the reason for that person's action, refute the idea by saying that there is a limit to what one can do even for a person in that particular position.

例 1.
友人	上級生だからね、僕たちが言わないことでも言うんじゃない？	He's an upperclassman, so isn't that why he says things that we wouldn't say?
あなた	たとえ上級生でも、言っていいことと悪いことがありますよ。	Even for an upperclassman, there are things one can and cannot say!

例 2.
友人	部長だからね、僕たちが黙っていないことでも黙っているんじゃない？	She is a division chief, so isn't that why she keeps quiet about things that we wouldn't keep quiet about?
あなた	たとえ部長でも、黙っていていいことと悪いことがありますよ。	Even as division chief, there are things one can and cannot keep quiet about!

18-6-3P Summarizing in a word 一言(ひとこと)でまとめる

When your friend explains what happened, summarize it in a word, using one of the selections provided below. Use each item once.

例 1.
友人	ひどいんですよ。カバンの中に変な物いれられたり、お金盗まれたり……。	It's awful. She had to go through having strange things put in her bag, having her money stolen . . .
あなた	へえ、まるで子供のいじめですね。	Wow, that sounds like bullying.

例 2.
友人	とても親切でね、薬くれたり、しっかり寝るためのアドバイスしてくれたり……。	He was really kind, offering medicine, giving me advice on how to sleep well . . .
あなた	へえ、まるで医者ですね。	Wow, he sounds like a medical doctor.

子供(こども)のいじめ　　不平(ふへい)　　台風(たいふう)　　競争(きょうそう)
送別会(そうべつかい)　　医者(いしゃ)　　面接(めんせつ)

18-6-4RCP Making an observation 観察(かんさつ)を述(の)べる (BTS 6)

You overheard various people making comments to someone else. Report what you heard to your associate, using the illustrations as the basis of your observation. Then listen to your associate's reaction and indicate whether she is sympathetic to the person being discussed, unsympathetic, or neither.

例 1.
あなた	政治家が、新しい開発が肝心だと言っているらしいです。	The politician is apparently saying that new developments are a key.
同僚	そう。政治家はみんなそう言うよね。でも本当にそう考えているかどうかはわからないんだよね。	Right. All politicians say that, right? But we don't know whether they are really thinking that way or not.

例 2.
あなた	上司が、顔を潰されたと言っているらしいです。	The superior is apparently saying that she feels humiliated.
同僚	聞いたよ、私も。まあね、あんなことされたんだから、黙ってはいないでしょうね。	I heard, too. Well, given that she suffered that kind of thing, I suspect she won't stay quiet.

	Sympathetic to the person being discussed	Unsympathetic to the person being discussed	Neither sympathetic nor unsympathetic to the person being discussed
例 1.		○	
例 2.	○		
3.			
4.			
5.			
6.			
7.			
8.			
9.			
10.			

18-6 腕試し

1. Discuss the actions of well-known people in relation to their societal roles. Is the person's action typical, slightly unusual, or completely out of the ordinary?
2. When a Japanese associate/friend describes someone's experience or situation, try summarizing it with a word.

◆ シーン 18-7R 練習

18-7-1R Passive? Honorific? Potential? 受け身？尊敬？可能？

Determine whether the underlined verbs are passive, honorific, or potential.

例1.	雨に<u>降られて</u>びしょびしょになってしまいました。	☒ Passive ☐ Honorific ☐ Potential
例2.	社長が<u>考えられた</u>案について話し合いたいと思います。	☐ Passive ☒ Honorific ☐ Potential
例3.	すみません。ちょっと先約があって今日は僕は<u>来られない</u>んです。	☐ Passive ☐ Honorific ☒ Potential
4.	やりたくなかったのに先生に<u>頼まれちゃった</u>から仕方がないなあ。	☐ Passive ☐ Honorific ☐ Potential
5.	明日は曇りになるらしいから、雲が多くて<u>見られない</u>でしょうね。	☐ Passive ☐ Honorific ☐ Potential
6.	だって早く帰ろうとしたところを服部君に<u>見られちゃった</u>んだもん。参ったよ。	☐ Passive ☐ Honorific ☐ Potential
7.	私は7時に参りますが、部長は何時に<u>来られる</u>おつもりですか。	☐ Passive ☐ Honorific ☐ Potential
8.	お客様はご自分のお洋服代に毎月どのぐらい<u>使われて</u>ますか。	☐ Passive ☐ Honorific ☐ Potential
9.	だれにも<u>気が付かれない</u>ように気を付けてくださいね。	☐ Passive ☐ Honorific ☐ Potential
10.	もう少し涼しくなってからやりたいと思っているのですが、イベントの日付ってまだ<u>変えられます</u>か。	☐ Passive ☐ Honorific ☐ Potential
11.	失礼なことを何度も<u>言われて</u>やる気がなくなりました。	☐ Passive ☐ Honorific ☐ Potential
12.	明日は晴れて暖かくなるらしいから外に<u>出られ</u>そうですね。	☐ Passive ☐ Honorific ☐ Potential

18-7-2R It seems that... 様子の表現

Select the appropriate expression by paying attention to what precedes or follows. For some items, either option is plausible, but one is preferred over the other due to the formality of the sentence.

例1. 読んだ本全部出しっぱなしの (らしい・**よう**) ですね。
例2. 来週は晴れる (よう・**みたい**) だから、ピクニックにでも行こうよ！
3. これが明日のステージでみんなが着なくちゃいけない服 (らしい・よう) ね。
4. 雨が降り出した (よう・みたい) なので、車で参ります。
5. それにしても何とも言えない天気ですね。涼しい (らしい・よう) な暖かい (よう・みたい) な……。
6. 雨に降られた (らしい・みたい) でビショビショになって大変だったそうですよ。
7. 午後になってどんどん曇り出した (らし・みた) くて何も見られなかったそうですよ。
8. 以前に一度できた (らしい・よう) んだけど、これ以上はもうできないみたいですね。
9. 電気代が高かったのはエアコンを付けっぱなしにしてたから (よう・みたい) だよ。
10. ２０度以下っていうのは8月にしては涼しい (よう・らしい) だ。

18-7-3RW Journal entries about weather
気候について記述する

Fill in the blanks with appropriate expressions about weather in the following journal entries. For #9, add your own journal entry about the weather.

暖かい服	涼しい服	晴れる
曇り	０度	降られて
涼しい	~~３０度~~	降られなかった
~~涼しく~~	暖かく	降らなかった

例1. せっかく旅行に来たのに、ハワイの天気にしてはめちゃくちゃ寒い！もっと＿＿暖かい服＿＿を着てくればよかった。
例2. 今週は毎日＿＿３０度＿＿以上！めちゃくちゃ暑くて大変だった。来週からはもっと＿＿涼しく＿＿なるといいな。
3. 明日の天気は＿＿＿＿＿＿のようだけど、雨にならないといいな。
4. 昨日の天気は＿＿＿＿＿＿が多かったけど、雨が＿＿＿＿＿＿＿＿からよかった。
5. ２５度。１０月にしては暑い方だ。もう少し＿＿＿＿＿＿＿＿を着てくればよかったな。
6. 先週はほとんど毎日＿＿＿＿＿＿＿＿以下！めちゃくちゃ寒くて大変だった。今週はもっと＿＿＿＿＿＿＿＿なってほしい。
7. 今日はきれいに＿＿＿＿＿はずだったのに雨に＿＿＿＿＿＿＿＿参った。
8. 日本の友人によると１８度ぐらいっていうのは、8月にしては＿＿＿＿＿＿＿＿方らしい。
9. ＿＿＿＿＿＿＿＿＿＿＿＿＿＿＿＿＿＿＿＿＿＿＿＿＿＿＿＿

◆ シーン 18-8R 練習

18-8-1R Expressions associated with temperature
温度の表現

Select the appropriate expression by paying attention to what precedes or follows.

例1. 本当に (㊤春・夏) らしい暖かい天気！こんな時はみんなでハイキングにでも行くしかないでしょ！
例2. (㊤温かい・暖かい) コーヒーでも飲みながら話しましょう。
3. あの子、(冷たい・涼しい) 物を飲みたがってるみたいなんだけど……。
4. バランスをよくするためには赤とか黄色とかの (温かめ・暖かめ) の色を使うしかないでしょう。
5. こんなに寒いんだからもっと (秋・冬) らしい服を着るべきですよ。
6. 先日は家に (温かく・暖かく) 入れてくれて本当にありがとう。助かったよ。
7. 今週はまだ秋らしい (寒い・涼しい) 天気だけど、来週からは気温が下がって冬みたくなるらしいよ。
8. また文句言われたの？っていうか本当に (寒い・冷たい) 家族だね。

18-8-2R 俳句？川柳？

Determine whether the following poems are 俳句 or 川柳. Circle the seasonal word and the season for each 俳句. The composers of famous 俳句 are listed in the answer key. Make use of collocations to work around expressions and kanji that have not been introduced.

例1. ㊤雪とけて㊦　村いっぱいの　子どもかな　　俳句 (㊤春・夏・秋・冬) ・川柳
例2. 明日まで　がんばるしかない　仕事ナウ！　　俳句 (春・夏・秋・冬) ・㊤川柳
3. 秋の雲　ちぎりちぎれて　なくなりぬ　　俳句 (春・夏・秋・冬) ・川柳
4. 寒けれど　富士見る旅は　羨まし　　俳句 (春・夏・秋・冬) ・川柳
5. 聞こえるよ　シャワーでいつも　歌う君　　俳句 (春・夏・秋・冬) ・川柳
6. フルコース　さすがグルメの　神田さん　　俳句 (春・夏・秋・冬) ・川柳
7. 覚えてる？　スマフォじゃなくて　スマホだよ　　俳句 (春・夏・秋・冬) ・川柳
8. 五月雨を　あつめてはやし　最上川　　俳句 (春・夏・秋・冬) ・川柳
9. したくない　意見というか　文句だけ　　俳句 (春・夏・秋・冬) ・川柳
10. らしくない　雪も降らない　クリスマス　　俳句 (春・夏・秋・冬) ・川柳
11. 夏休み　暑がりだけど　アウトドア　　俳句 (春・夏・秋・冬) ・川柳

18-8-3W Warm or cold? 温度(おんど)について言及(げんきゅう)する

Write a simple thank-you note or instruction as indicated. Use appropriate styles for the indicated addressees.

例1. The warm milk was tasty　　(to your host mother)
　　温かいミルク、おいしかったです

例2. It's tasty if you drink it after cooling it　　(to your friend)
　　冷やしてから飲むとおいしいよ

3. Please drink it before it gets cold (lit. 'while it is still not cooled down')　　(to your teacher)
　　_____

4. Please be sure to come having worn warm clothing　　(to your classmate)
　　_____

5. Please eat it after you warm it up　　(to your younger host brother)
　　_____

6. Thank you for the cold beer (you just finished it)　　(to your friend)
　　_____

18-8-4W What season? 季節(きせつ)を限定(げんてい)する

Determine and write down the seasons that are associated with the following *haiku*. Do your best to work around expressions and kanji characters that have not been introduced. Then write two *haiku* of your own.

例1.　帰り道　　　　　　　冷たい雪舞う　　　　　__冬__の空
例2.　__夏__　終わり　　　涼しい風に　　　　　　花火散る
3.　暖かな　　　　　　　_____のそよ風　　ピクニック
4.　３０度！　　　　　　_____だビーチだ　　バーベキュー！
5.　_____の夜に　月を見ながら　　　　　　お酒かな
6.　_____なのに　雨でびしょぬれ　　　　　サンタさん
7.　_____　　　　_____　　　　　　_____
8.　_____　　　　_____　　　　　　_____

◆ シーン 18-9R 練習

18-9-1R What particle? 疑問文の助詞を使いこなす

Which particle is better in the following sentences?

例 1. 残念ながら何があったか (が・**は**) 覚えていないようです。
例 2. 台風が来るか来ないか (で・**に**) よってスケジュールが変わってきます。
3. できるできないじゃなくて、自分を信じられるかどうか (が・は) 大切なんです。
4. 何個買わなくちゃいけないか (を・が) 早く決めてもらっていい？
5. あの大学に入れるかどうかは、学費がいくらカバーされるか (で・に) 決めようと思っています。
6. シンプルな言い方でもどんな風に言うか (で・に) よって伝わり方が変わります。
7. 申し訳ないけど、ここに入れるかどうかはお金を持っているかいないか (で・に) 決まっちゃうから……。
8. インタビューでどんなことを聞かれるか (を・は) もう一度教えてもらえませんか。

18-9-2R Even if... 条件・状態に関わらず……

Select the most suitable expression for the passages that follow. You may use each option once.

文句を言われたとしても	台風が来なくても	もう２、３個買ったとしても
~~下手であったとしても~~	~~日本に行けなくても~~	メッセージを送ったとしても
気温があまり高くなくても	暑くなったとしても	

例 1. たとえ＿＿＿日本に行けなくても＿＿＿、日本風の料理ならアメリカでも食べられますよ。
例 2. たとえ＿＿＿下手であったとしても＿＿＿まずはやってみることが大切です。
3. たとえ＿＿＿＿＿＿＿＿＿＿＿＿＿＿＿、夏の間外に出る時には水を持って行ったほうがいいですよ。
4. 申し訳ないけど、うちの父は気が付かないと思いますよ。たとえ＿＿＿＿＿＿＿＿＿＿＿＿＿＿……。
5. たとえ＿＿＿＿＿＿＿＿＿＿＿＿＿＿＿、涼しい服を来てくればいいだけのことです。

6. 残念ながら、明日のバーベキューはたとえ＿＿＿＿＿＿＿＿＿＿＿＿＿＿＿＿キャンセルになるでしょうね。
7. 全部食べられちゃうと思いますよ。たとえ＿＿＿＿＿＿＿＿＿＿＿＿＿＿＿＿……。
8. たとえ＿＿＿＿＿＿＿＿＿＿＿＿＿＿＿＿＿＿＿私はかまわないで自分風にアレンジするつもりです。

18-9-3RW How many? 数の表現

Provide an appropriate classifier for each item on the list.

例1.	例2.	3.	4.
シュークリーム １０個	黒い紙 ５０枚	青いノート 5＿＿＿	赤ペン 10＿＿＿
5. 消しゴム 3＿＿＿	6. Tシャツ 2＿＿＿	7. テレビ 1＿＿＿	8. 車 3＿＿＿
9. ブルーシート 2＿＿＿	10. ネクタイ 4＿＿＿	11. フォルダー 10＿＿＿	12. メニュー 5＿＿＿

18-9-4RW Expressing apology and disappointment
謝罪や残念な気持ちを述べる

Fill in the blanks by placing an appropriate expression of apology (申し訳ありませんが) or disappointment (残念ながら). If both apology and disappointment are possible, express disappointment.

例1. ＿＿＿申し訳ありませんが＿＿＿どういう風に作ればいいかもう一度教えてもらえますか。

例2. ＿＿＿＿残念ながら＿＿＿＿、そのサイズの紙はあと２枚しかございません。

3. ＿＿＿＿＿＿＿＿＿＿＿＿＿＿その本をあと３冊ほどいただいてもよろしいですか。
4. ＿＿＿＿＿＿＿＿＿＿＿＿＿＿先生が来られるかはまだ決まっていないようです。
5. ＿＿＿＿＿＿＿＿＿＿＿＿＿＿あと１０個ほど買ってきてもらえますか。
6. ＿＿＿＿＿＿＿＿＿＿＿＿＿＿明日のスポーツ会は台風のためキャンセルいたします。

◆ **Act 18　評価**

🎧 **聞いてみよう**

Read the context, listen to the audio, and then answer the questions. If you hear something unfamiliar, rely on what you know to choose the correct answer.

1. It's June and Brian is talking with his homestay mother.

    a. What is apparently going to happen, according to Brian?
    b. What is the situation in Kyushu?
    c. Where did Brian's homestay mother get this information from?
    d. How is the situation in Brian and his host mother's location different from the situation in Kyushu?
    e. What is Brian's homestay mother's advice?

2. Brian is talking with Suzuki-san, his aikido senior, as they are about to go on a club outing.

    a. What are things like today? How does Brian feel about the situation?
    b. What does Suzuki-san think feels good?
    c. How does the situation today compare with the norm?
    d. What does Brian say they need to be careful about? What situation does this warning apply to?

3. The aikido club members have reached their hiking destination. Suzuki-san is talking to a fellow club member.

    a. How does Suzuki-san describe their destination? Is her next comment positive or negative?
    b. What does Brian point out to Suzuki-san about their location?
    c. What does Suzuki-san point out in response to Brian?
    d. What seems unreal, according to Suzuki-san?
    e. What is Brian's suggestion?

4. Yamada-san works as a staff member of a community school and she stops her supervisor to report an issue.

    a. What is the issue that Yamada-san reports to her supervisor?
    b. What did the supervisor forget to tell Yamada-san?
    c. What was the supervisor's intention?
    d. What does Yamada-san say that she cannot do?
    e. What does her supervisor tell her to do?

怒られた。

5. Mizuno-san, Kanda-san's colleague at Ogaki Shokai, comes to Kanda-san for a conference.
   a. Who is the topic of this conference?
   b. What is the issue with this person?
   c. What does Kanda-san suppose might be the reason for the person's behavior?
   d. How does Mizuno-san describe emails from this person?
   e. What does Kanda-san think needs to be done?
   f. Why is Mizuno-san surprised?

6. Kanda-san approaches his colleague, Terada-san, to follow up on his earlier conversation with Mizuno-san.
   a. What does Kanda-san ask Terada-san to do?
   b. What does Terada-san think of the situation?
   c. What kind of comment did Mizuno-san make? What was her comment?

7. Brian notices that his homestay brother Ichiro seems down at the aikido club. He talks to their *senpai*, Suzuki-san.
   a. What is Brian's guess as to the reason for Ichiro's mood?
   b. What is the actual reason? How did Ichiro's actions affect others?
   c. What does Brian think of Ichiro's behavior?
   d. How does Suzuki-san explain Ichiro's behavior?

8. Ogaki Shokai has a new piece of office equipment and Kanda-san is being briefed about it from his colleague.
   a. What does Kanda-san's colleague tell him to do?
   b. Why is it okay for Kanda-san to do this?
   c. What does Kanda-san think his colleague's explanation means?
   d. What positive comment does Kanda-san's colleague make about the new piece of equipment?
   e. What negative comment does Kanda-san make about the new piece of equipment?

9. Mizuno-san is commenting on something that Kanda-san just finished.
   a. How does Kanda-san react to Mizuno-san's comment?
   b. How does Kanda-san explain what he did?
   c. In addition to the job being well done, how does Mizuno-san compliment Kanda-san?
   d. How does Kanda-san respond to this compliment?
   e. How does Mizuno-san say she is different from Kanda-san?

10. Yagi-bucho is talking with Kanda-san about another worker at Ogaki Shokai.
    a. How does Kanda-san describe this worker?
    b. What is Yagi-bucho thinking of doing?
    c. What does Kanda-san think of this idea?
    d. What does Kanda-san suggest they do?

11. Sasha's fellow intern has been in an accident and is hospitalized. She goes to see him.

    a. What does Sasha ask the intern?
    b. What does the intern apologize for?
    c. What was the intern doing when the accident happened?
    d. Where is the intern's injury?
    e. Why does the intern mention two to three weeks?
    f. Why does the intern mention two months?

12. Mizuno-san is talking with her colleague who is upset.

    a. What question does Mizuno-san's colleague ask her?
    b. What has happened that Mizuno-san's colleague is upset about?
    c. How do the managers want to handle the situation, according to Mizuno-san?
    d. What comment does Mizuno-san's colleague make regarding managers?
    e. What does Mizuno-san think they should do?

13. Eri, a graduate student, is talking to one of the professors at school.

    a. Who will be visiting Germany?
    b. What will this person be doing in Germany?
    c. Which part of Germany will this person visit?
    d. Where does this person also want to visit?

14. Eri, a graduate teaching assistant in the Japanese program, talks to Brian about something she has been reading.

    a. What kind of material has Eri been reading? What is it about?
    b. What comment does Eri make about the weather?
    c. What examples of this weather does Brian provide?

15. Kanda-san is visiting his parents in Hokkaido for the New Year's holiday. His mother is going out.

    a. Why does Kanda-san tell his mother to be careful?
    b. What is the weather situation today? Be specific.
    c. After hearing about the weather, what does Kanda-san's mother say she will do?

16. Mizuno-san asks one of the new interns in the office about something she has noticed.

    a. What did Mizuno-san notice?
    b. What is the reason for the situation?
    c. What does Mizuno-san ask the intern to do?

17. The intern at Ogaki Shokai and Mizuno-san are about to leave the conference room.

    a. What does the intern confirm with Mizuno-san?
    b. What tasks does Mizuno-san ask the intern to do?
    c. How does Mizuno-san reprimand the intern?

18. Sasha is visiting a farm on her day off and talking to the farm owner in his work shed.

   a. How does the farmer explain why the tomatoes turned out as they did?
   b. What does the farmer do with the tomatoes after picking them? Why does the farmer do this?

19. Takashi is talking to Amy about Kevin, another member of their student organization.

   a. What is Kevin's major?
   b. What is Kevin's career goal?
   c. How does Amy explain how Kevin's major relates to his career goal?

20. Kanda-san has gone out with his school friend from many years ago and brings up another classmate in their conversation.

   a. Who are they talking about? When did they know this person?
   b. How does Kanda-san describe this person?
   c. What happened to this person?
   d. What additional information does Kanda-san provide regarding what happened to this person?

使ってみよう

For each of the following, listen to the audio, and respond to what was said based on the context. Then listen to the sample response.

1. Tell a friend that even for the rainy season, this is a lot of rain.
2. Tell a friend that because it was clear weather when you left, you left your umbrella, but then it suddenly started raining.
3. Takayuki, your roommate, got mad at you because you always inadvertently leave the air conditioning on. You are talking to a different friend.
4. Tell a co-worker that because the division chief is the only one that can do it, there's nothing to do but ask the division chief to do it.
5. Comment to a friend that not saying anything and not showing up is not like Yuya-kun, and that you wonder if something happened.
6. When a friend asks if you are going to the U.S., clarify that you have been given permission to visit New York University.
7. When a friend asks if you talked to the teacher, respond that you did, then clarify that you just sent an email.
8. Tell a friend that Suzuki-san also wanted to go.
9. Ask a *senpai* how (i.e., in what manner) you should say something.
10. Tell a work *senpai* that the division chief said she wanted to know how many clients are coming.
11. Tell a work *kohai* even if it's slow, it's fine as long as she does a little at a time.

Now it's your turn to start the conversation based on the given context. Listen to how the other person reacts to you. For some items, you may not get a verbal response. Don't be concerned if you hear things you have not yet learned.

12. Tell a friend that the following happened, implying that you were negatively affected: (a) Tomoda-san went home early; (b) Ichiro-kun got angry; (c) a lower-level student said something terrible; (d) your teacher changed the time of the lecture many times.
13. Tell a friend that you were (a) scolded by the division chief; (b) teased a lot when you were a child; (c) trained strictly when you did sports in high school.
14. A package has just arrived, and you haven't opened it yet. Comment to a friend that it's too small to be a book.
15. Tell a friend that, based on evidence, it seems that (a) the snow is piling up; (b) the time of Sakamoto-sensei's lecture was changed; (c) Mima-san was also invited; (d) Murata-san is sick; (e) this is inexpensive for New York.
16. Tell a fellow teacher that the problem is whether or not lower-level students will also join.

読んでみよう

Consider the context provided and read the passage to answer the questions that follow. Do your best to work around the expressions and kanji characters that have not been introduced.

1. You found the sign on a busy street near the elementary school.

   a. What type of sign is it? Can you guess what 子供飛び出し means?

   [パフォーマンス] You are in the passenger seat. Inform the driver about the sign.
2. You found the following handwritten sign next to some snacks sold at a supermarket.

a. What season is this product available in?
b. How delicious is it?

[パフォーマンス] Talk about local specialties or food items that are only available in certain seasons. Ask your conversation partner if they tried the food you are talking about.

3. Below is an online weather forecast for today and tomorrow in Tokyo.

今日明日の気温と天気					11月27日　7時００分発表				
11月27日（水）					11月28日（木）				
曇時々雨　11℃　8℃					雨のち曇　12℃　7℃				
時間	0-6	6-12	12-18	18-24	時間	0-6	6-12	12-18	18-24
降水	-----	50%	80%	80%	降水	60%	40%	20%	10%
風：北の風					風：北西の風やや強く				

a. What will the weather be like tomorrow? Highest and lowest temperature? During what time is the highest chance of rain? From what direction is the wind blowing?
b. What is the weather the day after tomorrow? Highest and lowest temperature? During what time is the highest chance of rain? From what direction is the wind blowing?

[パフォーマンス] Decide whether to visit Tokyo either tomorrow or the day after tomorrow with your conversation partner. Talk about what you are planning to wear and what items to bring.

4. A weather forecast for the upcoming week you found online.

週間天気							11月27日　7時００分発表
日付	11月29日（金）	11月30日（土）	12月1日（日）	12月2日（月）	12月3日（火）	12月4日（水）
天気	晴れ	晴れ	晴時々曇	曇一時雨	晴時々曇	晴れ
気温（℃）	11 / 5	12 / 3	14 / 4	17 / 8	15 / 6	12 / 4
降水確率（％）	0	0	10	60	20	0

a. Which day is the warmest? What is the weather like on that day?

[パフォーマンス] Plan an outdoor activity with your conversation partner and decide when you are going based on the weather forecast.

5. Below is a text exchange between Sasha and her client.

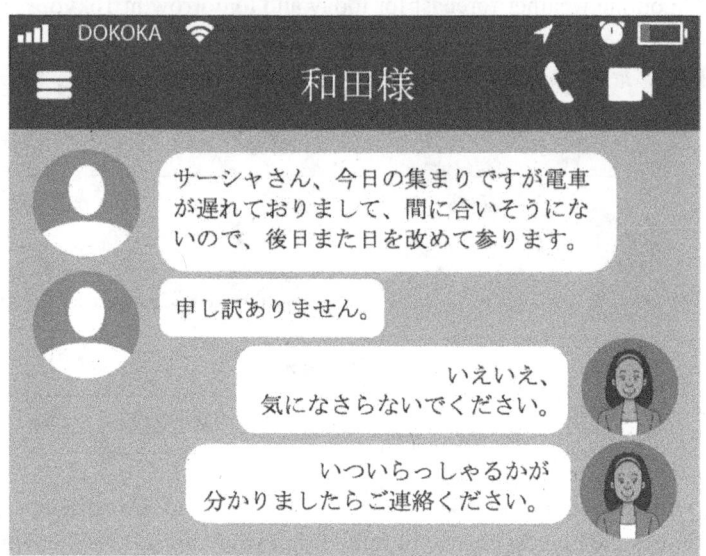

a. Why does the client apologize?
b. How does Sasha react to her client's apology?

[パフォーマンス] Assume the role of Sasha's client and give Sasha a call.

6. Brian found a list of haiku that Ichiro wrote when he was in elementary school.

白井一郎

春	夏	秋	冬
雲のない 晴れた日の下 チューリップ	台風で 学校休みだ うれしいな	マンガ本 読み出したら とまらない	大人でも 開けたがっちゃう プレゼント

a. What is チューリップ? Where is it located?
b. Why is Ichiro happy in the summer?
c. What does Ichiro say about マンガ本?
d. How does Ichiro describe 大人?

[パフォーマンス] Assume the role of Brian and tell Ichiro which haiku you think is the best.

7. Below is Brian's journal entry.

> 今日は冬にしては暖かかったので窓を開けっぱなしにしていた。そしたら学校に行っている間に雨に降られたらしく、部屋の中にあったオレの服がびっしょびしょ。オレの大切にしているトレカも！しかも残念なことにレアカード3枚グシャグシャ。たとえ今日のテストが100点でもこれはめちゃくちゃショック。雨を降らせた曇りの天気さん、僕からあなたに文句を言わせてください。っていうかもうこんな風に言うしかない。バカヤロー！！
> byブライアン

a. What is 窓? What did he do to it? Why?
b. What is トレカ? What happened to them? How does Brian feel about it?
c. What does テストで１００点 have to do with his journal entry?
d. What's the intention of saying バカヤロー at the end of his entry? To whom is it addressed?

[パフォーマンス] Talk about a recent experience that made you want to say バカヤロー.

 書き取り

Listen to the audio, repeat silently what you hear, then write it down. What do you think the context is?

1. _____。
2. _____。
3. _____。
4. _____。
5. _____。
6. _____。
7. _____。
8. _____。

書いてみよう

Consider the context provided and compose a text according to the directions.

1. You made Japanese-style soup for your classmate who is sick. Tell him what it is. Tell him to warm it up and have it (lit. 'drink').

2. The refrigerator door in your office is loose. Write a warning note about leaving it open.

3. You are shipping something you are selling online. Write a short apology note for sending it out late.

4. Your co-worker asked you to pick up some pictures she ordered online from a print store, but the print store did not have any of her pictures. Leave the following note to your co-worker.

It seems that it hadn't been ordered properly, so unfortunately not even one (picture) was being printed.

_____
_____
_____
_____

5. Write your own *haiku*.
6. Write your own *senryu*.

知ってる?

Select the most appropriate option and write the letter on your answer sheet.

1. You're upset that the teacher warned you about your study habits.
   先生に注意＿＿＿＿＿＿いやだったんだよ。(BTS 1)

   a. されて
   b. して
   c. させて

2. You're worried that your friend read a confidential email.
   あのメール、友だち＿＿＿＿＿＿読まれて心配してる。(BTS 1)

   a. が
   b. に
   c. は

3. You're surprised that the new student from France knows so much about Japan.
   フランス人にして＿＿＿＿＿＿日本のこと、よく知っていますねぇ。(BTS 2)

   a. も
   b. は

4. You think it's been an unusually hot summer this year.
   夏にして＿＿＿＿＿＿ちょっと暑すぎると思う。(BTS 2)

   a. も
   b. は

5. だす combined with a Verb stem means the action will _____. (BTS 3)

   a. be completed soon
   b. occur slowly
   c. begin to happen

6. っぱなし combined with the Verb stem means that something _____. (BTS 5)
   a. began without warning
   b. was left in an undesirable state
   c. ended quickly with a flourish

7. According to your weather app, it seems it will snow tomorrow.
   あしたは雪_____です。(BTS 6)
   a. らしい
   b. よう
   c. そう

8. You comment that working the night shift seems pretty hard.
   大変な_____だ。(BTS 6)
   a. よう
   b. みたい
   c. らしい

9. You comment that there are few teachers like Sakamoto-sensei.
   坂本先生_____な先生は少ない。(BTS 8)
   a. よう
   b. みたい
   c. らしい

10. You're sure that the only thing you can do is wait. (BTS 7)
    待つ_____ない。
    a. しか
    b. だけ
    c. は

11. You comment that it seems like autumn (even though it's winter) today.
    今日は秋_____ですねぇ。(BTS 8)
    a. よう
    b. らしい
    c. みたい

12. You can use って言うか when you _____. (BTS 9)
    a. misunderstand something
    b. ask about the meaning of a word
    c. add a stronger opinion

13. You think your friend may be feeling embarrassed about her old dress.
    あの古いドレス_____恥ずかしがってるでしょう。(BTS 10)
    a. が
    b. を
    c. の

14. You can attach the suffix 〜がる to some adjectives, 〜たい forms of verbs, and na-Nouns to _____. (BTS 10)

    a. confirm another's opinion
    b. express your concern
    c. describe someone else's feelings

15. You describe the new restaurant in your neighborhood.
    イタリア_____で、とっても美味しいです。(BTS 11)

    a. 風
    b. らしい
    c. よう

16. You tell your friend how to mix the cake batter.
    こういう風_____混ぜて。(BTS 11)

    a. で
    b. に
    c. の

17. You suggest that you and your co-worker decide who to invite to the meeting.
    誰を呼ぶか_____決めましょう。(BTS 12)

    a. で
    b. に
    c. を

18. You advise your roommate to say something even if it's outrageous.
    たとえひどいと_____、言わなかればならない。(BTS 13)

    a. 思っても
    b. 思いながら
    c. 思うのに

19. 四字熟語 are often used for _____. (BTL 1)

    a. word games
    b. proverbial sayings
    c. newspaper headlines

20. 俳句 always include a word that refers to _____. (BTL 3)

    a. the time of year
    b. an historical era
    c. a traditional event

21. 冷たい can be used to describe a cold _____. (BTL 4)

    a. morning
    b. color
    c. person

Appendix A: 文字練習 Symbol practice

Introduction

For each symbol, study the overall shape (top left) and stroke order, then complete every box to the right of it.

Act 13

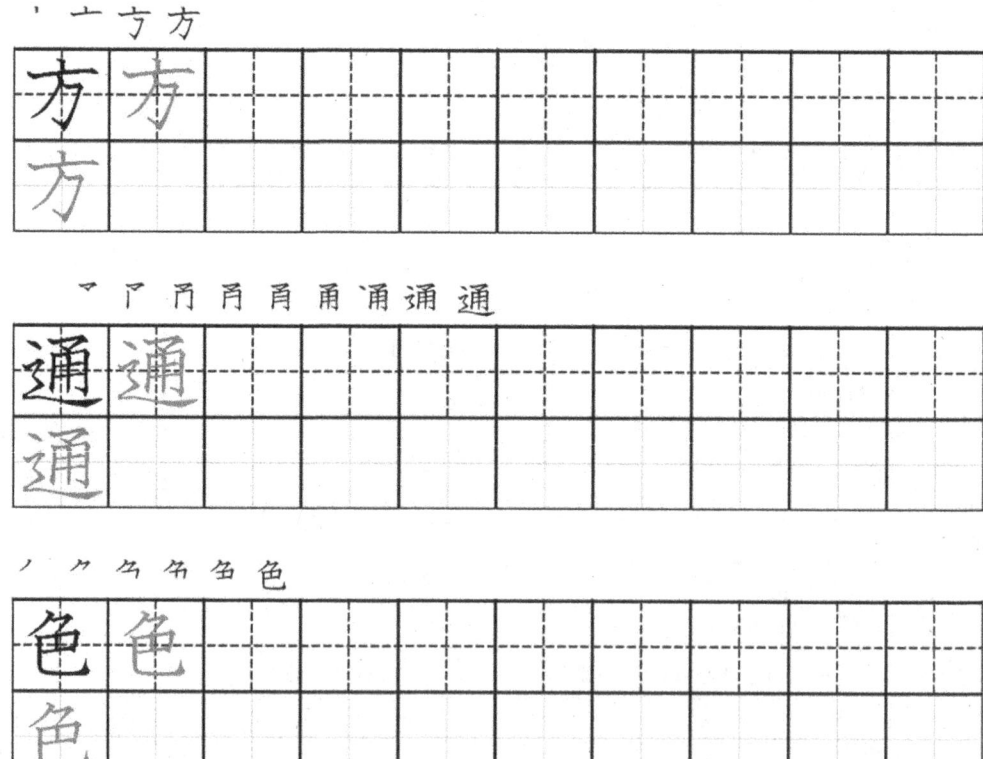

一 十 キ 丰 青 青 青

青 青

青

一 十 土 キ 亣 赤 赤

赤 赤

赤

一 十 艹 共 艹 芢 带 苗 黄 黄

黄 黄

黄

ノ 亻 白 白 白

白 白

白

丶 口 日 日 甲 甲 里 里 黑 黑 黑

黑 黑

黑

ノ 人 ㅅ 亽 牟 余 余 金 金「 金ㄱ 金ㅋ 鈤 鈤 銀 銀

銀 銀

銀

一 二 ㄐ 井

井 井

井

ノ 亻 仁 伊 佈 伢 例 例

例 例

例

丨 冂 冂 囲 困 困 困

困 困

困

一 ナ 方 友

友 友

友

ノ ノ 彳 彳 彳 彳 彼 彼

彼

彼

ノ 丨 冂 白 白 自

自

自

丨 丨 丷 当 当 当

当

当

一 十 十 古 古

古

古

フ ユ 尸 尸 尼 居 屖 屋

屋

屋

一 十 才

才

ノ ハ グ 父

父

し 口 口 口 母

母

丿 口 口 尸 兄

兄

く 女 女 女' 女一 女亡 姉 姉

姉

丶丶丷丷弟弟弟

ㄑㄑ女女妇妌妹妹

丶丷宀宀宀宁宇宇家家

丶亠方方扩扩扩於族族

Act 14

｜冂冂冃冃門門門問開開

丨 冂 冂 冃 門 門 門 門 閉 閉

、 ゛ ゛ 丷 半 米 米 米 料 料

一 丁 干 王 刊 玑 玾 理 理 理

フ カ 刀 召 召

丨 冂 内 内 肉 肉

ノ ク 刍 匂 甪 角 魚 魚 魚 魚

丶 丷 ⺍ 半 米 米

米 米
米

丿 入 人 今 全 全

全 全
全

丿 亻 亻 ⺅ 什 仆 伴 隹 焦 隼 集 集

集 集
集

丶 亠 广 广 庁 庄 店 店

店 店
店

丨 冂 冂 冋 冋 丹 咼 咼 咼 过 过 过

过 过
过

丶 亠 宀 宇 主

主

一 十 扌 扩 扩 拌 拌 持 持

持

丿 ⺧ 牛 牛 牜 牞 物 物

物

丨 冂 冂 皿 皿

皿

フ ㄋ 彐 习习 羽 羽 羽 習 習 習

習

くㄠㄠ幺幺糸糸紅紅細細紳紳練練

練 練

練

丶ㄧ冫厂冫丬汁汁消消消

消 消

消

丶ㄧ冫厂冫冲決

決 決

決

丶ㄧ冫冫氵汁汁洋洋

洋 洋

洋

丶ㄧ冫冫氵汀汀洒洒酒酒

酒 酒

酒

丿 二 千 禾 禾 和 和 和

一 十 艹 艹 芋 芙 苯 茶 茶

〰 幺 幺 糸 糸 糸 紅 紀 紀 紀 綠 綠 綠

丨 口 日 日 甲 甲 里 野 野 野 野

一 十 艹 艹 芋 芋 芋 荦 菜 菜

Act 15

一 十 土 丬 圹 坍 坍 場 場 場 場

場 場

場

丆 亍 戶 戶 所 所 所 所

所 所

所

亠 宁 方 方 扩 扩 扩 扩 旅 旅

旅 旅

旅

丿 人 今 今 今 今 食 食 食' 食' 食' 飣 飣 館 館

館 館

館

丨 冂 冂 冈 図 図

図 図

図

フ 引 引 引 引 引 引 張 張 張 張

一 二 三 千 壬 垂 垂 乗 乗

丶 丷 ⺅ ⺅ 羊 芦 美 着 着 着

フ ヌ ブ ブ ブ ブ 癶 発 発

丶 冫 冫 冫 汐 次 次

丶丷丬关关关送送送

送 送
送

丶丷宀宀宀空空空

空 空
空

丶冫氵氵汁汁汁洪洪港港港

港 港
港

丶丷宀宀宅宅

宅 宅
宅

ノクク多鱼鱼急急急

急 急
急

ノ 亻 亻 亻 佢 佢 便 便

便 便
便

ノ 二 千 千 禾 利 利

利 利
利

一 フ 才 不

不 不
不

ノ 厂 斤 斤 沂 䜣 近

近 近
近

フ ヲ ヨ 尹 尹 君 君

君 君
君

丶 冂 口 囗 日 目 目 冒 員 員

員

丶 丶 宀 宀 宀 宀 灾 客 客

客

丶 ㅏ 누 ㅓ 北

北

一 十 十 内 肉 南 南 南 南

南

一 丆 厂 丙 西 西

西

丿 𠂉 𠂊 牛 失

失 失

礼 礼

Act 16

呼 呼

伝 伝

付 付

丶 亠 亡 忘 忘 忘 忘

忘 忘

丶 丷 丷 ﾂﾞ 𭕄 𰀁 㝉 ﾂﾎﾞ 骨 覚 覚

覚 覚

一 十 扌 扣 扣 扣 招 招

招 招

丨 冂 冂 冋 冋 回

回 回

一 二 キ 才 末

末 末

ノ 八 ハ 今 今 合 合

舎

一 十 广 亡 古 肖 直 直

直

一 厂 厂 万 百 亘 車 連 連 連

連

く 乡 幺 幺 糸 糸 紗 絞 絡 絡

絡

ノ 〈 〃 ニ 平 乎 采 采 番 番 番 番

番

丶 ㄇ ㄖ 号 号

号

号

丶 丶 宀 宀 安 安 安 室 室 案

案 案

案

丨 ㄇ 内 内

内 内

内

丶 丶 宀 宀 宀 宀 宀 容 容

容 容

容

丶 亠 亣 亣 亦 亦 亦 变

变 变

变

く 幺 幺 纟 糸 糸 糽 紬 細 細

細 細

細

一 ナ 大 太

太 太

太

一 十 土 耂 考 考

考 考

考

一 十 土 壱 声 声 売

売 売

売

、 亠 广 広 広

広 広

広

一 セ 切 切

切 切
切

く 幺 幺 糸 糸 糸 糸 約 約

約 約
約

一 厂 厅 戸 束 束 束

束 束
束

Act 17

ノ イ イ' イ'' イ'' イ'' イ'' イ'' 僕 僕 僕 僕

僕 僕
僕

一 十 艹 艹 苎 芇 若 若

若 若
若

丶 亠 广 产 庁 产 庐 序 席 席

一 二 三 手

丨 冂 冂 月 月 且 助 助

一 二 弓 弓 弗 弗 弗 費 費 費 費

一 十 土 士 吉 吉 吉 声 袁 袁 遠 遠

丶 ー ー ー 冒 冒 官 官 軍 軍 運 運

運 運
運

丿 丨 以 以 以

以 以
以

一 十 土 耂 耂 者 者 者

者 者
者

丿 亻 亻 代 代

代 代
代

丶 ー ー 写 写

写 写
写

一 十 广 丙 肖 肖 直 直 真 真

真 真
真

ノ 亻 亻 仁 仁 信 信 信 信

信 信
信

一 厂 厂 厅 束 束 束 刺 刺 刺 頼 頼 頼 頼

頼 頼
頼

一 ノ 幺 玄 幺 糸 系

系 系
系

丶 宀 宀 宀 宀 宀 宿 宿 宿

宿 宿
宿

丨 冂 冃 日 旦 早 early 是 是 是 题 题 题 题 题 题

题 题

丨 冂 口 口" 口三 吽 呀 味

味 味

丶 亠 扩 立 产 产 产 音 音 音 意 意 意

意 意

丨 冂 冃 日 旦 早 里 昇 昇 暑 暑 暑

暑 暑

丶 冖 宀 宀 宀 宇 审 寒 寒 寒 寒 寒

寒 寒

243

Appendix A

、亠广广广疒疒病病病

病

、了阝阝'阝'阝广阶陀陀院院

院

一十艹艹艹甘甘甘甘苗苗菏蓮華薬薬

薬

、丶氵氵汁汁治治治

治

く幺幺幺糸糸糸紆紆紗絆絆絡緒緒

緒

Act 18

丶 广 广 广 广 广 庐 度

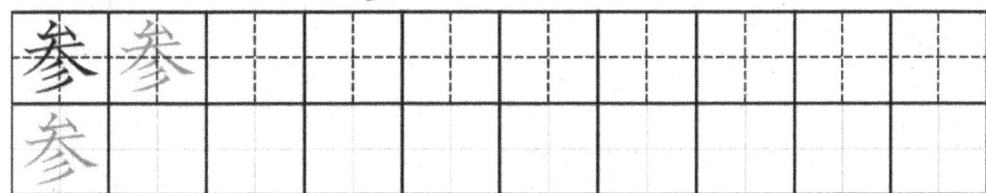

⺈ ⺁ ⺐ ⺐ 夂 夅 参 参

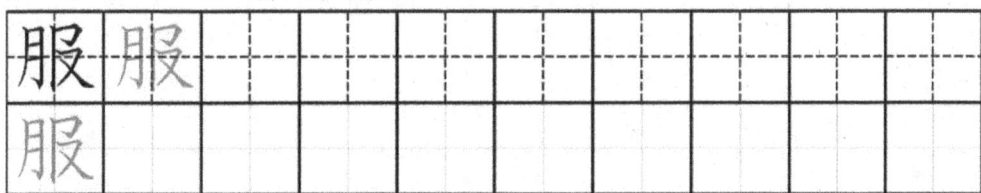

丿 几 月 月 刖 肌 服 服

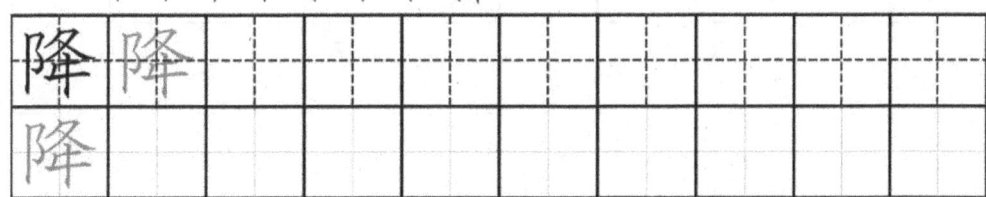

㇇ ㇌ 阝 阝 阡 阡 降 降 降

丨 冂 冃 日 旷 旷 旷 晴 晴 晴

一ㄧㄧ币币雨雨雨雲雲雲雲

雲

一ㄇㄇ日日旦旦早界界累累景暴暴暴

暴

丶丶氵氵汁汁泸泸涼涼涼

涼

丨冂円日日'日″日″日″日″眇眇暖暖

暖

丶丶氵氵汁汁注注

注

丶 亠 ナ 文

文

丿 勹 勹 句 句

句

一 二 三 声 夫 表 春 春 春

春

一 一 丆 丙 丙 百 百 頁 夏 夏

夏

一 二 千 チ 禾 禾 利 秋 秋

秋

ノ ク 夂 冬 冬

冬

丶 ⺀ 氵 氵 汩 汩 沪 沪 泗 温 温 温

温

丶 ⺀ 冫 冫 冷 冷 冷

冷

一 丆 ず 歹 歹 歼 残 残 残

残

ノ 人 ᐱ 今 今 念 念 念

念

丨 冂 日 日 申

申 申
申

丶 亠 亠 亍 言 言 訁 訃 訳 訳
訳 訳
訳

丿 几 凡 凡 凨 同 風 風 風
風 風
風

𠂊 厶 𠂊 台 台
台 台
台

丿 亻 個 個 個 個 個 個 個
個 個
個

丨 冂 冂 冊 冊

冊 冊

一 十 才 木 朴 柠 枋 枚

枚 枚

Appendix B: Assessment answer sheets

聞いてみよう

Write your answers to the Listening comprehension questions.

ACT # _____   Date: _____   Name: _____

No.	Q	Your answer
1	a	

読んでみよう

Write your answers to the Contextualized reading questions.

ACT # _____   Date: _____   Name: _____

No.	Q	Your answer
1	a	

書き取り

Write what you hear.

ACT # _____   Date: _____   Name: _____

No.	Your answer
1	

書いてみよう

Write your responses to the Contextualized writing items.

ACT # _____   Date: _____   Name: _____

知ってる?

Write your answers to the "What do you know?" questions.

ACT # _____   Date: _____   Name: _____

1		11		21	
2		12		22	
3		13		23	
4		14		24	
5		15		25	
6		16		26	
7		17		27	
8		18		28	
9		19		29	
10		20		30	

Appendix B

Appendix C: Answer keys

Act 13

13-1-1C Discussing the division chief's activities 部(ぶ)長(ちょう)の活(かつ)動(どう)について話(はな)す (BTS 1)
3. 面(めん)接(せつ); 4. 心(しん)配(ぱい); 5. 案(あん)内(ない); 6. 運(うん)転(てん)

13-1-2C Which perspective? どんな見(み)方(かた)? (BTS 3)
3. 8 new members, abundant; 4. 5 hours of running, abundant; 5. 10 cakes per day, limited; 6. 1,000 respondents, limited; 7. 10-minute commute, limited; 8. 2 people, limited

13-2-1C What is being suggested? どんな助(じょ)言(げん)? (BTS 4, 7)
3. it'd be better if one didn't come late to class; 4. it'd be dangerous to drive when one is sleepy; 5. it'd be better to leave it as is here; 6. one shouldn't stay up this late, as it'd be bad for the body; 7. one shouldn't bring pets here; 8. one shouldn't speak so loudly, as it'd be a nuisance; 9. one shouldn't sleep here; 10. it'd be better to practice language every day, even if a little at a time

13-3-1C According to what? 何の通(とお)り? (BTS 9)
3. a report, written according to what Yagi-bucho said; 4. cookies, made according to what was written in the book; 5. visitors, showed around according to what the president said; 6. a plan, attempting to write according to what they decided at the meeting the other day; 7. an event next month, do according to what the document from above indicates

13-3-2C What happened to that? 例(れい)の、どうなった? (BTS 8)
3. Yoshida-san doesn't know about it; 4. the younger character got worn out toward the end; 5. they closed it as of June 30th; 6. the intern went home to Brazil last month

13-4-1C. Scanning for 気「気(き)」を探(さが)そう (BTS 13)
3.ご気分、気を遣って; 4. 疲れ気味、気分; 5.平気、平気、気をつけて; 6. 気にならない、気がつかなかった; 7. 合気道、緊張気味、気に入って

13-4-2C. When does the call occur? いつの話? (BTS 14)
3. when he feels like he has a cold, habitual; 4. when he submits a proposal, habitual; 5. when he took the test, past; 6. when she first looked at it, past; 7. when it's during exams, habitual

13-5-1C What's wrong? どこが悪いのでしょう。(BTS 15)
3. fever doesn't go down; 4. has a runny nose; 5. has a stomachache; 6. is constipated

13-6-1C What did they do? 先輩がしたことは? (BTS 16)
3. meeting clients, attending meetings; 4. crying, laughing; 5. laughing as if having a good time, saying kind things; 6. receiving good wishes from everybody, receiving cards; 7. getting lost, forgetting bus tickets

13-6-2C Why not? なぜ? (BTS 16)
3. expensive, long; 4. very hot, it rained; 5. was surprised, was scared; 6. small, noisy; 7. weather was good, food was tasty

13-7-1R Person or comparison? 人?比較?
3. comparison; 4. person; 5. comparison; 6. person

13-7-2R Inventory counts 在庫を調べる
3. 24; 4. blue whiteboard markers; 5. white sticky notes; 6. black whiteboard markers

13-7-3R Half-full or half-empty? だけ?しか?
3. しか; 4. だけ; 5. しか; 6. だけ; 7. だけ; 8. しか

13-7-4W Using mnemonics お客様の特徴を記す
3. 車 (黄); 4. かばん (黒); 5. パソコン (白)

13-8-1RW Expressing concerns and prohibitions 気をつけること
3. 通って; 4. 自分一人; 5. もらわないと; 6. 気分; 7. 行っていないと; 8. 部長; 9. ３万円

13-8-2RW When statements こんなときは……
3. 本当にうれしかったですね; 4. 全部やってしまいましたよ。; 5. 友だちに来てもらってくださいね。; 6. ちゃんと休まないといけませんよ。; 7. ちゃんと話を聞かないとだめですよ。; 8. 例の話でもしようか。

13-8-3RW Potluck party assignments 持ち寄り品の割り当て
3. ブライアン; 4. 自分; 5. 古田先生; 6. 土屋さん; 7. 白井くん; 8. 青木さん

13-9-1R Family hobbies 家族の趣味
3. younger sister, SNS; 4. older sister, she is an OL (office lady = office worker); 5. father, he eats out frequently due to his busy schedule with only one or two

days off a month, but he is worried about being overweight (metabolic syndrome); 6. mother; she doesn't use things that she buys; 7. the blogger; she is doing an internship at a phone company; 8. younger brother; he is good at sports and academics

13-9-2R How is everyone in the family? ご家族(かぞく)は？
3. still resting in her room; 4. doing well; 5. doing things like reading manga and watching television all day

13-9-3W Describing family members 家族(かぞく)の紹介(しょうかい)
4. 姉（２４才）好きな色は赤。何でも赤じゃないとだめ; 5. 自分（２２才）日本語を勉強したり、日本のドラマを見たりするのが好き; 6. 妹（１８才）部屋にいる時はブログしかしない; 7. 弟（１３才）ゲームをしたり、友だちとサッカーをしたりするのが好き

聞いてみよう

1a. keeping it just in case; 1b. throw it away; 1c. it's worn out; Yuya won't use it; 2a. half day; 2b. long time; 2c. worked on a similar program; couldn't finish it; 3a. save it; 3b. deleting it because it seemed unnecessary; 3c. he hasn't done anything yet; 4a. what something is; 4b. it's something that the bucho left; 4c. last month's report; 5a. to take a shower; 5b. it was really hot; he walked a lot; 5c. yes; 6a. how well Kanda-san wrote it; 6b. Sasha, too, made the program quickly; 7a. runny nose, stomachache, and fever; 7b. a cold (not his usual allergy); 7c. to have a doctor take a look; it's no big deal; 7d. to not give the cold to others; 8a. it's comfortable; 8b. he wants something like this; 8c. it allows her to study a lot; 8d. sleep; 9a. furniture is on the 6th floor and places to eat (restaurants) are on the 7th and 8th floor and there is a café on the 1st basement floor; 10a. a planning document; 10b. it was approved; 10c. the higher-ups happened to be thinking the same thing; 10d. that the plan will proceed as written in the document that they turned in

読んでみよう

(1) a. red, blue, yellow, and black; white and silver color are missing; b. for someone to buy the missing colors on their way home since everyone is busy tomorrow; 2 or 3 since 1 is not enough

(2) a. Nagoya with older and younger sister; 3; b. *misokatsu*; it means 'very tasty'; c. they did things like going to Legoland and seeing a good-looking gorilla, so they walked all day long

(3) a. how is your family doing (are they well)?; b. there are places that you can't go through by car and places that are narrow and difficult to enter; c. be careful; call if something goes wrong

書き取り

1. お父さんもお母さんも早目に来られるんですか。
2. 友だちとゲームしたり家族とご飯食べたりしました。
3. 本当に困った時は彼のお兄さんに言ってくださいね。
4. 例の話、まだ白井さんの妹さんしか知らないんですよ。
5. お姉さんが言った通りに作らないといけないよ。
6. 黒じゃだめだから、赤と黄色にした方がいいですよね。
7. 青木さん、弟さんのご気分はよくなりましたか。
8. 名古屋の銀行までは自分一人で行っちゃだめ？

書いてみよう

1. この中に入ってはいけません。
2. 白井先生、明日のイベントには出られますか？
3. See 13-8-3W for samples.
4. 今週は名古屋に行ったり、京都に行ったりしました。せっかく日本に来たので友だちと2人で例のラーメンを食べて来ました。みんなが言ってた通り、本当においしかった！また日本に来る時は家族と来たいな。

知ってる？

1	A	11	B
2	C	12	A
3	B	13	B
4	A	14	B
5	B	15	C
6	C	16	B
7	A	17	A
8	B	18	B
9	C	19	A
10	A	20	C

Act 14

14-1-1C Transitive or intransitive? 他動詞？自動詞？ (BTS 1)
3. a; 4. b; 5. a; 6. a; 7. a; 8. b; 9. a; 10. b

14-1-2C Action to exert change or not? したこと？起こったこと？ (BTS 1)
3. cleaning, yes; 4. becoming free, no; 5. getting fixed, no; 6. putting in, yes

14-2-1C Hearsay or not? 聞いたこと？ (BTS 4)
3. hearsay; 4. not hearsay; 5. not hearsay; 6. hearsay; 7. hearsay; 8. not hearsay; 9. hearsay; 10. not hearsay

14-3-1C When did it happen? いつのこと？ (BTS 9, 10)
3. before; 4. after; 5. after; 6. during; 7. before; 8. before

14-4-1C When did it happen? いつの話？ (BTS 9, 10, 13, 14)
3. before forgetting what we did / while remembering what we did; 4. after returning home; 5. before going to physics class; 6. before going to bed; 7. after eating; 8. while they are still inexpensive / before they get expensive; 9. after throwing it away

14-6-1C Necessity or prohibition? 必要？禁止？ (BTS 18)
3. go see a doctor, necessity; 4. take a day off, prohibition; 5. be the division manager, necessity; 6. get delivered, necessity; 7. show, prohibition; 8. attend, necessity; 9. do one's best, necessity; 10. begin, prohibition

14-6-2C What's going on? 何があったの？
3. (h) taking responsibility; 4. (e) taking responsibility; 5. (g) not taking responsibility; 6. (a) taking responsibility; 7. (b) not taking responsibility; 8. (d) not taking responsibility; 9. (j) taking responsibility; 10. (f) not taking responsibility

14-7-1R Transitive or intransitive? 対象のある行動？ない行動？
3. 閉めよう; 4. つけて; 5. 見える・見える 6. 出ません; 7. 入れよう; 8. 出よう

14-7-2R Resulting state or action? 結果の状況？過程？
3. action; 4. action; 5. resulting state; 6. resulting state; 7. resulting state; 8. action

14-7-3W Writing down what to buy 買い物リスト
3. タイ料理の本; 4. 米、5 キロ; 5. 魚 (サーモン)、1000 円分; 6. すきやき肉、300 g

14-8-1R Transitive or intransitive? 対象のある行動？ない行動？
3. 閉まらない; 4. 集まって; 5. 開ける; 6. 集めている; 7. 集まって; 8. 出そう

14-8-2R When? いつ？
3. 入る; 4. 飲み過ぎる; 5. 見ている; 6. 閉まらない; 7. 話した; 8. 買った

14-8-3W Adding a time frame タイミングを明らかにする
3. お店が開いているうちに; 4. 今日は練習する前に; 5. 8時を過ぎるまでに; 6. みんなが集まったあとで(みんなが集まってから)

14-9-1R Transitive or intransitive? 対象のある行動?ない行動?
3. 入れる; 4. 出て; 5. 決まって; 6. 消して; 7. 集まった; 8. 出よう

14-9-2R Should or should not? するべきか否か
3. should not; 4. should; 5. should; 6. should not; 7. should not; 8. should

14-9-3W Writing names for a game 名前を書く
3. 酒井さん; 4. 七菜ちゃん; 5. 野田先生; 6. 茶山さん; 7. 和男くん; 8. 和田さん

聞いてみよう

1a. express delivery service; 1b. the gift is big and they have other baggage; 1c. order some flowers; 1d. immediately after drinking her tea; 1e. how much money was collected (to purchase the flowers); 2a. empty one side of the shelf; 2b. she wants to put her tools there; 2c. a box big enough to hold the things in front of him; 3a. the money she put in the drawer is missing (100,000 yen); 3b. money must be placed somewhere that can be locked; 3c. she's normally careful; 3d. because it was just for an hour; 4a. to pack a lunch for her; 4b. will deliver after he is finished with cleaning; 4c. why are you so nice; 5a. it's a toy; 5b. it's well made / it's a real keyboard; 5c. there is a switch on this (Kanda-san's) side; 6a. 400 meters; 6b. she thought it was going to be impossible to win; 6c. no more races this year; 6d. get some rest; 7a. there are two big meetings, one before lunch and another one after lunch; 7b. he is getting a ride from his division manager; 7c. before returning to the office; 8a. pass the soy sauce; 8b. is it weak; 8c. it is tasty but . . . ; 8d. mix it; 8e. the sauce had solidified beneath the food; 9a. if it is inside out; 9b. it is a reversible type of clothing; 9c. there is no inside or outer side; 10a. it's cold; 10b. the water he was holding would turn into ice; 10c. turn on the stove (room heater); 10d. where the switch (on/off button) is; 10e. it looks like the switch is about to break; 11a. get the plates out; 11b. one big plate and four small plates, and rice bowls and chopsticks; 11c. it smells good; 11d. it will warm you up when you eat it; 11e. eat it before it gets cold; 12a. when she put the money (100,000 yen) in the drawer; 12b. around 10 o'clock, a little before she opened the meeting room; 12c. that there was no one in the room around that time

読んでみよう

(1)a. a
(2)a. Osakana Kitchen Restaurant; b. it's okay to have fish every day; the restaurant attracts fish lovers (lit. 'fish lovers gather'); c. have some fish before you go home

(3) a. meat dish that uses wine (lit. 'alcohol') and soup with lots of vegetables; b. gather at Shirai Restaurant (1st floor) by 7 p.m.; bring your own plate; c. he thought it was going to be a western-style dish but he heard they are practicing a Japanese-style dish; d. Chayama-san, the rice can be cooked while making the dish; e. Sakai-san

(4) a. casual (they rarely use です・ます); b. it was deleted; when she got her new smartphone; c. she has work tomorrow; d. Midori will do Nana's part in the lesson until she arrives (after 7:30); e. Nana will call Midori after she leaves work

書き取り

1 和食だけじゃなくて、洋食も作らなくちゃ。
2 お茶会でもするとしたら、あのお店がいいかな。
3 緑さんが来る前に全部決まったそうですよ。
4 魚が集まってきたことは集まってきたけど……。
5 となりの方、ついさっきまでご主人かと思ってました。
6 お酒はあまり飲み過ぎないようにしてくださいね。
7 このお料理、あたたかいうちに召しあがってください。
8 部屋の電気、使った後で消したっけ？

書いてみよう

1. ドアは開けたら閉めましょう。
2. 持ち物リスト
   ☐ お米(1カップ)
   ☐ お皿
   ☐ 肉 (1人100g)
   ☐ 野菜
   ☐ お酒
3. 大学では自分で料理しなくちゃいけないけど、練習しているうちにおいしくできるようになってきた☺

知ってる？

1	A	11	C	21	A
2	B	12	A	22	B
3	A	13	C	23	C
4	B	14	A	24	B
5	B	15	C	25	A

6	A	16	A	26	B
7	B	17	B	27	B
8	C	18	A	28	A
9	B	19	C	29	C
10	A	20	C		

Act 15

15-1-1C Can you do it? できますか? (BTS 1)
3. b; 4. a; 5. b; 6. a; 7. b; 8. b; 9. a; 10. b; 11. a; 12. a; 13. b; 14. a; 15. b

15-2-1C Intention or expectation? 意図(いと)?前提(ぜんてい)? (BTS 2)
3. intention; 4. assumption; 5. intention; 6. intention; 7. assumption; 8. assumption; 9. intention; 10. assumption; 11. assumption; 12. intention

15-3-1C Hearsay or not? 伝言(でんごん)か否(いな)か (BTS 6)
3. hearsay; 4. not hearsay; 5. hearsay; 6. not hearsay; 7. hearsay; 8. not hearsay; 9. not hearsay; 10. hearsay; 11. hearsay; 12. not hearsay; 13. not hearsay; 14. hearsay

15-4-1C Follow the procedures 指示(しじ)に従(したが)う (BTS 7, 8)
来月の会は「銀屋」でします。銀屋は魚がおいしい店です。ご家族も友だちもどうぞごいっしょに。来れるか来れないか、ベンさんにテキストしてください。よろしくお願いします。

15-5-1C Intention or assumption? 意図(いと)?思(おも)い込(こ)み? (BTS 2, 11)
3. assumption; 4. assumption; 5. intention; 6. assumption; 7. intention; 8. assumption; 9. intention; 10. intention

15-7-1R Potential or honorific passive? 可能(かのう)?尊敬(そんけい)の受(う)け身(み)?
4. potential; 5. potential; 6. either; 7. honorific passive; 8. potential; 9. either; 10. either; 11. honorific passive; 12. honorific passive

15-7-2R Potential or intransitive? 可能(かのう)?自動詞(じどうし)?
3. another entity; 4. speaker; 5. another entity; 6. speaker; 7. another entity; 8. speaker

15-7-3W Filling out a schedule 予定表(よていひょう)に書(か)き込(こ)む
3. 酒井所長 3時; 4. 出張(東京 8時発、名古屋 10時着); 5. 練習場所 (302 → 201); 6. 勉強会 (図書館4時); 7. 旅行 (バス乗り場１０時)

15-8-1RW Organizing explanations 手順(てじゅん)を示(しめ)す
3. 最初にパンの上にケチャップをつけて、で、その上にチーズと好きな野菜を乗せて、最後にトースター（２００℃）に入れて１０分〜１２分待ったら

できるよ。; 4. まず空港に着いてからチェックインしなくちゃいけません。次にセキュリティーチェックです。それからゲートに行って、フライトに乗りますので、パスポートは出しやすいところに持っていた方がいいですよ。; 5. 最初に和食にするか洋食にするか決める。次にどちらかに決まったら、好きなレシピの本を見て、自分が作れる料理を見つける。で、作る料理が決まったら買い物かな、私だったら。; 6. まずみんなで集まって不便なことをリストアップしまていきます。それから、どうして不便なのかをブレーンストーミングして、で、どうやったら「不便」なことを「便利」にできるかアイディアを出していきます。

15-8-2R する？なる？
3. して; 4. なり; 5. して; 6. なって; 7. なり; 8. しよう; 9. なり; 10. なった

15-8-3W Convenient? Inconvenient? 便利か不便か
3. 私がよく使う空港はゲートの場所がわかりにくいから、不便だと思います; 4. 私が買い物をするお店はすぐ食べられる物が安く買えるから便利だと思います; 5. 私が使う宅急便はオーダーした次の日に家に送ってもらえるから便利だと思います

15-9-1R Intention or mistaken assumption? 意図？思い違い？
3. 会う; 4. 話した; 5. 会わない; 6. 送った; 7. 乗る; 8. 待つ

15-9-2R Whose opinion matters? 誰の意見？
3. 部長; 4. 店員さん; 5. 上; 6. 社長; 7. 子ども; 8. 家族; 9. 部長; 10. 客

15-9-3W Filling out a schedule 予定表に書き込む
3. (お客様に) お礼を送る (近くのコンビニ); 4. 白井君と練習 (7時); 5. 西田さんアポ (9時半); 6. 社員旅行 (東京駅南口、午前8時); 7. 社員旅行

評価

聞いてみよう

1a. to fill the empty space with something; 1b. so that it won't hit other things and break; 1c. paper or anything is fine; 2a. she can't deliver the document as is; 2b. separate things that are absolutely necessary from things that are okay to be deleted (lit. 'okay not be on the document'); 3a. is the third or fourth good for the client's schedule next month; 3b. either date is fine but the 4th fits better with his schedule; 3c. around 2 in the afternoon; 4a. were you able to get some rest; 4b. he was able to relax in the hot spring; 4c. Kanda-san's business trip overlapped with the company outing; 4d. that he was able to make it; 5a. the other company's person hasn't showed up yet; 5b. that they hurry and catch up with the *bucho* since they can still make it in time; 5c. that there is a special express train that they can ride; 6a. the remote is broken; 6b. she will buy a new one today; 6c. to go buy it; 6d. that it would help her; 7a. an accident; 7b. it is the time the client's flight departs; 7c. the client wants to arrive at the airport by 18:00; 7d. to take the train; 7e. the flight has been cancelled; 7f. it looks like he won't be able to return home today; 8a. he planned to do it in the morning; 8b. people normally don't forget something like that; 8c. he wrote a memo in his notebook that said "I should register"; 8d. the intern didn't actually write the memo (though he thought he did); 8e. the intern forgot to look at his notebook; 8f. he will do it over from the beginning; 9a. how (Sasha) Morris-san is doing recently; 9b. she has learned how to do her job quite a bit; 9c. she's become reliable to the point that he can leave things to her; 9d. have Sasha be in charge of the editing next month; 9e. he will talk to Sasha, with the plan to have her be in charge of the editing next month; 10a. it's handy and easy to see (read); 10b. to write things like plans and procedures; 10c. he thought she was the type of person who only used her cellphone; 10d. the same things she writes on her planner; 10e. she likes writing things by hand; 10f. once she got used to it she couldn't stop writing things in her planner by hand

読んでみよう

(1) a. Nishida; b. something edible; to eat it with others in the company; c. just a little (as a means to downplay the act of giving a gift)

(2) a. the location of the inn for the business trip; the fact that there is a library nearby; b. Kanda-san was planning to ride the train departing at 4 p.m., but the arrival time is past 9 (which is a little too late); c. to ride the train departing at 3 p.m.; Kitada-san uses 乗れますか to ask if it's possible for him to ride the 3 p.m. train

(3) a. a client; to change the next appointment with Nishida-san from 8/18 (T) to 8/17 (M); b. he is taking a vacation that week starting on Wednesday and going on a family trip; their flight leaves at 8 in the morning so they need to be at the airport by 6, which means they leave their home at 4:30; c. he needs to do things like going to get his passport and calling the delivery service, so it will be very hectic (バタバタ) and he worries that he might offend the client; d. to call Nishida-san and talk to him

書き取り

1. 西田君、次の5時発の電車には乗れますか？
2. 近くの図書館で勉強するつもりだそうです。
3. あのカメラマン、全国どこにでも出張するそうですよ。
4. 旅館の場所、ちょっと不便なんじゃない？
5. あの社員、英語が話せるようになったんですか？
6. 送ったつもりだったのですが、送れてなくて失礼しました。
7. 宅急便が使えるようになったから便利になりましたね。
8. お客様ですが、先ほど空港に着かれたとのことです。

書いてみよう

1.
西田さん
先日はお会いできなくて失礼しました。
こちら、よろしければ
ご家族で召し上がってください。
　　　　　　　　　　　　　Your name

2.
北田君
明日空港に行くんだけど、これ、宅急便で送っておいてもらえますか？
Your name

3.
南さん
東京３時発、名古屋５時１５分着です。
出張お気をつけて！
Your name

4.
まず、バスで「図書館前」まで行ってください。次に近くの学校の方に歩いて行くとコンビニがあるので、そこで右です。そのまままっすぐ行くと旅館です。

知ってる？

1	C	11	A
2	C	12	C
3	A	13	B
4	B	14	A
5	B	15	C
6	C		
7	A		
8	B		
9	A		
10	C		

Act 16

16-1-1C Declining invitations 誘いを断る (BTS 2)
3. a, e; 4. a, c; 5. e; 6. a, b, c, d

16-1-2C A reflection session 反省会 (BTS 1)
3. should have thought more seriously about the poster design; 4. should have helped out more; 5. should have asked people to wait until seats became available; 6. should have had seats for people who were waiting; 7. should have stayed to help with the clean-up; 8. should be happy that it went as well as it did

16-2-1C Enlisting help to continue 話を続けるための助けを求める (BTS 6)
3. ぼうぼう; ボロボロ; 4. まつまつ; ますます; 5. バタバタ; バラバラ; 6. うえがき; うわがき; 7. ガタンガタン; ガタガタ

16-3-1C Just happened or about to happen? どんなところ? (BTS 5, 7)
3. about to fail; 4. just finished; 5. about to submit; 6. about to refuse; 7. just arrived; 8. about to call; 9. about to leave; 10. about to delete; 11. just heard

16-3-2C Like what? たとえて言うと (BTS 8)
3. the lecture by that professor; no available seats, like a restaurant that you went to without making a reservation; 4. the section chief's explanation today; completely unintelligible, like the phrase "a strong-minded cat"; 5. the exam last week; okay at first, but the result was terrible, like a demolished Mt. Fuji; 6. hair; messy, like a proposal that you forgot to edit

16-3-4CP Expressing envy うらやましさ (BTS 8)
3. Kato-san, takes beautiful pictures; 4. Mori-san, takes care of even complicated issues; 5. Sasaki-san, keeps doing her favorite hobbies while keeping a part-time job; 6. Kobayashi-san, knows about hot springs all over Japan; 7. Yamaguchi-san, is able to research anything; 8. Minamida-san, is curious about things even outside of his specialization

16-4-1C Just happened or about to happen? (BTS 5, 7, 9) 今あったこと?それともこれから?
3. about to forget; 4. about to be in an accident; 5. just returned; 6. about to leave; 7. about to leave; 8. just gathered; 9. just finished writing

16-5-1C Reason or purpose? 理由? 目的? (BTS 10)
3. purpose; 4. reason; 5. reason; 6. purpose; 7. reason; 8. purpose; 9. reason; 10. purpose; 11. reason

16-5-2C Doing something for a purpose 目的を持って行動する (BTS 10)
3. to go to Tokyo station; 4. to deliver a package; 5. to enroll in a class; 6. to study sociology; 7. to lend an old textbook

16-6-1C Listening to opinions and taking notes 意見を書き取る (BTS 11)
3. there seem to be many people who are interested, the registration process is too complicated, not many people have registered; 4. the division chief said it was a good plan, there may not be enough people, Tomoda-san and Yoshida-san seem to be busy with another project; 5. it's good that it's not expensive, it may be difficult to use, the place you hold it is too large for a child's hand; 6. it's cheap enough that college students can come, it's too long, even on weekends people usually don't have that much time

16-6-2C Writing down opinions that you hear 意見を聞き書きする (BTS 11)
3. the school president's comment differs from the advanced meeting; 4. a single person should re-read the whole thing; 5. same as Suzuki's point and is willing to do the editing; 6. discuss as a group after Hayashi edits the whole thing; 7. shorten the president's comments by cutting the bottom portion

16-7-1R Contrast or reason? 逆接？理由？
3. に; 4. で; 5. で; 6. に; 7. で; 8. に

16-7-2RW Things that I should do or should have done . . . やるべきこと、後悔してること。
3. 覚えて; 4. 招待する; 5. 気をつけて; 6. やめた; 7. 使って; 8. 呼んだ

16-7-3W Writing down reminders 忘れないよう記録する
3. 漢字を覚える（１０回ずつ書く）; 4. 酒田さんを呼ぶ; 5. 黒い紙に書けるペン; 6. かさを忘れないように気を付ける; 7. 招待メールを送る; 8. 部長に週末のスケジュールを伝える

16-8-1R Provisional expressions 仮の表現
3. 合えば; 4. 直せば; 5. 聞けば; 6. 話してあげれば; 7. 社長なら; 8. 覚えなければ

16-8-2R Explaining what happened 何が起こったか説明する
3. 仕事の付き合いが入って; 4. 雨がふってきて; 5. プログラムがフリーズして; 6. 番号が消えて; 7. 部長が部屋に入って来て; 8. みんなびっくりして

16-8-3W Asking a favor by leaving a note お願いをメモする
3. 野口様、よろしければプレゼンの内容も伝えていただけますか。; 4. 洋子ちゃん、よかったら連絡先をメールしてもらえますか。; 5. 緑ちゃん、よかったら電話番号を教えてもらえますか。; 6. 八木部長、よろしければお客様に会社を案内していただけますか。

16-9-1R Expressing cause, reason, and purpose 原因、理由、目的の表現
3. 約束; 4. 細くなる; 5. 物を売る; 6. 部屋が広い; 7. 売り切れ; 8. 太った; 9. 変える; 10. 招待する

16-9-2R Which statement is softer? より柔らかい表現は？
3. b; 4. a; 5. a; 6. b; 7. b; 8. b

16-9-3RW Softening your statements and opinions 供述・意見を和らげる
4. この案、もう少し変えた方がいいように (いいかと) 思いますけど……。; 5. ちょっと考え過ぎのように (考え過ぎかと) 思いますけど……。; 6. 太いのはちょっと売り切れみたい (売り切れのよう) だよ。; 7. 細川さん、ちょっと考えてみると言ってたみたい (言ってたよう) だよ。; 8. 雪の天気でちょっと大変みたい (のよう) なので……。

評価

聞いてみよう

1a. messy, disorganized; 1b. he should have explained the process beforehand; 2a. to accompany her in the afternoon, if Kanda-san doesn't have any prior appointments; 2b. the publisher wants to apologize; 2c. the publisher caused some kind of trouble; 2d. the publisher shouldn't be so concerned; 3a. having a serious look on her face; 3b. playing a game; 3c. don't tell the division chief about it; 3d. he's not going to tell the division manager; 3e. it seems that you can learn things from playing the game; 4a. that we should try hard without giving up even when we fail; 4b. there are similar sayings in English; 4c. the second one with もと; 4d. the essence; 5a. it's hard to get used to onomatopoeia; 5b. it's easy for Japanese people to understand onomatopoeia; 5c. why does it have to be *gatagata* instead of *gatogato*?; 5d. he doesn't know, he hasn't really thought about it seriously; 6a. talk to Ikebe-san if Sasha has time; 6b. Ikebe-san is acting timid lately; 6c. Ikebe-san messed up the copies of reports the other day; 6d. capable; 7a. the company didn't match what Ikebe-san had imagined (her ideals); 7b. continue to work hard and not give up; 7c. she is doing well lately; 7d. (she can help Kanda-san) anytime if he finds something like this helpful; 8a. to follow the procedure as discussed the other day; 8b. Sasha will talk about the overall concept and Kanda-san is in charge of talking about the details; 8c. that it is the revised version; 8d. she just reprinted it; 9a. it seems that she is doing better; 9b. Sasha saw Ikebe-san smiling with the other interns as they showed their bentos to each other; 10a. it sold well; 10b. because it didn't sell well in the beginning but started to do much better when summer break started; 10c. he will check on the details again and he will share that with everyone in next week's meeting; 11a. it was fun; 11b. Sakamoto-sensei's failure story; 11c. that Sakamoto-sensei doesn't give up; 11d. Brian hasn't seen Sakamoto-sensei being timid; 11e. he gets motivated somehow

読んでみよう

(1) a. Brian needs to print an important assignment, but the printer is not working; b. he could have taken a look at it if Brian had told him about the issue when he was at home

(2) a. Hiroaki Hosokawa; b. about inviting Brian's for today's appointment to get together; c. Brian remembered that he forgot something as he was getting on the train, so he is probably on his way home; d. Tanaka-san has told Brian to be careful not to forget things a number of times; the other person guesses that Brian has forgotten to bring cash and comments that they should have sent Brian a reminder

(3) a. this is Brian's second time forgetting something today; b. Brian is going to contact the train station later; c. Hiroshi thinks Brian should talk to someone at the station if he is still near the station; d. to the lost and found, which is next to the station *kiosk*; not having a bag is terrible and the lost and found might be closed for the weekend; e. to tell everyone that they do not have to wait for him, in case he doesn't make it on time

(4) a. Monday through Friday 9 a.m. to 5 p.m.; 050-5555-3920; b. contents of the item; the date and time you lost the item; the location of where you suspect you lost the item; characteristics of the item (color, size, brand, maker, etc.); c. an exemplary list of things that people frequently lose such as cellphones/smartphones, bags, pass cases, paper bags, and wallets

(5) a. someone that wishes that they had cash because they have to use cash, but they do not have it; b. the convenience of the ATM machine is full time and is available every day (i.e., 365 days a year); you can use the ATM machine like a wallet and do things like withdrawing and depositing; c. there is no fee; d. 120 yen

書き取り

1. 洋太君、呼んであげれば来ると思うよ。
2. おり紙、全部売り切れだったようです。
3. 週末まで考えるための時間をください。
4. 約束してたのに覚えてなかったみたい。
5. 忘れるところでしたが気が付きました。
6. プレゼンの内容を直そうと思っていたところです。
7. 日付が変わってしまって間に合いませんでした。
8. 伝言、もう1回伝えるべきだと思います。

書いてみよう

1. 忘れ物、気を付けてね。
   (your name)

2.

JLCメンバー連絡先		
名前	電話番号	メールアドレス
例. 細川　広明	614-555-2918	h.hosokawa@fukuzawadaigaku.edu

3.

> クリスマスパーティーのご案内
> クリスマスなのに家族も大切な人も近くにいない。
> そんなみんなのためのパーティー！
> 日時：１２月２３日(土)　１９時〜２１時半
> 場所：フレンドホール２０１
> 内容：ゲーム、デザート、プレゼント！
> 連絡先：Amy Johnson（amyjohnson555@cu.edu）

4. Sample

今日はみんなで集まる約束があったんだけど、電車に乗ろうとしたところでカバンを忘れた事に気が付いて家に帰らなければならなかった☺　で、その後急いで行ったんだけど、急いでたからそのカバンを電車に忘れてしまって……☹せっかく呼んでもらったのに間に合わなかった☺

知ってる？

1	A	11	C
2	B	12	A
3	B	13	C
4	C	14	B
5	A	15	A
6	A		
7	B		
8	C		
9	A		
10	B		

Act 17

17-1-1C Meanings of ながら (BTS 1)

3. contradiction; 4. simultaneous activities; 5. contradiction; 6. simultaneous activities; 7. simultaneous activities; 8. simultaneous activities; 9. contradiction; 10. contradiction

17-2-1C What's the expectation? 予想されていること (BTS 3)

3. the test is not that difficult for college students, even for first-year students. 4. Saya and Soichi are asleep; 5. the item can be sold for a good price; 6. it will take 1 or 2 months by sea mail; 7. Murakami-san will not use the ordinary train; 8. Ichiro will arrive in 10 minutes

17-3-1C Who did it? したのは誰? (BTS 5)

3. Yoshino-san, helped; 4. Morikawa-san, greeted; 5. Fukumoto-san, paid; 6. Watanabe-san, carried; 7. Murakami-san, saw; 8. Kobayashi-san, decorated the room; 9. Eguchi-san, invited; 10. Takahashi-san, closed; 11. Ito-san, called; 12. Omura-san, chose

17-4-1C Who did it? したのは誰? (BTS 7)

3. someone else, copy; 4. someone else, close; 5. the speaker, send; 6. someone else, go; 7. someone else, help; 8. the speaker, borrow; 9. someone else, go home; 10. someone else, rewrite; 11. the speaker, stay behind; 12. someone else, inform; 13. the speaker, invite

17-4-2C According to what? 何によると? (BTS 8)

3. his grades are among the top, what I heard from Ichiro-kun; 4. his approval rating is high among senior citizens, this newspaper article; 5. there are over 10,000 hits each day, the information Matsuda-san looked up; 6. the U.S. is number one, this graph; 7. the performance/efficiency is the best, a magazine I was reading yesterday

17-5-1C Qualified responses 〜次第?情報源? (BTS 8, 11)

3. it depends on the test results; 4. according to this article; 5. according to information Furuta-san gave; 6. it depends on the household; 7. it depends on things like grades and attendance; 8. according to what the division chief said

17-6-1C When? いつ? (BTS 13)

3. interesting opinions, compile into a document once everybody's opinions are expressed; 4. support ratio, report to the division chief once the overall ratio begins to go up; 5. this task, have a completion party once it's completely done

17-7-1R "Time" or "notwithstanding"? 並行か矛盾か

3. time; 4. notwithstanding; 5. notwithstanding; 6. notwithstanding; 7. time; 8. time

17-7-2R Reasonable expectations 妥当な予想

3. 助からない; 4. 知らない; 5. 安かった; 6. 運べる; 7. ならない; 8. 下手な

17-7-3RW Responding ambiguously 曖昧に答える

3. 料理ですか。まあ上手でもないけど、下手でもないですよ; 4. あの場所ですか。まあ、便利ではないけど、不便でもないですよ; 5. あの席ですか。ま

あ遠くはないけど、近くもないですよ; 6. 僕 (私) ですか。いえ、運べなくはないですよ; 7. 遠野先生ですか。まあ、若くはないけど、若くなくもないですよ; 8. 僕 (私) ですか。いえ、助けられなくはないですよ; 9. 白井君ですか。いえ、強気ではないけど、弱気でもないですよ。

17-8-1R Making requests 依頼の内容
3. 待たせない; 4. 頼り過ぎない; 5. 信じない; 6. 出る; 7. 見せない; 8. あげる

17-8-2R Identifying the source 情報源は？
3. 新聞; 4. 神田さん; 5. 昨日読んだ本; 6. 若者の話

17-8-3RW Using causatives 使役表現
3. 宿題を持たせて; 4. 勉強させて; 5. １０代の子に飲ませて; 6. 来させて; 7. 子どもに乗らせて; 8. 漢字を覚えさせ; 9. だれかに頼らせて

17-8-4RW Thank you messages 感謝のことば
3. 宿題をやり直させて; 4. IT系の仕事の話を聞かせて; 5. 弟を待たせて; 6. ２０代のころの事を思い出させて; 7. 僕にも出席させて; 8. 妹にも聞かせて; 9. 写真を使わせて

17-9-1R To or with each other? 〜合う
3. 通じ; 4. 付き; 5. 連絡し; 6. 言い; 7. 出し; 8. 分かり

17-9-2R Depending on what? 何によって？
3. 場合; 4. 薬; 5. スケジュール; 6. 天気; 7. 日; 8. ライフスタイル

17-9-3RW Writing short memos メモを書く
3. 宿題; 4. 病院; 5. 一緒に; 6. 薬; 治る; 7. 意味; 8. 暑く

聞いてみよう

1a. it's bad manners; 1b. don't talk while chewing gum; 2a. how much profit it made; 2b. the marketing was successful; 2c. it was broadly supported, from young people to elderly people in their 60s; 3a. whether Janet Ota is second or third generation; 3b. Takashi doesn't know the details, but she is third generation according to the introduction given by his teacher; 3c. that the person knows about Japan but doesn't speak the language; 4a. the biggest project of the year ended; 4b. for helping each other; 4c. to have a party to celebrate the success of the project; 4d. to eat as much as they can; 4e. to have a toast; 4f. it is expected that the head of the company will come later; 5a. it's wasteful; 5b. Sasha asks Eri if she was going to throw the herbs into the trash without using all of them; 5c. that there are some left; 5d. Eri will use all of it (until the very end); 6a. he plans to attend it; 6b. she can't decide, she wants to attend it but she thinks it's a little expensive; 6c. it's not cheap, but the meal cost is included in the fee; 6d. she will register for it by the end of the day; 7a. the graph on the page is one from two years ago; 7b. Sasha thanks the visitor for letting her know; 7c. she will have someone in her company replace it with a new one; 8a. it has become cold; 8b. the grade for his history class is worse than he thought; 8c. grades are nothing really, you should enjoy your everyday life; 8d. he feels uplifted listening to her voice (advice); 9a. what the article is about; 9b. the article is about problems associated with elderly people; the number of accidents caused by elderly people is increasing; 9c. it is increasing rapidly especially in recent years; 10a. sleeping while driving and hitting something; going forward (by hitting the gas) thinking it's the brake pedal; (driving while) trying to get something from the back and not looking ahead; 10b. it depends on the person; 10c. he agrees, you can't say that every elderly person's driving is dangerous; 11a. how to study English effectively; 11b. summarize the lecture; 11c. it's not okay to not work hard, but if your English is not getting better even when you put a lot of effort into it then your study method is not effective; 12a; he's the person who made an appointment with division manager Ono at 2; 12b. who he is / which company he belongs to; 12c. to wait over there; 12d. he'll wait here; 13a. for making Kanda-san wait; 13b. for visiting her when she is busy; 13c. this person, Hayashi, will accompany them today

読んでみよう

(1) a. there are delays due to cancellations caused by a snowstorm
(2) a. he went to a hospital in Japan by himself without relying on anyone; b. he can get better right away if he takes the medicine, so he's going to take it
(3) a. to work on his own to an extent possible; b. 4 hours because there were kanji characters he hadn't studied and he was working on his homework while watching TV
(4) a. attended a digital art class with Amy; b. they were allowed to use tablets; they completed their art project in about 2 hours; c. to be a professional artist in the not-so-distant future; d. digital generation, young artists; unbelievable; the room was hot; his hand is tired; his eyes are also tired
(5) a. $750; b. $360; c. do not spend more than $50 eating out; d. as much as possible, don't use up all the smartphone data; e. no, because he is paying fees for the bus and a ride service; f. dating, digital art class, photography class, eating and drinking, and an online streaming service; g. delivery fees and clothing (socks and T-shirts)
(6) a. kanji characters that students have not studied yet; b. students should be able to follow the content; c. she wants her students to do the assignment on their own as much as possible, but it is okay to work on it with classmates and help each other; d. she tells students to be careful not to get sick because it's getting cold

書き取り

1. 僕たちにも出席させていただきありがとうございました。
2. 遠野さんがスキャンするように言ってた写真です。
3. 先日の集まりの会費と飲み物代は以上となります。
4. 困った時は助け合って一緒にがんばりましょう。
5. 学者によると、この病気は薬で治せるとのことです。
6. 大学によっては理系学部がないところもあるみたいですよ。
7. まだ若いんだから頼れるだけ頼ってもいいと思いますよ。
8. テレビを見ながら宿題してもあまり意味ないんじゃないの。

書いてみよう

1. Sample

   遠野さん
   病院からもらった薬です。飲んで休めば早く治るはずです。お大事に。
   Your name

2. Sample

   件名：１２月２日の宿題

   西田先生
   今日はカゼがまだ治りきっていなくてクラスに出席できなくてすみませんでした。宿題で意味の分からないところがあるのですが、明日のクラスの後で少しお時間いただけませんか。
   よろしくお願いします。
   Your Name

3. Sample

   僕たちにもできるボランティア！
   #困った時は助け合い　#若者だってがんばります#一緒にがんばろう　#いい写真　#信じ合える友人

4. Sample

   昨日はボランティアとしてガーディングの仕事を手伝わせてもらった。あまり上手にはできなかったけど、プランターを運びながら色々なことを考えさせてもらいました。暑くも寒くもなくて気持ちのいい天気だったなあ。

5. Sample

１１月	金額	メモ
食費	$250	お酒に３０ドル以上使わないようにする
アパート代	$400	

電気代	$35	
水代	$25	
電話代	$75	できるだけデータを使い切らないようにする

知ってる?

1	A	11	B	21	C
2	C	12	C	22	A
3	C	13	B	23	B
4	B	14	C	24	A
5	A	15	A		
6	C	16	A		
7	A	17	C		
8	B	18	B		
9	B	19	B		
10	C	20	A		

Act 18

18-1-1C Who did it? 誰がした? (BTS 1)

3. Murakami-san; 4. Uchida-san; 5. Yamaguchi-san; 6. Yoshino-san; 7. Omura-san; 8. Tanaka-san; 9. The speaker; 10. Shimizu-san; 11. The speaker; 12. Yamazaki-san

18-1-2C Listening to the weather forecast 天気予報を聞く (BTS 4)

3. a; 4. j; 5. g; 6. i; 7. f; 8. e; 9. b; 10. c

18-2-1C What's going on? どういうこと? (BTS 6)

3.polite; 4. uncertain; 5. uncertain; 6. polite

18-3-1C Meanings of Noun + らしい (BTS 6 & 8)

3. typical of a class; 4. evidence-based conjecture; 5. typical of a class; 6. evidence-based conjecture; 7. evidence-based conjecture; 8. typical of a class

18-4-1C Who is she talking about? 誰のこと? (BTS 10)
3. another person; 4. the speaker; 5. the speaker; 6. another person; 7. another person; 8. the speaker; 9. another person; 10. another person; 11. the speaker; 12. another person; 13. the speaker; 14. the speaker

18-5-1C What are they talking about? 話題は? (BTS 12)
3. who to invite; 4. how to increase the efficiency; 5. what kind of content to have; 6. whether to submit it this month or next month; 7. why they are opposed; 8. what to eat; 9. when it would be good to get together; 10. whether to increase or decrease the cost

18-6-1C Even supposing that . . . 条件の不足を指摘する (BTS 13)
3. even a superior student; 4. even a weak effect; 5. even if we had detailed information; 6. even something small; 7. even if you lose

18-6-4RCP Making an observation 観察を述べる (BTS 6)
3. unsympathetic; 4. neither; 5. unsympathetic; 6. sympathetic; 7. sympathetic; 8. sympathetic; 9. unsympathetic; 10. sympathetic

18-7-1R Passive? Honorific? Potential? 受け身?尊敬?可能?
4. passive; 5. potential; 6. passive; 7. honorific; 8. honorific; 9. passive; 10. potential; 11. passive; 12. potential

18-7-2R It seems that . . . 様子の表現
3. らしい; 4. よう; 5. よう・よう; 6. みたい; 7. らし; 8. らしい; 9. みたい; 10. よう

18-7-3RW Journal entries about weather 気候について記述する
3. 曇り; 4. 雲; 降らなかった; 5. 涼しい服; 6. 0度 (or other cold temperature); 暖かく; 7. 晴れ; 降られて; 8. 涼しい; 9. your own journal entry

18-8-1R Expressions associated with temperature 温度の表現
3. 冷たい; 4. 暖かめ; 5. 冬; 6. 温かく; 7. 涼しい; 8. 冷たい

18-8-2R 俳句?川柳?
3. 俳句 by 内藤鳴雪 (秋); 4. 俳句 by 正岡子規 (冬); 5. 川柳; 6. 川柳; 7. 川柳; 8. 俳句 by 松尾芭蕉 (春); 9. 川柳; 10. 俳句 (冬); 11. 俳句 (夏)

18-8-3W Warm or cold? 温度について言及する
3. 冷めないうちに召し上がってください; 4. 暖かい服を着てくるようにしてください; 5. 温めてから食べてね; 6. 冷たいビール、ごちそう様

18-8-4W What season? 季節を限定する
3. 春; 4. 夏; 5. 秋; 6. 冬

18-9-1R What particle? 疑問文の助詞を使いこなす
3. が; 4. を; 5. で; 6. に; 7. で; 8. を

18-9-2R Even if... 条件・状態に関わらず……
3. 気温があまり高くなくても; 4. メッセージを送ったとしても; 5. 暑くなったとしても; 6. 台風が来なくても; 7. もう2、3個買ったとしても; 8. 文句を言われたとしても

18-9-3RW How many? 数の表現
3. 冊; 4. 本; 5. 個; 6. 枚; 7. 台; 8. 台; 9. 枚; 10. 本; 11. 枚; 12. 冊/枚

18-9-4RW Expressing apology and disappointment 謝罪や残念な気持ちを述べる
3. 申し訳ありませんが; 4. 残念ながら; 5. 申し訳ありませんが; 6. 残念ながら

聞いてみよう

1a. a typhoon is approaching; 1b. it's raining a lot already and windy; 1c. the weather forecast; 1d. it is raining like the rainy season (just drizzling); 1e. it's better not to go outside; 2a. there's no wind, it's sunny; great; 2b. the sun; 2c. it's relatively warm for October; 2d. heat stroke; in the afternoon when the temperature gets higher; 3a. pretty; positive (her heart is cleansed); 3b. the sunlight is intense because they are at the top of the mountain; 3c. the temperature is not that high and it feels good; 3d. the exhausted feeling she had seems like a lie; 3e. let's walk once we are feeling better; 4a. there is a complaint that the air conditioning in room 200 isn't working; 4b. that they can't use the room today; 4c. he intended to tell her but ended up forgetting ; 4d. she can't take any further responsibility; 4e. please don't get so angry; 5a. a new part-time student worker; 5b. she can't do anything; the only thing she does is complain; 5c. that she was spoiled growing up; 5d. she only considers her own convenience and has no training (in how to be) a working adult; 5e. that they should train her here; 5f. because Kanda-san is passing (the responsibility to train her) to Mizuno-san; 6a. to tell him her honest feelings; 6b. it's impossible to work together on this team anymore; 6c. a complaint; that the person is not responsible at all; 7a. maybe Ichiro was scolded by his teacher; 7b. Ichiro made a mistake at a crucial point the other day; Ichiro thinks that his action caused his teacher to lose face; 7c. Ichiro is worrying too much; 7d. It is very Ichiro-like; 8a. to leave the AC on; 8b. it changes the (set) temperature depending on whether there are people or not and when people are not moving; 8c. that it's okay if you forget to turn it off; 8d. that it's earth-friendly; 8e. it may cause humans to stop using their heads; 9a. being praised like that is a problem; 9b. he had no choice but to do it; 9c. he did a good job being patient with simple (boring) tasks; 9d. he actually likes doing simple things; 9e. for her it would be unthinkable, she'd probably quit halfway through; 10a. cooperative and excellent; she doesn't show signs of unwillingness when doing simple tasks; she speaks politely and she doesn't offend customers; 10b. having her be in charge of the next lecture; 10c. it would be no problem; 10d. because it's a good opportunity they should have her do it with Morris-san; 11a. how is his condition; 11b. for causing Sasha to worry; 11c. just walking normally down a street; 11d. his legs; 11e. he can't walk for two to three weeks; 11d. it will take two months to be completely healed; 12a. why he has to stay silent; 12b. his idea was stolen; 12c. they seem like they don't want to make a big deal out of it; 12d. there are things that are good to do and bad to do even for superiors; 12e. to speak honestly; 13a. the professor; 13b. do one lecture and do some traveling by himself for about two weeks; 13c. the north; 13d. the Mediterranean Sea; 14a. an article about global warming; 14b. the recent weather has been abnormal; 14c. there are many instances of heavy rain and snow; 15a. there is ice on the road; 15b. it has started snowing already; there will be a snowstorm in the afternoon with 4 centimeters of snow; 15c. she will return home as soon as possible; 16a. the table is very wet; 16b. the ice in the cup melted; 16c. to put the cup away instead of leaving it out; 17a. that no one is using the conference room anymore; 17b. to lock the room and turn the lights and the AC off; 17c. she wants him to notice these things on his own without her telling him everything; 18a. he took good care of them; 18b. he wraps each one and places them in a box so that they don't get damaged during delivery; 19a. economics; 19b. to be the president of the country; 19c. he said that (people) should study politics if (they) want to be a member of the Diet/Parliament/Congress, but not (if they are planning to be) the president; 20a. Kinoshita-kun from middle school; 20b. he was a bully; 20c. he became a member of the Diet; 20d. Kinoshita-kun appears on things like TV and is quite famous

読んでみよう

(1) a. a warning; children jumping out suddenly
(2) a. summer; b. it's so tasty that you can't stop eating it once you start eating it
(3) a. cloudy and sometimes rainy; 11° Celsius is the high; 8° Celsius is the low; highest chance of rain is 12 p.m.–12 a.m.; wind is blowing from the north; b. rainy then cloudy; 12° Celsius is the high; 7° Celsius is the low; highest chance of rain is 12 a.m.–6 a.m.; wind is blowing from the northwest (a little strong)
(4) a. December 2nd (Monday); the high is 17° Celsius and the low is 8° Celsius; cloudy and rainy for a short while (60% chance of rain)
(5) a. the train is running late and he can't make it to the gathering today; b. she says not to worry and please contact her when he figures out when he is coming
(6) a. a tulip under a sunny sky with no clouds; b. there is no school because of a typhoon; c. he can't stop reading it once he starts reading; d. even adults want to open their presents
(7) a. window; he left it open because it was a warm day for winter; b. trading cards (three rare ones); they got soaked because they were in the clothing he left in his room that got rained on while he was at school; Brian is disappointed; c. even if he got 100% on today's test he would feel very bad (shocked); d. to complain to the cloudy weather that caused the rain to fall

書き取り

1. 冬らしい　風が冷たい　白い朝
2. お茶飲めば　暖かい日の　春の午後
3. イニシヤチブ？　言ってください　もう一度
4. 雨に降られて服がびしょびしょで参りました。
5. 夏にしては雲が多くて涼しい天気ですね。
6. 今は晴れてるけど午後から曇り出すらしいよ。
7. って言うかこれは文句を言うしかないでしょう。
8. うちの子、たとえ台風でも外に行きたがるんですよ。

書いてみよう

1. Sample 和風のスープです。温めて飲んでください。
2. Sample ドアの開けっぱなしに注意！
3. Sample 発送が遅くなってしまい、申し訳ありませんでした。
4. Sample ちゃんと注文されてなかったようで、残念ながら一枚もプリントされてませんでした。
5 & 6. make sure your *haiku* and *senryu* have the 5, 7, 5 structure and the *haiku* has a word associated with one of the four seasons

知ってる？

1	A	11	C	21	C
2	B	12	C		
3	B	13	B		
4	A	14	C		
5	C	15	A		
6	B	16	B		
7	A	17	C		
8	A	18	A		
9	B	19	B		
10	A	20	A		